Learn Spanish at Your Own Pace

Step-by-Step Course for Beginners

by Maria Fernandez

SPANISH COURSES BY MARIA FERNANDEZ - kerapido.com

- Learn Spanish at Your Own Pace - Online course
- Learn Spanish at Your Own Pace - Book & audiobook
- Spanish Verb Course - Online course
- Spanish Verb Series - Books & audiobooks
- Spanish Audio Lessons for Complete Beginners - Audiobook & transcript
- Spanish Online Lessons - Live
- Fluent in Spanish - Book & audiobook
- Sherlock Holmes Bilingual Story - Book & audiobook
- Sherlock Holmes Bilingual Story - Online course
- Spanish Course for Kids - Online course
- Spanish Video Lessons on YouTube
- Speak Spanish with Maria Fernandez - Podcast

ENGLISH COURSES BY MARIA FERNANDEZ - learnenglishwithmaria.com

- 30-Day English Speaking Challenge - Online course
- Get a Better English Accent in 1 Hour - Online course
- Complete British English Pronunciation Course - Online course
- 30-Day English Writing Challenge - Online course
- English Online Lessons - Live
- English Video Lessons on YouTube

Credits

Written by: Maria Fernandez
Book design by: Maria Fernandez (with thanks to Simon King)
Cover design by: Maria Fernandez
Proofreading by: Susanna Flett
Editor: Maria Fernandez

© Maria Fernandez, 2012
© Maria Fernandez, this edition, 2023

All rights reserved. The content of this book may not be copied, distributed, loaned, extracted, published, recorded, displayed, modified or transferred in any form or by any means except with prior permission.

ISBN 978 − 0 − 9545320 − 8 − 6

Typeset in Times with LaTeX by Maria Fernandez (with thanks to Simon King)

To get this course recordings, go to: kerapido.com/book

To contact Maria Fernandez, go to: kerapido.com/contact

To see all the Spanish courses created by Maria Fernandez, go to: kerapido.com

To see Maria Fernandez's English courses, go to: learnenglishwithmaria.com

A mi hermana Matilde, tejedora de sueños

To my sister Matilde, weaver of dreams

Contents

	How to make the most of this course	1
1	Numbers: 0 to 30	3
2	Greetings	8
3	At the hotel	18
4	At the restaurant	28
5	The alphabet	36
6	Ordering drinks	40
7	At the apartment	48
8	At the supermarket 1	56
9	The family	64
10	Numbers: 31 to 100	74
11	Telling the time	78
12	Ordering tapas	86
13	Transport	96
14	Shops and eating places	106
15	At the chemist's	116
16	On holiday	124

17 At the supermarket 2	132
18 Days, months and dates	140
19 Asking for directions	150
20 101 to 1000, and more	158
21 At the tourist office	164
22 Clothes and shoes	174
23 Renting a car	182
24 At the bank	192
Solutions to the exercises	201
Nicholas's family tree	229
Clothes and shoe sizes	229
Map of Spain	230
Map of the World	231
Verb tables	233
Spanish - English Glossary	239
English - Spanish Glossary	265
Where to find Maria Fernandez's courses	299

How to make the most of this course

There are many ways of studying a foreign language. Some are tedious, impractical and fruitless; others are fun, useful and effective. This book (together with its recordings) will help you enjoy the challenge of learning Spanish. To give you a head start, here are some of the tips I can offer from decades of studying and teaching languages:

- Be positive. Don't talk yourself down, and don't listen to anyone who may discourage you.
- Study regularly. Ideally, you should do at least one lesson per week, spread over three or four days.
- If possible, book a holiday to a Spanish speaking country. The prospect of communicating with native speakers is the biggest incentive to study a language.
- Take this book with you when commuting by public transport, and read it.
- Concentrate on the skills you most want to develop. If it's speaking that you most want to master, go through each new speaking exercise several times, and revise the old ones frequently.
- Make notes on your book whenever you have a query or want to highlight something, rather than using a separate notepad. This will save time and make your revising easier.
- Go through this Spanish book from cover to cover. It will not only take you up to an intermediate level, it will also boost your confidence and self-esteem regarding communicating in Spanish.
- Don't allow yourself to forget words you've learned in previous dialogues. As you go on, you should put as much time into revising old lessons as into learning new things.
- If possible, join a Spanish class or, even better, get a native private tutor.
- Be realistic about your goals. Don't set yourself too much work.
- Different people find different learning tips useful, so try and choose the tips that suit you.

Lesson 1. Numbers: 0 to 30

Welcome to your first Spanish lesson! To start off, we are going to learn to count from zero to thirty. You can listen to these numbers, as well as the other sections in this course, in the recordings that accompany this book. You can find them at **kerapido.com/book**

0	cero	8	ocho	16	dieciséis	24	veinticuatro
1	uno	9	nueve	17	diecisiete	25	veinticinco
2	dos	10	diez	18	dieciocho	26	veintiséis
3	tres	11	once	19	diecinueve	27	veintisiete
4	cuatro	12	doce	20	veinte	28	veintiocho
5	cinco	13	trece	21	veintiuno	29	veintinueve
6	seis	14	catorce	22	veintidós	30	treinta
7	siete	15	quince	23	veintitrés		

1.1 Very important tips

→ Listen to the audio material as many times as you feel necessary to get familiar with all the numbers. Once you are happy with your pronunciation, cover up the Spanish words and try to come up with the numbers you have just learned.

→ Don't be harsh on yourself! You will make lots of mistakes before you can get things right. It is inevitable!

→ Going through the lessons in order will help you minimise having to look words up in the glossary in the back of the book. New words and their translations are listed after the dialogue where they first appear.

1.2 Watch out for your pronunciation

→ Spanish pronunciation is very regular.

→ The secret of how to communicate successfully is not only in mastering each individual letter, but also in getting familiar with certain groups of letters. In the case of the numbers above, for instance: *ce, ci, qui* are the most important letter groups. Throughout these 24 lessons, the 'Watch out for your pronunciation' section will highlight the most common pronunciation mistakes that English speakers tend to make, and will show you how to avoid them.

→ So, let's start by practising the letters 'b' and 'v'. Repeat after the Spanish speaker: *ba, be, bi, bo, bu, va, ve, vi, vo, vu.*

→ Notice that the Spanish 'v' sounds just like the Spanish 'b'. To practise this sound, listen carefully to the numbers 20 to 29 and repeat them.

→ Now listen to these other numbers and practise saying them, as they are the most difficult ones to pronounce correctly: *cero, seis, siete, nueve, diez, doce, quince, dieciséis, diecisiete, veinte, treinta.*

→ Finally, you will find that some numbers sound very similar. Pay particular attention to the following groups: 2/10/12; 6/7; 16/17; 20/30.

→ Good news! Once you have learned these thirty numbers, all other numbers are going to be easy to learn. Why? Because most of them will resemble the ones you have seen in this lesson.

1.3 You may wonder...

How important is it to get the pronunciation right? You do not have to pronounce things perfectly in order to be understood by native speakers, but there are certain mistakes that you should avoid. These will be highlighted in the 'Watch out for your pronunciation' section throughout this book.

I can't tell the difference between some numbers when I hear them. What can I do? Don't only practise listening to them, but also saying them. The better you pronounce the numbers yourself, the better you will understand them when other people say them. Practise them over several sessions. Start other lessons and then come back to the numbers in Lesson 1 regularly, until you are totally familiar with them.

What is the accent in words like* dieciséis *or* veintidós *for? The accent is there to tell you where to put the stress. Many Spanish words are stressed on the second last vowel or group of vowels, like: *uno, cuatro, nueve, catorce, veinte*. These words do not need an accent when written because they belong to the norm. *Dieciséis* and *veintidós* have an accent to remind you that they do not belong to the norm.

1.4 Spanish words with something in common

→ Just looking at the words for the thirty-one numbers in this lesson, you can find similarities that will help you remember them more easily. Notice, for example, that numbers 16 to 19 in Spanish literally mean 'ten and six' (*dieciséis*), 'ten and seven' (*diecisiete*), 'ten and eight' (*dieciocho*) and 'ten and nine' (*diecinueve*).

→ 21 to 29 also have other numbers in them, just like in English: *uno, dos, tres, cuatro, cinco, seis, siete, ocho, nueve.* 11 to 15, however, are quite different: *once, doce, trece, catorce, quince.*

1.5 Tip of the day

> The way in which you use this book will make a big difference to how fast and how well you learn Spanish. To make the most of your time and energy, follow the tips I give you in every section.

1.6 Exercises

(See solutions on p. 201)

Tip: When you finish an exercise, check your answers and then write down your marks and the current date next to the exercise. Do likewise each time you repeat the exercise. It is a good way to keep track of your progress.

Exercise 1: Read these numbers out loud in Spanish:

$a.$10 $b.$13 $c.$7 $d.$30 $e.$8 $f.$15 $g.$20 $h.$9 $i.$11 $j.$16

Exercise 2: Which of the two numbers is being said?

$a.$ 2 - 12 $b.$ 2 - 10 $c.$ 10 - 12 $d.$ 3 - 13 $e.$ 4 - 14

$f.$ 6 - 7 $g.$ 16 - 17 $h.$ 5 - 15 $i.$ 20 - 30 $j.$ 24 - 25

Exercise 3: Match the Spanish words with the figures:

a. tres	11
b. veinticinco	14
c. trece	29
d. veintiséis	25
e. catorce	15
f. veintisiete	3
g. once	26
h. veinticuatro	27
i. quince	13
j. veintinueve	24

Exercise 4: Write down the figures for the numbers you hear:

a. ....   b. ....   c. ....   d. ....   e. ....

f. ....   g. ....   h. ....   i. ....   j. ....

1.6 Exercises

Do you want to get more drills, line by line dialogues, and interactive vocabulary flashcards? Go to **kerapido.com/book**

Lesson 2. Greetings

Tip: Before you read the dialogues, or their translation, close the book and listen to the recordings twice. That will help you improve your listening skills a lot faster.

Diálogo 1

María:	Buenos días, Ana, ¿qué tal estás?
Ana:	Bien, gracias, ¿y tú?
María:	Bien.

Diálogo 2

Juan:	Hola, buenas tardes.
Ricardo:	Hola, me llamo Ricardo, y tú ¿cómo te llamas?
Juan:	Juan. ¿De dónde eres?
Ricardo:	De Inglaterra.

Diálogo 3

José:	Hola, buenas noches, te presento a mi amigo Pedro.
Margarita:	Encantada.
Pedro:	Encantado.
Margarita:	¿Estás de vacaciones?
Pedro:	Sí.
Margarita:	¿En qué hotel estás?
Pedro:	En el "Sol y Playa".
Margarita:	¡Yo también!
Pedro:	Entonces, ¡hasta pronto!
Margarita:	¡Hasta la vista!
José:	¡Adiós!

DIALOGUE 1

Mary:	Good morning, Anne, how are you?
Anne:	Fine, thanks, and you?
Mary:	Fine.

DIALOGUE 2

John:	Hello, good afternoon.
Richard:	Hello, my name is Richard, and you, what's your name? (literally[1]: Hello, I'm called Richard, and you, how are you called?)
John:	John. Where are you from?
Richard:	England (lit: From England).

DIALOGUE 3

Joseph:	Hello, good evening, this is my friend Peter (lit: I introduce you to my friend Peter).
Margaret:	Pleased to meet you (lit: pleased).
Peter:	Pleased to meet you (lit: pleased).
Margaret:	Are you on holiday?
Peter:	Yes.
Margaret:	Which hotel are you in?
Peter:	The 'Sun and Beach'
Margaret:	Me too!
Peter:	Then, see you soon!
Margaret:	See you!
Joseph:	Goodbye!

---

[1] The word 'literally' will from now on be abbreviated as 'lit'.

2. Greetings

2.1 New words

adiós	goodbye	hola	hello, hi
amigo (m[2])	(male) friend	hotel (m)	hotel
Ana	Anne	Inglaterra	England
bien	fine, well	José	Joseph
buenas	good	Juan	John
buenas noches	good evening, good night	la	the (f)
		Margarita	Margaret
buenas tardes	good afternoon, good evening	María	Mary
		me llamo	my name is
buenos días	good morning	mi	my
cómo	how	noche (f)	night
de	from, of	Pedro	Peter
día (m)	day	playa (f)	beach
diálogo (m)	dialogue	presento	I introduce
dónde	where	qué tal estás	how are you [tú]
el	the (m)	qué	what, which
en	in, at, on	Ricardo	Richard
encantada	pleased (f[3])	sí	yes
encantado	pleased (m)	sol (m)	sun
entonces	then	también	too, also
eres	you [tú] are	tarde (f)	afternoon, evening
estás	you [tú] are	te	to you
gracias	thank you	tú	you (singular, col[4])
hasta	until, till	vacaciones (f/pl[5])	holidays
hasta la vista	see you	y	and
hasta pronto	see you soon	yo	I, me

---

[2] m = masculine
[3] f = feminine
[4] col = colloquial
[5] f/pl = feminine plural

2.2 Watch out for your pronunciation

Tip: To master speaking, it is good to practise reading out each dialogue several times along with the recordings, trying to keep up with the Spanish speaker. This will be hard at first, but you will soon make remarkable progress.

→ Let's practise the letter 'h'. Repeat these two groups of letters after the Spanish speaker. Notice that the 'h' is silent, so they sound the same: *ha, he, hi, ho, hu; a, e, i, o, u.*

→ Now practise saying: *hola, el hotel, hasta.*

→ Remember to pronounce 'v' like 'b'. Practise saying: *bien, veinte, buenas, vacaciones, también, nueve.*

→ You may have noticed that some words sound very fast. That is because Spanish speakers tend to join words together whenever possible. Listen to these sentences: *¿qué tal estás? ¿de dónde eres? ¿en qué hotel estás?* (how are you? where are you from? which hotel are you in?). You will see more about this throughout this book.

→ Here are the most difficult words in this lesson. Listen to them and practise saying them: *qué, me llamo, te llamas, Inglaterra, presento, vacaciones, hotel, playa.*

2.3 Important notes

→ *Qué* is a very common Spanish word which most often means 'what' or 'which'. Questions often start with *qué*.

→ *Cómo* is also a very common word. Most often it means 'how'. In the case of *¿cómo te llamas?* what you are asking is 'how are you called?'

→ Words like *qué* and *cómo* may seem difficult at first, because they are not always used in the way we expect. The odds are, however, that you will soon get used to them, because they come up all the time.

2. Greetings

→ Now let's have a look at *¿Cómo te llamas?* and *me llamo Pedro*. Here we are literally saying: 'How do you call yourself?' and 'I call myself Peter'. When you are learning a foreign language it is essential that you find a balance between understanding things literally and learning in a more intuitive way. In the dialogues, I will give you the literal translation when I think it will help you learn a particular phrase. Your goal, however, must be to learn to use words in context rather than individually. Remember, more often than not words have more than one translation, and their meaning will be determined by context.

→ *Eres* and *estás* both mean 'you are'. The main difference between them is that *eres* is used to refer to facts that change very slowly or do not change at all (like where you are from), whereas *estás* refers to situations that can change at any point (like where you are).

→ *Tú* means 'you', where 'you' is just one person, the one I am talking to. When talking to two or more people, we will use a different word (vosotros) that you will practise later on.

→ *Yo* (I) and *tú* (you) are often dropped in Spanish. Why? Because when you say, for instance, *presento* (I introduce) or *estás* (you are) it is clear that you are talking about *yo* and *tú*, so you do not need to say them. Occasionally *yo* and *tú* are used for emphasis, just like when you say in English 'I, myself, ...'. Once again, you will see more about this in the next few lessons, so don't worry about it just now.

→ *Me, te* - you will come across these two small words very frequently. *Me* refers to *yo* (I or me), and *te* refers to *tú* (you - as explained above).

→ Other useful expressions: *¿qué tal estás?* (how are you?), *te presento a ...* (this is... - when introducing someone), *yo también* (me too), *buenos días* (good morning), *buenas tardes* (good afternoon, good evening), *buenas noches* (good evening, good night), *hasta pronto* (see you soon), *hasta la vista* (see you).

2.4 Tip of the day

> If you have any queries about the dialogues, translations, important points, exercises, etc. in this book, visit Maria Fernandez's website **kerapido.com**

2.5 You may wonder...

Can you say ¿qué tal? instead of ¿qué tal estás?? Yes, you can, and it also means 'how are you?', but it is a bit more colloquial.

What are the ¿ and ¡ for? They are there to indicate that a question or exclamation is starting.

Can you say the 'c' of **gracias** *with a /ss/ sound instead of a /th/ sound?* Yes, you can. In fact, that is the way most people pronounce the *ci* in Central and South America, and in the south of Spain.

When do you use **buenos días, buenas tardes** *and* **buenas noches***?* *Buenos días* (good morning) is used during the period between getting up and lunch (whenever that is). *Buenas tardes* (good afternoon, good evening) is used between lunch and sunset or dinner (whenever they are). Buenas noches (good evening, good night) is used between sunset or dinner and going to bed. So, as you can see, these phrases are quite flexible in Spanish and ruled by food rather than the clock.

Doesn't **buenos días** *mean 'good day'?* Literally, it means 'good days', but since you use it more or less like 'good morning' in English that is the way it is going to be translated throughout this book.

2.6 Spanish words with something in common

→ *Buenos* and *buenas*. Many Spanish describing words have four forms. In this case they are: *bueno, buena, buenos, buenas*. They all translate as 'good' in English. For the moment, let's just say that Spanish describing words have to agree (i.e. be masculine or feminine, singular or plural) with the noun they describe. If you want to see some examples of describing words in use, go to p. 67

→ *Encantado* and *encantada*: if you are male, you say *encantado* (pleased to meet you), and if you are female you say *encantada* (which also means 'pleased to meet you'). The reason for having two words is because they have to agree with the gender of the person they refer to. This will become clear in the next few lessons.

2.7 Building up new sentences

Tip: To build up your confidence in a foreign language, it's good to practise putting together your own sentences with the words you have learned so far. You can start with sentences that are very similar to the ones in the dialogues, only changing a word or two. In no time, you will find yourself able to say a lot more than you thought! Here are some new sentences:

Me llamo Ana.
My name is Anne.
Te presento a mi amigo Juan.
This is my friend John.
¿Dónde estás?
Where are you?
¿Estás en el hotel?
Are you at the hotel?
¿Estás en la playa?
Are you on the beach?
Tú también.
You too.

2.8 Exercises

(See solutions on p. 201)

Exercise 1: Say these phrases in Spanish:

1. Are you on holiday?
2. Good afternoon
3. Good morning
4. Hello, how are you?
5. Me too
6. My name is John
7. See you soon!
8. What's your name?
9. Where are you from?
10. Which hotel are you in?

Exercise 2: Which of the two is the answer to each question you hear?

1. De Inglaterra   or   En el hotel
2. Margarita   or   Sol y Playa
3. Gracias   or   Bien, gracias
4. Sí   or   También
5. Sol   or   En el Hilton
6. De Margarita   or   En la playa
7. En el Inglaterra   or   De Inglaterra
8. Sí   or   Juan
9. En la playa   or   De Inglaterra
10. Bien   or   Sí

2. Greetings

Exercise 3: Match the Spanish phrases with their English translations:

1. Hola, ¿qué tal estás?	Are you from England?
2. ¿Eres de Inglaterra?	My name is Mary.
3. Buenos días, María.	What's your name?
4. ¿Qué tal estás?	This is my friend Mary.
5. ¿Cómo te llamas?	Good morning, Mary.
6. ¿Dónde estás?	Hello, how are you?
7. Hasta luego, María.	Where are you?
8. Te presento a mi amiga María.	Are you on holiday?
9. Me llamo María.	See you later, Mary.
10. ¿Estás de vacaciones?	How are you?

Exercise 4: Write down the words you hear:

1. .... 2. ....

3. .... 4. ....

5. .... 6. ....

7. .... 8. ....

9. .... 10. ....

Lesson 3.   At the hotel

You can listen to this lesson's dialogues, new words, pronunciation section, sentences and exercises in the recordings that accompany this book. You can find them at **kerapido.com/book**

Diálogo 1

Sra. Martínez: Buenos días, tengo una reserva a nombre de Martínez.
Recepcionista: Un momento, por favor. Rosa Martínez. Aquí está. ¿Puedo ver su pasaporte?
Sra. Martínez: Aquí tiene.
Recepcionista: Muchas gracias. Tiene reservada una habitación individual con baño para tres noches.
Sra Martínez: Eso es. ¿Puedo mandar un mensaje por correo electrónico?
Recepcionista: Sí. Hay un ordenador en la cafetería.
Sra Martínez: Ah, ¿y me puede dar la llave de mi habitación?
Recepcionista: Aquí tiene.

Diálogo 2

Sr Rodríguez: ¿Tienen habitaciones libres?
Recepcionista: No, lo siento, está todo ocupado.
Sr Rodríguez: Vale, muchas gracias.

Diálogo 3

Sr López: Buenas tardes, quiero una habitación doble.
Recepcionista: ¿Para cuántas noches?
Sr López: Para cuatro. ¿Tienen habitaciones con baño?
Recepcionista: Sí. Todas las habitaciones tienen baño, televisión, aire acondicionado, teléfono y radio.
Sr López: Vale. ¿A qué hora tenemos que dejar la habitación?
Recepcionista: Antes de las once.
Sr López: ¿Podemos dejar el equipaje aquí hasta las cinco? Tenemos dos maletas.
Recepcionista: Sí, claro. Firme aquí, por favor. El desayuno se sirve de siete a nueve.

Dialogue 1

Mrs Martínez:	Good morning, I have a reservation in the name of Martínez.
Receptionist:	One moment, please. Rosa Martínez. Here it is. May I see your passport?
Mrs Martínez:	Here you are (lit: here you have).
Receptionist:	Thank you very much. You have a single room with bathroom reserved for three nights.
Mrs Martínez:	That's it. Can I send a message by email?
Receptionist:	Yes. There is a computer in the cafeteria.
Mrs Martínez:	Oh, and can you give me my room key? (lit: ... the key of my room?)
Receptionist:	Here you are.

Dialogue 2

Mr Rodríguez:	Do you have any rooms free? (lit: do you have rooms free?)
Receptionist:	No, I'm sorry, everything's full.
Mr Rodríguez:	OK, thank you very much.

Dialogue 3

Mr López:	Good afternoon, I want a double room.
Receptionist:	For how many nights?
Mr López:	Four (lit: For four). Do you have any rooms with bathroom?
Receptionist:	Yes. All the rooms have bathroom, television, air conditioning, telephone and radio.
Mr López:	OK. What time do we have to leave the room?
Receptionist:	By eleven o'clock (lit: before eleven).
Mr López:	Can we leave our luggage here till five? (lit: can we leave the luggage ...) We have two suitcases.
Receptionist:	Yes, of course. Sign here, please. Breakfast is served from seven till nine.

3. At the hotel

3.1 New words

a	to, at	ordenador (m)	computer
a qué hora	at what time	para	for
aire acondicionado (m)	air conditioning	pasaporte (m)	passport
antes de	before[1]	podemos	we can
aquí	here	por	for, through
baño (m)	bathroom	por favor	please
cafetería (f)	cafeteria	puede	he/she/it can, you [usted] can
claro	of course		
con	with	puedo	I can
correo (m)	mail, post	que	that
cuántas	how many (f/pl)	quiero	I want
dar	to give	radio (f)	radio
dejar	to leave	recepcionista (m)	receptionist
desayuno (m)	breakfast	recepcionista (f)	receptionist
doble	double	reserva (f)	reservation
electrónico	electronic	reservada	reserved (f)
equipaje (m)	luggage	Rosa	Rose
es	he/she/it is, you [usted] are	se sirve	is served
		señor (m)	man, gentleman
eso	that (thing)	señora (f)	woman, lady
está	he/she/it is, you [usted] are	Sr	Mr
		Sra	Mrs, Ms
firme	sign[2]	su	your[3], his, her, its, their
habitación (f)	room, bedroom		
hay	there is, there are	teléfono (m)	telephone
hora (f)	time, hour	televisión (f)	television
individual	individual, single	tenemos	we have
libres	free (m/pl, f/pl)	tenemos que	we have to
llave (f)	key	tengo	I have
lo siento	I'm sorry	tiene	he/she/it has, you [usted] have
maleta (f)	suitcase		
mandar	to send	tienen	you [ustedes]/ they have
mensaje (m)	message		
momento (m)	moment	todas	all (f/pl)
muchas gracias	thank you very much	todo	all (m/sing[4])
no	no	vale	OK
nombre (m)	name	ver	to see
ocupado	full, busy		

---

[1] *Antes de* can also mean 'by (a certain time)'.
[2] *Firme* is a command meaning 'sign', as in 'sign here, please'.
[3] For more details about *su*, go to p. 68
[4] m/sing = masculine singular.

20

3.2 Watch out for your pronunciation

→ Repeat after the Spanish speaker: rra, rre, rri, rro, rru.

→ Now, let's practise the 'r' sound in: *Rosa, reserva, correo, radio, Ricardo, Inglaterra.*

→ Have you noticed that you can only hear one 'a' in *una habitación*, and not two? That is because in Spanish you often link words together in such a way that you lose repeated letters, like here. In Lesson 4 you will see how words get linked in Spanish. For the moment I just wanted you to be aware of it.

→ Difficult words: listen to these words and practise saying them: *por favor, aquí, una habitación, electrónico, hay, la llave, vale, quiero, televisión, teléfono, radio, aire acondicionado, equipaje, desayuno.*

→ Watch out for words that look very similar in English and Spanish like: *televisión, teléfono, radio, aire, cafetería, electrónico, individual.* Notice the difference between the English and Spanish pronunciation.

3.3 Important notes

→ *El día/los días, la habitación/las habitaciones.* All Spanish nouns are either masculine or feminine, and their plurals are easy. The first thing you need to know is that the plural of *el* is *los*, and the plural of *la* is *las*. El, la, los and las all mean 'the'. As far as nouns go, there are two possible endings for the plural: 's' and 'es'. When the noun ends in a vowel (e.g., *día*), it takes an 's' (*días*). When it ends in a consonant (*habitación*), it takes an 'es' (*habitaciones*).

→ *Un* and *una*: *una habitación* (a room), *un momento* (a moment). *Un* and *una* both mean 'a' or 'one'. *Un* goes before masculine nouns, and *una* before feminine nouns.

→ *Un* and *uno*. The difference between *un* and *uno* is that *un* is used before a noun (*un pasaporte*, a passport), whereas *uno* is used without the noun it refers to (*quiero uno*, I want one). They are both masculine.

3. At the hotel

→ *Hay* means both 'there is' and 'there are'. It is a very useful word that will come up frequently.

→ Word order. *Una habitación individual* (a single room), literally translates as: a room single. In the majority of cases, the English 'describing word + noun' (e.g. single room) becomes 'noun + describing word' (*habitación individual*) in Spanish. You will soon get used to it, as there are plenty of examples throughout this book.

→ Other useful expressions: *a nombre de* (in the name of), *aquí tiene* (here you are), *muchas gracias* (thank you very much), *eso es* (that's it), *lo siento* (I'm sorry), *a qué hora* (at what time).

3.4 Tip of the day

The better your Spanish pronunciation, the more likely that Spanish people will want to talk to you!

3.5 You may wonder...

How can you tell that ¿tienen habitaciones libres? *(do you have any rooms free?)* **is a question and tiene reservada una habitación** *(you have a room reserved)* **is not? Is it just the '¿' that tells you? Are there no extra words like 'do' in English?** No, there are no extra words like 'do' to indicate questions. In written Spanish, the '¿' tells you where a question starts. When talking, questions go up at the end (*libres*) and statements go down (*habitación*). Listen carefully to the recordings to notice the difference.

What does* las once *really mean? *Las once* refers to *las once horas* (eleven o'clock; lit: the eleven hours). When telling the time in Spanish, you always say it like this: *las ocho* (eight o'clock), *las cinco* (five o'clock), etc. You will learn how to tell the time in Lesson 11.

What do **lo siento** *and* **muchas gracias** *mean word for word?* When it comes to expressions like *lo siento* (I'm sorry) and *muchas gracias* (thank you very much) it is better not to analyse them word for word. Learn them as a whole. That way you will always get them right. In the dialogues, I will give you the literal translation of a sentence when I think it will help you, but not otherwise.

What are **Sr** *and* **Sra** *short for?* *Sr* is short for *señor* (Mr), and *Sra* is short for *señora* (Mrs, Ms).

No doubt there are many other questions to be answered, but we have seen enough new material for one lesson. So, let's leave it for later.

3.6 Spanish words with something in common

→ *Todo* and *todas* both mean *all* or *the whole*. *Todo* is used with masculine singular words, as in *todo el equipaje* (all the luggage, the whole luggage). *Todas* is used with feminine plural words, as in *todas las habitaciones* (all the rooms). *Todo* also means 'everything': *está todo ocupado* (everything is full).

→ *Tengo* (I have), *tiene* (he/she/is has, you [usted] have), *tenemos* (we have), *tienen* (you [ustedes]/they have). So, what is the difference between *tiene* and *tienen*? First of all, let's see the difference between *usted* and *ustedes*. *Usted* means 'you', where 'you' refers to only one person, the one I am talking to, just like *tú* in the previous lesson, p. 12. However, *tú* is a colloquial form whereas *usted* is more formal. Roughly speaking, *tú* is the form you use with people you are in first name terms with, whereas *usted* is the form you use with people you call by their surname. *Ustedes* is simply the plural of *usted*, that is, the form you use to address two or more people in a formal way.

→ Now let's see *tiene* and *tienen* in context. In *tiene reservada una habitación ...* (you have a room reserved ...) the receptionist is referring to only one person, Mr López. In *¿tienen habitaciones libres?* (do you have any rooms free?) Mr López is referring to the hotel as a group of people, not just the receptionist he is talking to. The words *tiene* and *tienen* will come up frequently in this book, so there will be plenty of opportunity to master them.

3. At the hotel

→ *La reserva* (the reservation) and *reservada* (reserved). Notice the similarity between these two words. Making connections between words helps you build up your vocabulary and remember words more easily.

3.7 Building up new sentences

Note: All these new sentences are built with words you already know. Listen to them in the recordings and repeat them. When you're familiar with them, try building similar sentences yourself.

¿A qué hora podemos ver la habitación?
What time can we see the room?

¿Me puede dar su pasaporte?
Can you give me your passport?

¿Puedo ver su ordenador?
Can I see your computer?

¿Tienen ordenadores?
Do you have computers?

Hay dos teléfonos en el hotel.
There are two telephones in the hotel.

¿Dónde están las llaves de Juan?
Where are John's keys?

Quiero una habitación doble con baño.
I want a double room with bathroom.

Tengo que dejar la maleta en la habitación.
I have to leave the suitcase in the room.

3.8 Exercises

(See solutions on p. 202)

Exercise 1: Say these sentences in Spanish

1. Can I see the hotel?
2. How are you?
3. Do you have rooms with air conditioning?
4. Do you have any rooms free?
5. What's your name?
6. By four o'clock.
7. There are three radios in the room.
8. I have a reservation in the name of Miller.
9. Where are you from?
10. One moment, please.

Exercise 2: Which of the two sentences is being said?

1. ¿Puedo ver el baño?   ¿Puedo ver los baños?
2. Hay un ordenador   Hay dos ordenadores
3. Quiero una habitación   Quiero dos habitaciones
4. Antes de las dos   Antes de las doce
5. Tenemos seis maletas   Tenemos siete maletas
6. ¿Me puede dar la llave?   ¿Me puede dar las llaves?
7. Tiene una habitación   Tiene dos habitaciones
8. ¿Puedo mandar un mensaje?   ¿Puedo mandar dos mensajes?
9. Quiero una radio   Quiero dos radios
10. La llave de María   Las llaves de María

3. At the hotel

Exercise 3: Match the Spanish sentences with their English translations:

1. ¿Podemos ver su ordenador?	*I have two computers.*
2. ¿Puedo ver su ordenador?	*You (usted) have two computers.*
3. Tenemos un ordenador.	*I have a computer.*
4. Tenemos dos ordenadores.	*You (ustedes) have a computer.*
5. Tengo dos ordenadores.	*You (ustedes) have two computers.*
6. Tengo un ordenador.	*Can I see your (usted) computer?*
7. Tiene dos ordenadores.	*We have two computers.*
8. Tiene un ordenador.	*You (usted) have a computer.*
9. Tienen un ordenador.	*Can we see your (usted) computer?*
10. Tienen dos ordenadores.	*We have a computer.*

Exercise 4: Write down the plurals of these words (using *los* or *las*):

1. el amigo   *los amigos*
2. el hotel   ....
3. la playa   ....
4. el nombre   ....
5. el pasaporte   ....
6. la cafetería   ....
7. el baño   ....
8. la maleta   ....
9. el desayuno   ....
10. la llave   ....

Lesson 4. At the restaurant

Diálogo 1

Antonio:	Buenos días, ¿tiene una mesa para cinco?
Camarero:	Lo siento, está completo. ¿Pueden volver dentro de una hora?

Diálogo 2

Camarero:	¿Qué van a tomar?
Javier:	De primero, sopa de pescado y una ensalada mixta, y de segundo un filete de vaca con patatas fritas y pollo asado.
Camarero:	¿Y de beber?
Javier:	Una botella de vino tinto de la casa y agua mineral con gas.
Camarero:	¿Algo más?
Javier:	No, eso es todo, gracias. ¿Me puede decir dónde están los servicios?
Camarero:	Al fondo, a la derecha.

Diálogo 3

Teresa:	Buenas noches, tenemos una mesa reservada a nombre de Teresa García.
Camarera:	Por aquí, por favor. Aquí tienen la carta. (*Unos minutos más tarde*) ¿Qué van a cenar?
Teresa:	¿Qué nos recomienda?
Camarera:	La sopa de mariscos, las sardinas asadas y el atún, y si quieren carne les recomiendo el pavo asado y el pato.
Teresa:	¿Tienen algún plato vegetariano?
Camarera:	Sí, tenemos tortillas y espaguetis.
Teresa:	Pues vamos a tomar mariscos con mayonesa y salmón con patatas, y ensalada y una tortilla francesa con arroz.
Camarera:	¿Y qué van a beber?
Teresa:	¿Nos puede traer la carta de vinos?
Camarera:	¡Cómo no! Y les voy a traer también la sal y la pimienta.
Teresa:	(*Más tarde*) La cuenta, por favor.

Dialogue 1

Anthony:	Good morning, do you have a table for five?
Waiter:	I'm sorry, we're full (lit: it's full). Can you come back in an hour?

Dialogue 2

Waiter:	What are you going to have?
Javier:	As a starter, fish soup and a mixed salad, and for the main course a beef steak with chips (lit: fried potatoes) and roast chicken.
Waiter:	And to drink?
Javier:	A bottle of the house red wine and sparkling mineral water.
Waiter:	Anything else? (lit: anything more?)
Javier:	No, that's all, thank you. Can you tell me where the toilets are?
Waiter:	At the end, on the right.

Dialogue 3

Theresa:	Good evening, we have a table reserved in the name of Teresa García.
Waitress:	This way, please. Here you are, the menu (lit: Through here, please. Here you have the menu). (*A few minutes later*) What are you going to have for dinner? (lit: What are you going to dine?)
Theresa:	What do you recommend? (lit: What do you recommend us?)
Waitress:	The shellfish soup, the grilled sardines and the tuna, and if you want meat I recommend the roast turkey and the duck (lit: I recommend you the roast turkey ...).
Theresa:	Do you have any vegetarian dishes?
Waitress:	Yes, we have omelettes and spaghetti.
Theresa:	Then we're going to have shellfish with mayonnaise and salmon with potatoes, and salad and a French omelette with rice.
Waitress:	And what are you going to drink?
Theresa:	Can you bring us the wine list.
Waitress:	Of course! And I'm also going to bring you salt and pepper.
Theresa:	(*Later on*) The bill, please.

4. At the restaurant

4.1 New words

a la derecha	on the right	mineral	mineral
agua (f[1])	water	minuto (m)	minute
al	to the	mixta	mixed
al fondo	at the end	nos	us, to us
algo	something, anything	patata (f)	potato
algún	any, some (m)	pato (m)	duck
Antonio	Anthony	pavo (m)	turkey
arroz (m)	rice	pescado (m)	fish
asadas	grilled, baked, roasted	pimienta (f)	pepper (spice)
asado	grilled, baked, roasted	plato (m)	dish, plate
atún (m)	tuna	pollo (m)	chicken
beber	to drink	por aquí	this way
botella (f)	bottle	pueden	you [uds]/they can
camarera (f)	waitress	pues	then
camarero (m)	waiter	quieren	you [uds]/they want
carne (f)	meat	recomienda	he/she/it recommends, you [ud[2]] recommend
carta (f)	menu		
casa (f)	house	sal (f)	salt
cenar	to have dinner	salmón (m)	salmon
cómo no	of course	sardina (f)	sardine
completo	full	servicios (m/pl)	toilets
con gas	sparkling, fizzy	si	if
cuenta (f)	bill	sopa (f)	soup
de primero	as a starter	tarde	late
de segundo	for the main course	tenemos	we have
decir	to tell, to say	Teresa	Theresa
dentro de	in	tinto	red (wine)
derecha (f)	right	tomar	to take, to have
ensalada (f)	salad	tortilla (f)	omelette
espaguetis (m/pl[3])	spaghetti	traer	to bring
están	you [uds]/they are	unos	some
filete (m)	steak	vaca (f)	beef, cow
francesa	French	vamos	we go/are going
fritas	fried (f/pl)	van	you [uds[4]]/they go, are going
les	to you, to them		
marisco (m)	shellfish	vegetariano	vegetarian
más	more	vino (m)	wine
mayonesa (f)	mayonnaise	volver	to come back
mesa (f)	table	voy	I go/am going

---

[1] *El agua* is in fact a feminine word, but it takes 'el' because it starts with a stressed 'a'
[2] ud = usted (you - singular formal)
[3] m/pl = masculine plural
[4] uds = ustedes (you - plural formal)

4.2 Watch out for your pronunciation

→ Repeat after the Spanish speaker: *ra, re, ri, ro, ru*.

→ Now, let's practise the 'r' sound in: *tardes, eres, gracias, pronto, María, hora, claro, dar, ordenador, sirve*.

→ Notice the difference between the 'r' and the 'rr' sounds: *radio, cafetería, reserva, firme, recepcionista, ver*. Don't forget that an 'r' at the beginning of a word always has a 'rr' sound.

→ How to stress Spanish words: It is good to learn where the stress goes on each word. Many Spanish words are stressed on the second last vowel, or group of vowels, but not all of them. Practise saying: *adiós, también, estás, hotel, algún; teléfono, electrónico*.

→ Linking words. Practise saying these sentences like the Spanish speaker: *¿qué van a tomar?* (what are you going to have?), *¿dónde están los servicios?* (where are the toilets?), *las sardinas asadas y el atún* (the grilled sardines and the tuna), *¿tienen algún plato vegetariano?* (do you have any vegetarian dishes?). Notice that when a word ends in a consonant and the next one starts with a vowel (like *sardinas asadas*) these two words are run together and sound like one long word with no break. Also, when a word starts with the same letter that the previous word finishes with (like the 'e' in *dónde están*) you only say that letter once.

→ Difficult words: Listen to these words and practise saying them: *tiene, volver, primero, filete, pollo, vino, servicios, recomienda, vegetariano, tortilla, mayonesa, arroz, pimienta*.

4.3 Important notes

→ *El/la* and 'the': you may have noticed that sometimes you have *el* or *la* in the Spanish dialogue (as in *y les voy a traer también la sal y la pimienta*), but no 'the' in the English translation 'and I'm also going to bring you salt and pepper'. For the moment let's just say that it is more common to use *el* and *la* in Spanish than *the* in English, but there are also occasions in which you use 'the' but not *el* or *la*. We will see examples of this throughout the dialogues.

→ *De*: Notice the way you say fish soup, beef steak or wine list in Spanish: *sopa de pescado, filete de vaca, carta de vinos*. You are actually saying: soup of fish, steak of beef, list of wines.

→ *Al = a + el* (to the). That is why we say *al hotel* (to the hotel), but *a la playa* (to the beach).

→ Other useful expressions: *dentro de una hora* (in an hour), *de primero* (as a starter), *de segundo* (for the main course), *¿algo más?* (anything else?), *eso es todo* (that's all), *¿me puede decir ... ?* (can you tell me ...?), *al fondo* (at the end), *a la derecha* (on the right), *por aquí* (this way), *¿qué nos recomienda?* (what do you recommend), *¿nos puede traer ...?* (can you bring us ...?), *¡cómo no!* (of course!), *más tarde* (later on).

4.4 Tip of the day

If you find a Spanish word or phrase difficult to remember or understand, make a note of it in pencil 30 pages later and leave it. Next time you come across your note the odds are that it won't be a problem any more. If it is, do the same another 30 pages later.

4.5 You may wonder...

Are all nouns ending in 'o' masculine, and in 'a' feminine? No. The majority are but there are exceptions, like *la radio*.

Could you say perdón instead of lo siento? Yes. *Perdón* and *lo siento* both mean *I'm sorry*.

4.6 Spanish words with something in common

→ *Asado* and *asadas* (grilled, baked, roasted): *asado* is used with masculine singular words (*un pollo asado*) and *asadas* with feminine plural words (*las sardinas asadas*), just like *todo/todas*.

→ *Sí* (with an accent) (yes) and *si* (without an accent) (if).

→ *Nos recomienda* (he/she/it recommends [to us], you [ud] recommend [to us]) and *les recomiendo* (I recommend [to you - you = ustedes]).

→ *Voy a* (I go to, I'm going to), *vamos a* (we go to, we're going to) and *van a* (you [uds]/they go to, are going to).

→ *Quiero* (I want) and *quieren* (you [uds]/they want)

→ *Está* (he/she/it is, you [ud] are) and *están* (you [uds]/they are)

4.7 Building up new sentences

¿Tiene una mesa para dos?
Do you have a table for two?
¿Pueden volver dentro de tres horas?
Can you come back in three hours?
¿Qué van a ver?
What are you going to see?
¿Me puede decir dónde está la playa?
Can you tell me where the beach is?
Tenemos una habitación.
We have a room.
Les recomiendo la sopa de pollo.
I recommend the chicken soup (to you).
¿Tienen agua mineral con gas?
Do you have sparkling mineral water?
Tenemos una mesa en la habitación.
We have a table in the room.
Vamos a beber vino tinto.
We're going to drink red wine.

4.8 Exercises

(See solutions on p. 203)

Exercise 1: Say these phrases in Spanish:

1. Good afternoon, do you have a table for three? (you = usted)
2. What are you going to have? (you = ustedes)
3. Shellfish soup and a mixed salad.
4. Roast chicken with chips.
5. Can you tell me where the hotel is? (you = ud)
6. Do you have grilled sardines? (you = uds)
7. Can you bring me a bottle of water? (you = ud)
8. The bill, please.
9. Can I see the menu?
10. I want turkey with rice.

Exercise 2: What would you say before the words you hear: *el, la, los* or *las*?

1. .... 2. ....
3. .... 4. ....
5. .... 6. ....
7. .... 8. ....
9. .... 10. ....

4.8 Exercises

Exercise 3: Complete each sentence with one of the following missing words:

> Missing words: a, con, de, con, de, de, para, de, a, en

1. ¿Tiene una mesa .... cuatro?
2. ¿Pueden volver dentro .... dos horas?
3. ¿Qué van .... tomar?
4. Quiero un filete .... patatas fritas.
5. Están .... la derecha.
6. ¿Nos puede traer la carta .... vinos?
7. Hay un teléfono .... la habitación.
8. ¿Tienen habitaciones .... baño?
9. El desayuno se sirve .... siete a diez.
10. ¿Me puede dar la llave .... la habitación?

Exercise 4: How would you translate these sentences?

1. ¿Tiene radio? ....
2. ¿Podemos ver la carta de vinos? ....
3. ¿Me puede decir dónde están las botellas de agua ?
3. ....
4. Tenemos carne asada. ....
5. Les recomiendo el pollo frito. ....
6. Tenemos un amigo en Inglaterra. ....
7. Vamos a ver a Margarita. ....
8. ¿Me puede traer el desayuno? ....
9. ¿Me puede dar un pollo? ....
10. ¿Dónde están las patatas? ....

Lesson 5. The alphabet

Listen to the Spanish speaker in the recordings and repeat the letters you hear:

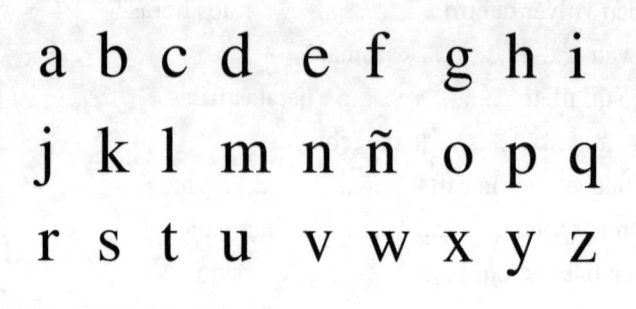

5.1 New words

tu	your [you = tú]	*se escribe*	one writes

Practise these two sentences:

➜ *¿Cómo se escribe?* How do you spell it? or How does one spell it?

➜ *¿Cómo se escribe tu nombre?* How do you spell your [you = tú] name? or How does one spell your [you = tú] name?

5.2 Watch out for your pronunciation

➜ Practise saying all the letters of the alphabet until you feel you sound like the native speaker in the recordings.

➜ Practise spelling out your name and address, using Spanish letters.

5.3 Important notes

→ The better you learn to say each letter of the alphabet, the better your pronunciation will be in general. This is particularly important in the case of the vowels (*a, e, i, o, u*).

→ The letters 'k' and 'w' are quite rare in Spanish.

5.4 Tip of the day

It's better to study for 15 or 20 minutes four or five times a week, than for three hours on Sundays. You'll remember things better and you'll get used to the language more naturally.

5.5 You may wonder...

How can I master the Spanish alphabet? Do the following: say each letter of the alphabet **after** the speaker in the recordings; repeat this exercise several times; then, say each letter of the alphabet **before** the speaker; once more, repeat this exercise several times; repeat the spelling exercises in this lesson until you get no mistakes in any of them; continue with your lessons and come back to the alphabet regularly; repeat the spelling exercises from time to time.

5.6 Spanish words with something in common

→ *Tu* (your [you = *tú*]) and *tú* (you). Notice the accent on *tú* (you).

5.7 Spelling names out

Practise spelling these names out using Spanish letters:

¿Cómo se escribe tu nombre? (How do you spell your name?)

Ricardo	Almudena	Carlos	Estefanía[1]	Luis
Susana	Ignacio	Beatriz	Gonzalo	Julia

5.8 Exercises

(See solutions on p. 204)

Exercise 1: Spell these names out in Spanish:

1. Michael
2. Emily
3. William
4. Samantha
5. Andrew
6. Elizabeth
7. Anthony
8. Jennifer
9. Alexander
10. Nicole

Exercise 2: Which of the two letters is being said?

1. a e
2. b t
3. g j
4. i e
5. c z
6. s c
7. f v
8. k q
9. b v
10. h j

Exercise 3: Write down the letters you hear:

1. .... 2. .... 3. .... 4. .... 5. ....
6. .... 7. .... 8. .... 9. .... 10. ....

---

[1] When spelling words out, it is uncommon to mention the written accent. You tend to assume that the other person knows if there is one. That is why the speaker in the recordings says only the letters for the name Estefanía.

5.8 Exercises

Exercise 4: Write down the names being spelt out:

1. .... 2. ....
3. .... 4. ....
5. .... 6. ....
7. .... 8. ....
9. .... 10. ....

Lesson 6. Ordering drinks

Diálogo 1

Camarero: Buenos días, ¿qué van a tomar?
Javier: Un café con leche, un café solo, un descafeinado, un batido, un té con leche y un zumo de naranja con hielo.
Camarero: Lo siento, no nos queda zumo de naranja.
Javier: Entonces una naranjada. Ah, y también un chocolate caliente. ¿Me puede decir cuánto es todo?
Camarero: Sí, nueve euros y veinticinco céntimos.
Javier: Aquí tiene. Diez euros. Quédese con el cambio.
Camarero: Muchas gracias.

Diálogo 2

Julia: Por favor, ¿nos puede traer otra tónica, una cerveza grande, una jarra de sangría y un vaso de agua mineral sin gas?
Camarero: Ahora mismo.

Diálogo 3

Camarera: ¿Qué les pongo?
Beatriz: Vamos a ver. Una caña, una copa de vino tinto, una Coca-Cola® con ron, una copa de jerez, un whisky doble y un vodka con limón.
Camarera: ¿Algo más?
Beatriz: No, eso es todo, gracias.

Diálogo 4

Camarero: ¿Qué desean?
Jorge: Una copa de vino tinto, dos de vino blanco, una de rosado y una cerveza.
Camarero: ¿Grande o pequeña?
Jorge: Pequeña.

Dialogue 1

Waiter:	Good morning, what are you going to have?
Javier:	A white coffee (lit: a coffee with milk), a black coffee (lit: a coffee on its own), a decaf, a milk shake, one tea with milk and an orange juice with ice.
Waiter:	I'm sorry, we don't have any orange juice left.
Javier:	Then, an orangeade. Oh, and also a hot chocolate. Can you tell me how much everything is?
Waiter:	Yes, nine euros and twenty-five cents.
Javier:	Here you are. Ten euros. Keep the change.
Waiter:	Thank you very much.

Dialogue 2

Julia:	Excuse me, (lit: please) can you bring us another tonic water, a large beer, a jug of sangria and a glass of still mineral water?
Waiter:	Right away.

Dialogue 3

Waitress:	What can I get you? (lit: what do I put you?)
Beatrice:	Let's see. A small beer, a glass of red wine, a rum and Coke® (lit: a Coke® with rum), a glass of sherry, a double whisky, and a vodka and lemon (lit: and a vodka with lemon).
Waitress:	Anything else?
Beatrice:	No, that's everything, thanks.

Dialogue 4

Waiter:	What would you like? (lit: what do you wish for?)
George:	One glass of red wine, two of white wine, one of rosé, and a beer.
Waiter:	Large or small?
George:	Small.

6. Ordering drinks

6.1 New words

ahora	now	leche (f)	milk
ahora mismo	right away, right now	limón (m)	lemon
batido (m)	milk shake	mismo	same
Beatriz	Beatrice	naranja (f)	orange
blanco	white	naranjada (f)	orangeade
café (m)	coffee	no nos queda ...	we don't have any ... left
café solo (m)	black coffee	otra	another, another one (f)
caliente	hot	pequeña	small (f)
cambio (m)	change	pongo	I put
caña (f)	small beer	por favor	excuse me, please
céntimo (m)	cent	quédese	keep (a command)
cerveza (f)	beer	ron (m)	rum
chocolate (m)	chocolate	rosado	rosé
Coca-Cola® (f)	Coke®	sangría (f)	sangria[1]
copa (f)	glass	sin	without
cuánto	how much	sin gas	still
descafeinado (m)	decaf	solo	on its own, alone
desean	you [uds]/they wish	té (m)	tea
euro (m)	euro	tónica (f)	tonic water
grande	big, large	vamos a ver	let's see
hielo (m)	ice	vaso (m)	glass
jarra (f)	jug	vodka (m)	vodka
jerez (m)	sherry	whisky (m)	whisky
Jorge	George	zumo (m)	juice

6.2 Watch out for your pronunciation

→ Let's practise the letter 'e'. Notice that the 'e' at the end of a word is never dropped in Spanish words: *filete, leche, chocolate, noche, grande, tarde, equipaje*. Notice also that, unlike in english, the Spanish 'e' always has the same sound: *euros, hotel, desean, céntimos, volver, pueden, recepcionista, reserva*.

---

[1] *Sangría*: A cold red wine punch

→ Now practise saying these words. Make sure you pronounce all the letters. *Descafeinado, ensalada, servicios, recomienda, francesa, pasaporte, televisión, teléfono.*

→ Difficult words: Listen to these words and practise saying them: *naranja, hielo, jarra, quédese, cerveza, jerez, pequeña.*

6.3 Important notes

→ Describing words ending in 'e'. Notice that *caliente* (hot) and *grande* (large) are both masculine and feminine: *el café caliente* (the hot coffee), *la leche caliente* (the hot milk), *el hotel grande* (the large hotel), *la cerveza grande* (the large beer). We have seen other describing words, like *asado* and *asadas*, which have different masculine and feminine forms. To revise them, go to p. 33

→ *Por, a, de, con, para, en.* These very common words called 'prepositions' are used in different ways depending on the context. However, they do generally have the following meanings: *por* (for, through), *a* (to, at), *de* (of, from), *con* (with), *para* (for), *en* (in, on, at).

→ Other useful expressions: *no nos queda ...* (we don't have any ... left), *¿cuánto es?* (how much is it?), *quédese con el cambio* (keep the change), *ahora mismo* (right away), *vamos a ver* (let's see).

6.4 Tip of the day

Do not hesitate to underline or highlight any words or phrases in this book that you find of special interest. That way, revising your lessons will be faster and more effective.

6.5 You may wonder...

What is the difference between **¿qué van a beber?** *(what are you going to drink?) and* **¿qué van a tomar?** *(what are you going to have?)?* *Beber* means 'to drink' and *tomar* means 'to have', so *¿qué van a beber?* is only used in a drinking context, while *¿qué van a tomar?* can be used in both an eating and a drinking context.

What is the difference between **una caña** *and* **una cerveza pequeña?** *Una caña* is a colloquial way of saying *una cerveza pequeña* (a small beer).

Why do you say **dos de vino blanco** *and not* **dos copas de vino blanco?** In Spanish you often drop nouns that have been said immediately before, like *copas* in the dialogue.

What is the difference between **una copa** *and* **un vaso?** *Una copa* is a glass with a stem, and *un vaso* a glass without a stem.

In Dialogue 4, when the waiter says **¿grande o pequeña?**, *does he refer only to the beer, or the wine too?* He refers only to the beer. You can tell because the words *grande* and *pequeña* are feminine singular (like *una cerveza*). If he was asking about the glasses of wine (*las copas de vino*), he would have said *¿grandes o pequeñas?*

6.6 Spanish words with something in common

→ *Puedo* (I can), *puede* (he/she/it/you [ud] can), *podemos* (we can), *pueden* (you [uds]/they can). For more information on this and other verbs, go to page 236

6.7 Building up new sentences

No nos queda café.
We don't have any coffee left.
¿Nos puede traer otra cerveza?
Can you bring us another beer?
¿Tienen vasos?
Do you have any glasses?
Voy a tomar leche caliente.
I'm going to have hot milk.
Vamos a beber agua con hielo.
We're going to drink water with ice.
Tenemos tres botellas de vino blanco de la casa.
We have three bottles of house white.
¿Me puede decir dónde está la cerveza?
Can you tell me where the beer is?
Quiero dos cervezas pequeñas.
I want two small beers.
Los cafés están calientes.
The coffees are hot.
¿Qué podemos tomar?
What can we have?

6.8 Exercises

(See solutions on p. 205)

Exercise 1: Say these sentences in Spanish:
1. I want two white coffees.
2. We don't have any sherry left.
3. Can you [ud] bring me another glass of red wine?
4. Do you [uds] have white wine?
5. I'm going to have a small beer [colloquial].
6. We're going to drink orangeade.
7. We have four bottles of beer.
8. Can you [ud] tell me where the rum is?
9. The soup is hot.
10. Do you [uds] have still mineral water?

6. Ordering drinks

Exercise 2: Which of the two words is being said?

1. café	cafés	2. batido	batidos
3. zumo	zumos	4. euro	euros
5. cerveza	cervezas	6. jarra	jarras
7. vaso	vasos	8. caña	cañas
9. copa	copas	10. limón	limones

Exercise 3: Match the Spanish sentences with their English translations:

1. Quiero cuatro cervezas grandes.	You want four large beers.
2. Quiero cuatro cervezas pequeñas.	We have four small beers.
3. Quieren cuatro cervezas grandes.	I have four small beers.
4. Quieren cuatro cervezas pequeñas.	You want four small beers.
5. Tenemos cuatro cervezas grandes.	I want four large beers.
6. Tenemos cuatro cervezas pequeñas.	You have four small beers.
7. Tienen cuatro cervezas grandes.	I want four small beers.
8. Tienen cuatro cervezas pequeñas.	I have four large beers.
9. Tengo cuatro cervezas grandes.	You have four large beers.
10. Tengo cuatro cervezas pequeñas.	We have four large beers.

Exercise 4: Dictation: write down the words you hear. You will hear each set of words twice:

1. .... 2. ....

3. .... 4. ....

5. .... 6. ....

7. .... 8. ....

9. .... 10. ....

Lesson 7.   At the apartment

Diálogo

Marta: Buenas tardes. Tenemos un apartamento reservado a nombre de Gómez.
Recepcionista: Vamos a ver. Sí, tienen el apartamento número veintisiete. Por aquí, por favor. (*En el apartamento*) Como pueden ver, tiene dos baños, dos habitaciones con dos camas, un salón con terraza y ésta es la cocina.
Marta: ¿Tiene lavadora y microondas?
Recepcionista: Sí. También tiene lavaplatos, cocina de gas, nevera y congelador. Las mantas y las toallas están en los armarios de las habitaciones.
Marta: ¿Qué día vienen a limpiar?
Recepcionista: Los lunes y los jueves.
Marta: ¿Dónde se deja la basura?
Recepcionista: En los cubos grises de la entrada.
Marta: ¿Y cuándo abren la piscina por la mañana?
Recepcionista: A las siete y cierran a las nueve de la noche. La piscina de los niños abre de ocho de la mañana a siete de la tarde.
Marta: ¿Dónde podemos aparcar el coche?
Recepcionista: En el garaje. Ahora les enseño dónde está.
Marta: ¿Hay algún supermercado cerca de aquí?
Recepcionista: Sí, hay varios. Aquí tienen toda la información que necesitan sobre la zona y también las instrucciones del apartamento.

Dialogue

Martha:	Good afternoon. We have an apartment reserved in the name of Gómez.
Receptionist:	Let's see. Yes, you have apartment number twenty-seven. This way, please. (*At the apartment*) As you can see, it has two bathrooms, two bedrooms with two beds, a sitting room with a balcony, and this is the kitchen.
Martha:	Does it have a washing machine and a microwave?
Receptionist:	Yes. It also has a dishwasher, gas cooker, fridge and freezer. The blankets and towels are in the bedroom wardrobes (lit: are in the wardrobes of the bedrooms).
Martha:	What day do they come to clean?
Receptionist:	On Mondays and Thursdays (lit: the Mondays and the Thursdays).
Martha:	Where should we leave the rubbish? (lit: where does one leave the rubbish?)
Receptionist:	In the grey bins at the entrance.
Martha:	And when do they open the swimming pool in the morning?
Receptionist:	At seven and they close at nine in the evening. The children's swimming pool opens from eight in the morning till seven in the evening.
Martha:	Where can we park the car?
Receptionist:	In the garage. I'll show you now where it is (lit: Now I show you where it is).
Martha:	Are there any supermarkets near here?
Receptionist:	Yes, there are several. Here you have all the information that you need on the area and also the instructions for the apartment.

7. At the apartment

7.1 New words

a las siete	at seven o'clock	instrucciones (f/pl)	instructions
abre	he/she/it opens, you [ud] open	jueves	Thursday
		lavadora (f)	washing machine
abren	you [uds]/they open	lavaplatos (m)	dishwasher
aparcar	to park	limpiar	to clean
apartamento (m)	apartment, flat	lunes	Monday
armario (m)	wardrobe, cupboard	mañana (f)	morning
basura (f)	rubbish	manta (f)	blanket
cama (f)	bed	Marta	Martha
cerca	near, nearby, close	microondas (m)	microwave
cerca de	near, close to	necesitan	you [uds]/they need
cierran	you [uds]/they close	nevera (f)	fridge
coche (m)	car	niño (m)	child, boy
cocina (f)	kitchen, cooker	número (m)	number
cocina de gas (f)	gas cooker	piscina (f)	swimming pool
como	as	que	that
congelador (m)	freezer	qué día	what day, when
cuándo	when	reservado	reserved
cubo (m)	bin	salón (m)	sitting room
deja	he/she/it leaves, you [ud] leave	se deja	one leaves
		sobre	on, about, on top of
del	of the	supermercado (m)	supermarket
enseño	I show	terraza (f)	balcony
entrada (f)	entrance	toalla (f)	towel
ésta	this, this one	toda	all (f)
garaje (m)	garage	varios	several
gris	grey	vienen	you [uds]/they come
hay	there is, there are	zona (f)	area, zone
información (f)	information		

7.2 Watch out for your pronunciation

→ Let's practise the letter 'a'. Notice that the Spanish 'a', unlike in English, always has the same sound: *apartamento, información, hay, mantas, Marta, zona, sangría, vegetariano, mayonesa, mineral.*

→ Now let's compare the letters 'a' and 'e'. Listen to these words and repeat them: *abren, cerca, deja, nevera, Beatriz, caliente, grande, botella, ensalada, pescado.*

7.3 Important notes

→ Let's also practise how to link words together in speech: *tenemos un apartamento, vamos a ver, por aquí, dos habitaciones, están en los armarios, vienen a limpiar, aparcar el coche*. To revise how to link words together, go to p. 31.

→ Difficult words: Listen to these words and practise saying them: *terraza, lavadora, microondas, lavaplatos, congelador, toallas, armarios, jueves, piscina, coche, garaje, supermercado, instrucciones*.

→ An effective way of improving your pronunciation is to record yourself and compare your pronunciation to that of the Spanish speakers.

7.3 Important notes

→ *Tiene* means: 'he/she/it has' and 'you have' (where 'you' is *usted*, one person only). So, *¿tiene agua?*, for instance, can mean: 'do you have water?', 'does he have water?', 'does she have water?', 'does it have water?'. It may sound confusing, but in a particular context you will always know what is being said.

→ *Ésta* and *está* mean: 'this' or 'this one', and 'is'. Compare these examples: *ésta es la terraza* (this is the balcony), *ésta es grande* (this one is big), *la mesa está en la cocina* (the table is in the kitchen).

→ *Es* and *está*. As we saw on p. 12, the main difference between these two verbs is that *es* (he/she/it is, you [ud] are) is used to refer to facts that do not change or change very slowly (like sizes), whereas *está* (he/she/it is, you [ud] are) refers to situations that may change (like where something or someone is).

→ *Del* = *de* + *el* (of the). Notice that we say *del* hotel (of the hotel), but *de la* terraza (of the balcony). Remember *al* (*a* + *el*) and *a la* which we saw on p. 32.

→ *De la mañana* and *por la mañana*. *De la mañana* is used when telling the time, for instance in *las ocho de la mañana* (eight in the morning), whereas *por la mañana* is used without giving an exact time, for instance in *¿cuándo abren por la mañana?*

7. At the apartment

→ Notice how you say 'on Mondays', 'on Thursdays' in Spanish: *los lunes, los jueves.*

→ Other useful expressions: *como pueden ver* (as you can see), *¿qué día?* (what day? when?), *cerca de aquí* (near here, nearby).

7.4 Tip of the day

> When going through the dialogues, read them out loud as if you were actually talking to someone. If you only read them quietly, you'll find it difficult to speak up when the time comes.

7.5 You may wonder...

What is the plural of el microondas *and* el lavaplatos? *Los microondas* and *los lavaplatos.* Notice that only *el* changes.

What is the difference between ¿qué día? *and* ¿cuándo?? *¿Cuándo?* is more general. It can refer to what time of day, or which day, month, year, etc., whereas *¿qué día?* means literally 'what day?'.

What is the difference between qué *and* que? Generally speaking, *qué* means 'what' and *que* means 'that'. Compare: *¿qué van a tomar?* (what are you going to have) and *la información que necesitan* (the information that you need).

7.6 Spanish words with something in common

→ *Reservado* and *reservada* both mean 'reserved'. *Reservado* is used with masculine singular words (*tengo un apartamento reservado a nombre de ...*, I have an apartment reserved in the name of...) and *reservada* with feminine singular words (*tengo una mesa reservada a nombre de ...*, I have a table reserved in the name of).

7.7 Building up new sentences

→ *Algo* and *algún*. *Algo* means 'anything' when asking a question ¿*algo más?* (anything else?) and 'something' when making a statement *tengo algo* (I have something). *Algún* means 'any' and 'some'. It's used before masculine singular nouns: ¿*hay algún supermercado?* (are there any supermarkets?), *algún día* (some day).

→ *Todo*, *toda* and *todas*: on p. 23 we saw that *todo* and *todas* both mean 'all' or 'the whole'. *Toda* means the same and is used with feminine singular words. Compare: *todo el apartamento* (the whole apartment), *todas las toallas* (all the towels), *toda la basura* (all the rubbish).

→ *Abre* (he/she/it opens, you [ud] open) and *abren* (you [uds]/they open).

7.7 Building up new sentences

Hay tres camas pequeñas en la habitación.
There are three small beds in the bedroom.

¿Qué día vamos a cenar con Margarita?
When are we going to have dinner with Margaret?

¿Dónde están las toallas de los niños?
Where are the children's towels?

¿Cuándo cierran la piscina?
When do they close the swimming pool?

¿Hay algún hotel cerca de aquí?
Is there a hotel near here?

Aquí tiene las instrucciones del microondas.
Here are the microwave instructions.

Es por la mañana.
It's in the morning.

7.8 Exercises

(See solutions on p. 206)

Exercise 1: Say these sentences in Spanish:

1. There is a large bed in the sitting room.
2. Can we see the apartment balcony?
3. They have a small kitchen.
4. Where are the blankets?
5. When do they open the swimming pool?
6. Are there any garages near here?
7. What day do the children come?
8. What do you [uds] want to have for dinner?
9. Do you [uds] have a car?
10. They open at nine in the morning.

Exercise 2: Which phrase is the answer to each question you hear? Read all the answers before you play the questions in the recordings:

1. Sí, hay dos.
2. En el cubo de la entrada.
3. Doce euros y veinte céntimos.
4. En el armario del baño.
5. Sopa de pescado y espaguetis.
6. El jueves por la mañana.
7. A las nueve de la noche.
8. Una tónica y un zumo de naranja.
9. Lo siento, está completo.
10. A las ocho.

7.8 Exercises

Exercise 3: Which is the odd one out in each group?

1. la mañana	la tarde	el coche	la noche
2. siete	dieciocho	treinta	nombre
3. el baño	el pavo	la cocina	el salón
4. la lavadora	el microondas	la botella	la nevera
5. el batido	la leche	el vino	el pollo
6. el ron	la mayonesa	la cerveza	la sangría
7. el vaso	la sopa	la ensalada	la tortilla
8. José	Inglaterra	Juan	Javier
9. la sardina	el atún	el salmón	la caña
10. el café	el descafeinado	la manta	el té

Exercise 4: What would you put before each of the words below: *el* or *la*?

1. ..... nombre
2. ..... salón
3. ..... habitación
4. ..... congelador
5. ..... noche
6. ..... tarde
7. ..... coche
8. ..... garaje
9. ..... información
10. ..... café

Lesson 8. At the supermarket 1

Diálogo 1

Francisco: Disculpe, ¿me puede decir dónde están los carritos y las cestas?
Dependienta: En la entrada principal.
Francisco: ¿Y sabe dónde puedo encontrar el aceite y la fruta?
Dependienta: El aceite está junto a la carne y la fruta en el pasillo central.
Francisco: (*En el puesto de la fruta*) Buenos días, ¿me puede poner un kilo de fresas, dos de plátanos y medio de kiwis?
Dependienta: ¿Algo más?
Francisco: Sí, dos kilos de manzanas, un melón y una sandía.
Dependienta: ¿Qué más?
Francisco: ¿Cuánto cuestan las uvas?
Dependienta: Dos con cincuenta el kilo.
Francisco: Vale. ¿Me puede poner medio kilo?
Dependienta: ¿Alguna cosa más?
Francisco: No. Eso es todo. ¿Pago aquí o en caja?
Dependienta: Se paga todo en caja.
Francisco: Muchas gracias. Hasta luego.
Dependienta: Hasta luego. ¿Quién es el siguiente?

Diálogo 2

Francisco: (*En el puesto de las verduras*) Hola, necesito medio kilo de cebollas, un pepino, una lechuga y dos pimientos verdes. ¿Tiene espárragos?
Dependienta: Sólo tenemos espárragos en lata. Están junto al azúcar y las galletas. ¿Qué más le pongo?
Francisco: Dos kilos de tomates, uno de zanahorias y medio de champiñones.
Dependienta: No me quedan champiñones. ¿Alguna otra cosa?
Francisco: No, eso es todo, gracias.
Dependienta: De nada.

Dialogue 1

Frank:	Excuse me, can you tell me where the trolleys and baskets are?
Shop assistant:	At the main entrance.
Frank:	And do you know where I can find the oil and the fruit?
Shop assistant:	The oil is next to the meat, and the fruit in the central aisle.
Frank:	(*At the fruit stall*) Good morning, can you give me one kilo of strawberries, two of bananas and a half of kiwis? (lit: can you put me ...)
Shop assistant:	Anything else? (lit: anything more?)
Frank:	Yes, two kilos of apples, a melon and a watermelon.
Shop assistant:	What else? (lit: what more?)
Frank:	How much do the grapes cost?
Shop assistant:	Two fifty per kilo.
Frank:	OK. Can you give me half a kilo? (lit: Can you put me ...)
Shop assistant:	Anything else? (lit: Anything more?)
Frank:	No. That's everything. Do I pay here or at the till?
Shop assistant:	Everything's paid at the till.
Frank:	Thank you very much. See you later.
Shop assistant:	See you later. Who's next? (lit: Who is the next?)

Dialogue 2

Frank:	(*At the vegetable stall*) Hello, I need half a kilo of onions, a cucumber, a lettuce and two green peppers. Do you have asparagus?
Shop assistant:	We only have tinned asparagus (lit: asparagus in tin). They're next to the sugar and the biscuits. What else can I give you? (lit: what more do I put you?)
Frank:	Two kilos of tomatoes, one of carrots and a half of mushrooms.
Shop assistant:	I don't have any mushrooms left. Anything else? (lit: any other thing?)
Frank:	No, that's everything, thanks.
Shop assistant:	You're welcome (lit: Of nothing).

8. At the supermarket 1

8.1 New words

aceite (m)	oil	manzana (f)	apple
alguna	any, some (f)	medio	half
azúcar (m)	sugar	melón (m)	melon
caja (f)	till, box	necesito	I need
carrito (m)	trolley	no	no
cebolla (f)	onion	pago	I pay
central	central	pasillo (m)	aisle, corridor
cesta (f)	basket	pepino (m)	cucumber
champiñón (m)	mushroom	pimiento (m)	pepper, capsicum
cosa (f)	thing	plátano (m)	banana
cuánto cuestan ...	how much are ...	poner	to put
cuestan	they cost	principal	main
de nada	you're welcome	puesto (m)	stall
dependienta (f)	shop assistant	qué más	what else
disculpe	excuse me	quién	who
encontrar	to find	sabe	he/she//it knows, you [ud] know
espárrago (m)	asparagus		
Francisco	Frank	sandía (f)	watermelon
fresa (f)	strawberry	se paga	it is paid, one pays
fruta (f)	fruit	siguiente	next
galleta (f)	biscuit	sólo	only
junto a	next to	tomate (m)	tomato
kilo (m)	kilo	uva (f)	grape
kiwi (m)	kiwi	verdes	green (m/pl, f/pl)
lata (f)	tin, can	verduras (f/pl)	vegetables
lechuga (f)	lettuce	zanahoria (f)	carrot

8.2 Watch out for your pronunciation

→ Let's practise the letter 'i'. Notice that, unlike in English, the Spanish 'i' always has the same sound: *microondas, varios, Francisco, pimientos, hielo, medio, cafetería*.

→ Now let's compare the letters 'i' and 'e'. Listen to these words and repeat them: *limón, té, aire, sirve, tiene, pepino, aceite, disculpe*.

8.3 Important notes

→ Stress: Make sure you know where to stress these words: *apartamento, habitaciones, principal, aparcar, supermercado, información, instrucciones, café, chocolate, jerez.*

→ Difficult words: Listen to these words and practise saying them: *carritos, cestas, plátanos, uvas, caja, siguiente, verduras, espárragos, azúcar, zanahorias, champiñones.*

8.3 Important notes

→ Nouns ending in 'e' can be either masculine or feminine. So, to know whether *aceite* or *leche* take *el* or *la*, the simplest thing is to learn *el aceite* and *la leche*, rather than just *aceite* and *leche*.

→ *No me queda* and *no me quedan*. Notice the difference: *no me queda* is used with mass nouns (i.e. those referring to things that cannot be counted), like 'water': *no me queda agua* (I don't have any water left). *No me quedan* is used with nouns that can be counted, like 'peppers': *no me quedan pimientos* (I don't have any peppers left).

→ Other useful expressions: *junto a* (next to), *¿me puede poner?* (can you give me?), *¿qué más?* (what else?), *¿cuánto cuestan ...?* (how much are ...?), *¿alguna cosa más?* (anything else?), *en lata* (tinned), *¿qué más le pongo?* (what else can I give you?), *no me quedan ...* (I don't have any ... left), *¿alguna otra cosa?* (anything else?), *de nada* (you're welcome).

8.4 Tip of the day

Reading the dialogues along with the Spanish speakers in the recordings will dramatically improve your pronunciation, intonation and speed.

8.5 You may wonder...

What is the difference between **sólo** *and* **solo**? *Sólo* means 'only', whereas *solo* (without the accent) means 'alone', 'on its own' or 'on his own'.

What is the difference between **algo más, alguna cosa más** *and* **alguna otra cosa**? Not much, really. They all translate as 'anything else', although the first two literally mean 'anything more', and *alguna otra cosa* literally means 'any other thing'.

What is the difference between **junto al** *and* **junto a**? *Junto al* (next to the) is used before *el* nouns: *junto al supermercado* (next to the supermarket). *Junto a* is used in all other occasions: *junto a los supermercados* (next to the supermarkets), *junto a la piscina* (next to the pool), *junto a las casas* (next to the houses), *junto a un supermercado* (next to a supermarket), etc.

Can you say **¿dónde están los carritos?** *(where are the trolleys?) without* **¿me puede decir?** *(can you tell me?)?* Yes, it is the same as in English. You can say 'where are the trolleys?' instead of 'can you tell me where the trolleys are?' The only difference is that it is not as polite.

Why does **champiñones** *not have an accent, unlike* **champiñón**? Roughly speaking, because *champiñones* is stressed on the second last vowel, which is the default, whereas *champiñón* is stressed on the last vowel, which is not the default. We have also seen: *habitación* and *habitaciones*.

8.6 Spanish words with something in common

→ *Se sirve* (is served, one serves), *se deja* (is left, one leaves), *se paga* (is paid, one pays). We will come back to this on p. 153.

→ *Verde* (green) and *las verduras* (vegetables, greens).

→ *Pongo* (I put) and *poner* (to put).

→ *Pago* (I pay) and *se paga* (is paid, one pays).

8.7 Building up new sentences

→ *Necesito* (I need) and *necesitan* (you [uds]/they need). See page 234

→ Looking at the verbs in this section, we can now tell that some patterns begin to merge. Verbs ending in 'o' refer to 'I', for example: *pongo* (I put) or *pago* (I pay); and those ending in 'n' to 'you' [*uds*] and 'they', for example: *necesitan* (you/they need) or *vienen* (you/they come). We will see more patterns as we progress. Alternatively, go to page 233

→ *Cuánto* (how much) is used when followed by a verb like *cuestan* or *es*, and *cuántas* (how many) is used when followed by a feminine plural noun, like *noches*.

8.7　Building up new sentences

¿Dónde están las sandías?
Where are the watermelons?

¿Me puede poner dos kilos de zanahorias?
Can you give me two kilos of carrots?

¿Cuánto cuestan las manzanas?
How much are the apples?

El melón se paga en caja.
The melon is paid for at the till.

No nos quedan uvas.
We don't have any grapes left.

No me queda leche.
I don't have any milk left.

¿Quién es?
Who is it?

8.8 Exercises

(See solutions on p. 207)

Exercise 1: Say these sentences in Spanish:

1. Where are the grapes?
2. The sugar is next to the oil.
3. How much are the biscuits?
4. We have tinned mushrooms.
5. I only have two euros.
6. I need the car.
7. I don't have any towels left.
8. When can I see the apartment?
9. Can you [ud] give me two kilos of strawberries?
10. Who is Margaret?

Exercise 2: Which of the two words is being said?

1. el carrito	los carritos	2. la cesta	las cestas
3. la fresa	las fresas	4. el plátano	los plátanos
5. la manzana	las manzanas	6. la uva	las uvas
7. el kilo	los kilos	8. la caja	las cajas
9. la cebolla	las cebollas	10. la lechuga	las lechugas

Exercise 3: Match the English with the Spanish expressions:

1. yo también	that's everything
2. eso es todo	let's see
3. cómo no	at the end
4. quédese con el cambio	me too
5. ahora mismo	as you can see
6. vamos a ver	of course
7. como pueden ver	you're welcome
8. cerca de aquí	keep the change
9. al fondo	near here
10. de nada	right away

8.8 Exercises

Exercise 4: How would you translate these sentences?

1. ¿Puedo ver las cestas?
1. *Translation:* ....

2. ¿Dónde están los espárragos en lata?
2. *Translation:* ....

3. Hay diez niños en la piscina.
3. *Translation:* ....

4. La fruta está en la nevera.
4. *Translation:* ....

5. Vamos a tomar fresas.
5. *Translation:* ....

6. Quiero un zumo de manzana.
6. *Translation:* ....

7. ¿Cuándo vienen al supermercado?
7. *Translation:* ....

8. La carne está en el congelador.
8. *Translation:* ....

9. ¿Qué día vamos a cenar con mi amigo?
9. *Translation:* ....

10. No me quedan sandías grandes.
10. *Translation:* ....

Lesson 9. The family

Monólogo

Hola, me llamo Nicolás. Vivo en Segovia con mi familia en una casa con jardín. Mi mamá se llama Beatriz y mi papá se llama Francisco. Mi hermano se llama Bernardo y mi hermana Carmen. El padre de mi mamá se llama Javier y la madre de mi mamá se llama Juana. Yo soy su nieto.

   El abuelo Javier y la abuela Juana tienen un hijo y dos hijas: el tío Joaquín, la tía Susana y mi mamá. El tío Joaquín está casado con Rocío y tienen dos hijos: Emilia y Tomás. Emilia es mi prima y Tomás mi primo. La tía Susana está divorciada y tiene un bebé. No sé cómo se llama su ex marido.

   Mi papá tiene tres hermanos: Enrique, Luis y Natalia. Enrique está separado y Luis está viudo, pero tiene un gato y un perro. El tío Enrique tiene una hija que se llama Clara. La tía Natalia está soltera pero se casa mañana. Vamos a ir todos a la boda. Su novio se llama Alfredo y es hermano de la tía Rocío, la mujer del tío Joaquín. Mi prima Emilia es sobrina de Alfredo y Tomás es su sobrino, y Clara es sobrina de Natalia. Ahora él va a ser tío de Clara, y ella va a ser tía de Emilia y Tomás. ¡Qué lío! Menos mal que estoy soltero.

MONOLOGUE

Hello, my name is Nicholas. I live in Segovia with my family in a house with a garden (lit: in a house with garden). My mum is called Beatrice and my dad is called Frank. My brother is called Bernard and my sister, Carmen. My mum's father is called Javier and my mum's mother is called Joanna. I'm their grandson.

Grandfather Javier and Grandmother Joanna have one son and two daughters: Uncle Joachim, Aunt Susan and my mum. Uncle Joachim is married to Rocio and they have two children: Emily and Thomas. Emily is my female cousin and Thomas is my male cousin. Aunt Susan is divorced and has a baby. I don't know what her ex-husband is called.

My dad has three siblings: Henry, Louis and Natalie. Henry is separated and Louis is a widower (lit: Louis is widowed), but he has a cat and a dog. Uncle Henry has a daughter who is called Clare. Aunt Natalie is single but she's getting married tomorrow (lit: but gets married tomorrow). We are all going to the wedding (lit: we're going to go ...). Her fiancé is called Alfred and is the brother of Aunt Rocio (lit: is brother of Aunt Rocio), Uncle Joachim's wife. My cousin Emily is Alfred's niece, and Thomas is his nephew, and Clare is Natalie's niece. Now he's going to be Clare's uncle, and she's going to be Emily's and Thomas's aunt. What a mess! It's just as well that I'm single.

⇒ Can you build Nicholas's family tree?   (See solution on p. 229)

9. The family

9.1 New words

abuela (f)	grandmother	Nicolás	Nicholas
abuelo (m)	grandfather	nieta (f)	granddaughter
abuelos (m/pl)	grandparents, grandfathers	nieto (m)	grandson
		nietos (m/pl)	grandchildren, grandsons
Alfredo	Alfred	no sé	I don't know
bebé (m)	baby	novia (f)	fiancée, girlfriend
Bernardo	Bernard		
boda (f)	wedding	novio (m)	fiancé, boyfriend
casado	married (m)		
Clara	Clare	padre (m)	father
divorciada	divorced (f)	papá (m)	dad
él	he	pero	but
ella	she	perro (m)	dog
Emilia	Emily	prima (f)	(female) cousin
Enrique	Henry	primo (m)	(male) cousin
estoy	I am	qué lío	what a mess
ex	ex	sé	I know
familia (f)	family	se casa	he/she/you get(s) married, is/are getting married
gato (m)	cat		
hermana (f)	sister	se llama	he/she/it is called, you [ud] are called
hermano (m)	brother		
hermanos (m/pl)	brothers and sisters, siblings, brothers	separado	separated
		ser	to be
hija (f)	daughter	sobrina (f)	niece
hijo (m)	son	sobrino (m)	nephew
hijos (m/pl)	children, sons	soltero	single
ir	to go	soy	I am
jardín (m)	garden	su	his, her, their, your[1]
Joaquín	Joachim	Susana	Susan
Juana	Joanna	tía (f)	aunt
Luis	Louis	tío (m)	uncle
madre (f)	mother	todos	all
mamá (f)	mum	Tomás	Thomas
mañana	tomorrow	va	he/she/it goes/is going, you [ud] go/are going
marido (m)	husband		
menos mal	it's just as well	viudo	widowed, widower
monólogo (m)	monologue	vivo	I live
mujer (f)	wife, woman		
Natalia	Natalie		

---

[1]For more details about *su*, go to p. 68

9.2 Watch out for your pronunciation

→ Repeat after the Spanish speaker: *ja, je, ji, jo, ju; ha, he, hi, ho, hu.*

→ Let's practise the letter 'j'. Notice the difference between the English and the Spanish 'j'. Listen to these words and repeat them: *jardín, caja, naranja, mujer, jerez, garaje, mensaje, Jorge, José, Juana, jueves, junto.*

→ Now let's revise the letter 'h'. Remember that it is silent. Listen to these words and repeat them: *hijo, hija, hermana, hotel, hay, zanahoria, hielo.*

→ Difficult words: Listen to these words and practise saying them: *bebé, vivo, nieto, Emilia, Enrique, divorciada, viudo, novio, pero, perro.*

9.3 Important notes

→ *Soy* and *estoy*. The main difference between these two words is that *soy* (I am) is used to refer to facts that change very slowly or do not change at all (like being someone's grandchild), whereas *estoy* (I am) refers to situations that can change at any point (like being single, or location). We have seen *eres* vs *estás* and *es* vs *está* on pp. 12 and 51 respectively.

→ *Soltero, soltera, solteros, solteras*. Remember that Spanish describing words have to agree (i.e. be masculine or feminine, singular or plural) with the noun they describe. Here are some examples of these describing words in use: *el tío Jorge está soltero* (uncle George is single), *la tía Ana está soltera* (aunt Anne is single), *los amigos de Cristina están solteros* (Christine's friends are single), *las amigas de Javier están solteras* (Javier's friends are single).

→ *Grande* and *grandes*, *principal* and *principales*. When the describing word does not end in an 'o' in the masculine form, there are only two possible forms of the word, instead of four. One is singular, and used with both masculine and feminine nouns (*grande, individual*), and the other one is plural, also used with both masculine and feminine nouns (*grandes, individuales*). Here are some examples of these describing

9. The family

words in use: *el coche grande* (the large car), *la mesa grande* (the large table), *los coches grandes* (the large cars), *las mesas grandes* (the large tables); *el garaje individual* (the single garage), *la habitación individual* (the single room), *los garajes individuales* (the single garages), *las habitaciones individuales* (the single rooms).

→ *Su* means his, her, their, your (where you = ud or uds). So, when you say, for example, *su apartamento*, you could be saying 'his apartment', 'her apartment', 'their apartment', 'your apartment'. This may look confusing at first, but in context it is usually clear who it refers to.

→ Negative sentences: Notice how the word *no* always goes before the verb: *no sé* (I do not know), *no me quedan* ... (I do not have any ... left).

→ Other useful expressions: *no sé* (I don't know), *¡qué lío!* (what a mess!), *menos mal* (it's just as well).

9.4 Tip of the day

Don't waste time making lists of words or flash cards. Instead, practise building up sentences with the words you've learned so far in this course. They're all listed under the dialogue they first come up in, and included in the glossary at the end.

9.5 You may wonder...

Where is Segovia? Segovia is a Spanish city. To find out where it is, look at the map on p. 230.

***In the monologue, why do you say* yo soy su nieto *and not simply* soy su nieto?** The word *yo* is used here to highlight the fact that I am talking about myself, and not about someone else mentioned in the same paragraph.

How do you say **the parents?** *Los padres*, which also means *the fathers*, the plural of *el padre* (the father).

Does **el novio** *mean both* **the boyfriend** *and* **the fiancé?** Yes, it does.

How do you say **the girlfriend?** *La novia*.

How do you say **see you tomorrow?** *Hasta mañana*.

How do you say **tomorrow morning?** *Mañana por la mañana*.

How do you say **your** *in Spanish?* 'Your' (referring to 'you' = *tú*) is *tu*, 'your' (referring to 'you' = *vosotros*) is *vuestro*.

9.6 Spanish words with something in common

- *Él* (he) and *ella* (she).

- *El pimiento* (the pepper, the capsicum) and *la pimienta* (the pepper [a spice]).

- *Todo, todos, toda* and *todas*. We can now guess that these four words mean 'all' or 'the whole'. Like all other describing words, they have to agree with the noun they describe. This is how you use them: *todo el supermercado* (the whole supermarket), *toda la piscina* (the whole swimming pool), *todos los supermercados* (all the supermarkets), *todas las piscinas* (all the swimming pools).

- *Me llamo* (my name is), *te llamas* (your [you = *tú*] name is), *se llama* (his name is, her name is, its name is, your [you = *ud*] name is). Can you guess how you would say 'they are called John and Emily'? Yes, that's right, it is: *se llaman Juan y Emilia*.

- *Soy* (I am), *eres* (you [tú] are), *es* (he/she/it is, you [ud] are). See page 237

- *Sé* (I know), *sabe* (he/she/it knows, you [ud] know). See page 236

- *Voy a* (I am going to), *va a* (he/she/it is going to, you [ud] are going to), *vamos a* (we are going to), *van a* (you [uds]/they are going to).

→ *Mañana* (tomorrow) and *la mañana* (the morning). Notice that *mañana* (tomorrow) comes on its own, never after *la*.

→ *El perro* (the dog) and *pero* (but).

9.7 Building up new sentences

Vivo en Inglaterra con mi hermana.
I live in England with my sister.

La prima de mi madre se llama Beatriz.
My mother's cousin is called Beatrice.

Su sobrina está casada con mi amigo Francisco.
His/her niece is married to my friend Frank.

¿Cómo se llama el bebé de tu prima?
What's your cousin's baby called?

Mañana por la mañana vamos a ir a la piscina de los abuelos.
Tomorrow morning we're going to the grandparent's swimming pool.

¿Qué día es la boda de tu sobrino?
What day is your nephew's wedding?

¿Dónde vive la mujer de tu primo?
Where does your cousin's wife live?

No sé qué quieren.
I don't know what they want.

¿Cón quién está casada Rocío?
Who is Rocio married to?

La boda va a ser en el hotel de mi tío.
The wedding is going to be at my uncle's hotel.

9.8 Exercises

(See solutions on p. 208)

Exercise 1: Say these sentences in Spanish:

1. I live in a flat with my wife.
2. My sister is called Clare.
3. My uncle John is married.
4. What's your niece called?
5. On Monday we have to go to the supermarket.
6. Where is your friend's dog?
7. How much are the strawberries?
8. I don't have any biscuits left.
9. Are there any peppers in the fridge?
10. Can we see grandmother?

Exercise 2: Which sentence is the question for each answer you hear? (Read all the questions before you listen to this exercise in the recordings.)

1. ¿Qué día es la boda de Juana?
2. ¿Cómo se llama el primo de tu amiga?
3. ¿Cómo se llama la prima de tu amigo?
4. ¿Dónde están las toallas?
5. ¿Cuánto cuestan los plátanos?
6. ¿Dónde está el coche de Luis?
7. ¿Con quién está casado Javier?
8. ¿Dónde vive el marido de tu sobrina?
9. ¿Vamos a ir en coche?
10. ¿Cuándo abren el supermercado?

9. The family

Exercise 3: Complete these sentences with the missing words given below:

> Missing words: mantas, cómo, armario, llama, mal, cerca, poner, con, hora, qué.

1. ¿Me puede decir cómo se .... su tía?
2. ¿Me puede .... tres kilos de manzanas?
3. Las copas están en el .... de la cocina.
4. ¿Dónde están las .... de los niños?
5. ¿A qué .... podemos ir a su casa?
6. ¿Hay algún supermercado .... de aquí?
7. ¡........................... lío!
8. Menos .... que tenemos coche.
9. Voy a tomar té .... leche.
10. No sé .... se llama su hermana.

Exercise 4: Write down the plurals of these words:

1. sobrino   ....
2. sobrina   ....
3. soltero   ....
4. separada   ....
5. padre   ....
6. madre   ....
7. principal   ....
8. lavaplatos   ....
9. salón   ....
10. grande   ....

Lesson 10. Numbers: 31 to 100

31	treinta y uno	54	cincuenta y cuatro	77	setenta y siete
32	treinta y dos	59	cincuenta y nueve	80	ochenta
38	treinta y ocho	60	sesenta	82	ochenta y dos
40	cuarenta	65	sesenta y cinco	87	ochenta y siete
43	cuarenta y tres	66	sesenta y seis	90	noventa
44	cuarenta y cuatro	70	setenta	91	noventa y uno
50	cincuenta	76	setenta y seis	100	cien

10.1 Watch out for your pronunciation

→ Let's practise the letter 'o': *uno, dos, cuatro, cinco, ocho, once, doce, catorce, dieciocho, veintiocho, ochenta, noventa.*

→ Make sure you say the 'o' short and clear like in *pot*, and not as in *cosy* or *folk* where the 'o' is lengthened.

→ Watch out for the vowels in these word pairs: *seis* but *sesenta*, *siete* but *setenta*, *nueve* but *noventa*.

→ Listen to these numbers and practise saying them: *treinta y tres, cuarenta y cuatro, cincuenta y cinco, sesenta y seis, setenta y siete, ochenta y ocho, noventa y nueve.*

10.2 Important notes

→ The word *y* (and): Notice that Spanish two-figure numbers have the word *y*, whereas their English translation does not have *and*. Compare: *treinta y siete*/thirty-seven, *cincuenta y ocho*/fifty-eight, *noventa y cinco*/ninety-five.

→ Feminine numbers: All Spanish numbers ending in *uno* also have a feminine form: *una, veintiuna, treinta y una, cuarenta y una, noventa y una,* etc. They are used just like any other number, but before feminine nouns: *tengo una mesa* (I have one table), *tenemos treinta y una llaves* (we have thirty-one keys), *tienen ochenta y una toallas* (they have eighty-one towels).

→ Let's now revise some useful expressions: *yo también* (me too), *lo siento* (I'm sorry), *dentro de una hora* (in an hour), *¿me puede decir ... ?* (can you tell me ...?), *a la derecha* (on the right), *¿nos puede traer ...?* (can you bring us...?), *ahora mismo* (right away), *vamos a ver* (let's see), *junto a* (next to), *no me quedan ...* (I don't have any ... left), *de nada* (you're welcome), *no sé* (I don't know), *menos mal* (it's just as well).

10.3 Tip of the day

Don't learn too many new things in one day. If you have time left after doing a whole lesson, go back and repeat some of the old exercises, or re-read previous dialogues, rather than starting a new lesson.

10.4 You may wonder...

Do any other numbers, apart from those with the word **uno** *in them, have a feminine form?* No. All other numbers are both masculine and feminine.

Are **treinta, cuarenta, cincuenta,** *etc. feminine numbers?* They are both feminine and masculine. Just because they end in 'a' it does not mean that they are only feminine.

Can you add an 's' to the numbers? No. As tempting as it may be to add an 's' to numbers like *cuatro* or *ocho*, all numbers, except for *uno*, are plural by definition.

Are there any other accents on Spanish letters apart from the á, Á, é, É, í, Í, ó, Ó, ú, Ú? No. Unlike French, Spanish has only the < ´ > accent.

10. Numbers: 31 to 100

How do you give phone numbers in Spanish? This is best explained with an example: 91 078 89 92. You can say: *noventa y uno, cero, setenta y ocho, ochenta y nueve, noventa y dos*; or, *nueve uno cero siete ocho ocho nueve nueve dos*.

10.5 Spanish words with something in common

→ Notice the similarity between: *tres/treinta, cuatro/cuarenta, cinco/cincuenta, seis/sesenta, siete/setenta, ocho/ochenta, nueve/noventa*.

10.6 Building up new sentences

Las manzanas cuestan un euro y setenta y nueve céntimos el kilo.
The apples cost one euro and seventy-nine cents per kilo.
Los niños quieren noventa céntimos.
The children want ninty cents.
En la casa de Emilia hay trece gatos.
In Emily's house there are thirteen cats.
Las toallas cuestan veintiún euros.
The towels cost twenty-one euros.
En el armario de la cocina hay treinta y seis vasos.
In the kitchen cupboard there are thirty-six glasses.
Tenemos cuarenta y ocho latas de tomate.
We have forty-eight tins of tomatoes.
Los pimientos en lata cuestan ochenta y nueve céntimos.
The tinned peppers cost eighty-nine cents.
Tengo cien mensajes.
I have one hundred messages.
Tienen setenta y una.
They have seventy-one.
Mi abuelo tiene quince nietos.
My grandfather has fifteen grandchildren.

10.7 Exercises

(See solutions on p. 209)

Exercise 1: Read these numbers out loud in Spanish:

a. 37	*b.* 49	*c.* 53	*d.* 66	*e.* 14
f. 71	*g.* 84	*h.* 0	*i.* 99	*j.* 100

Exercise 2: Which numbers have not been said in the recordings?

a. 22	28	21		*b.* 36	39	37
c. 13	15	11		*d.* 44	46	45
e. 51	52	56		*f.* 66	67	77
g. 77	76	66		*h.* 89	98	99
i. 42	52	92		*j.* 10	12	2

Exercise 3: Write down the figures for the numbers you hear:

a. .... b. .... c. .... d. .... e. ....
f. .... g. .... h. .... i. .... j. ....

Exercise 4: Write down the telephone numbers you hear:

a. .... b. ....
c. .... d. ....
e. .... f. ....
g. .... h. ....
i. .... j. ....

Lesson 11. Telling the time

This is how you tell the time in Spanish:

es la una
it's one o'clock

son las dos
it's two o'clock

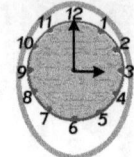
son las tres
it's three o'clock

son las cuatro
it's four o'clock

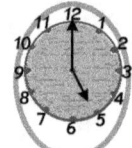
son las cinco
it's five o'clock

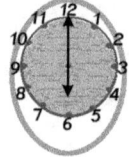
son las seis
it's six o'clock

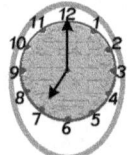
son las siete
it's seven o'clock

son las ocho
it's eight o'clock

son las nueve
it's nine o'clock

son las diez
it's ten o'clock

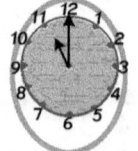
son las once
it's eleven o'clock

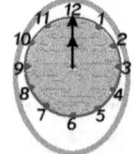
son las doce
it's twelve o'clock

This is how you ask the time:

¿Qué hora es?
What time is it?

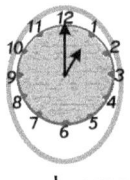 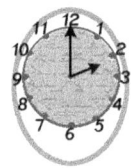 

    es la una   son las dos   son las tres

it's one o'clock   *it's two o'clock*   *it's three o'clock*

This is how you ask what time something is taking place:

¿A qué hora vienen?
What time are they coming?

 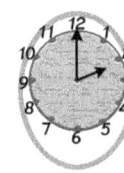 

    a la una   a las dos   a las tres

at one o'clock   *at two o'clock*   *at three o'clock*

11. Telling the time

This is how you tell other times:

es la una y veinticinco	son las dos y media
it's twenty-five past one	*it's half past two*
son las tres menos cinco	son las cuatro menos veinticinco
it's five to three	*it's twenty-fve to four*
son las cinco menos cuarto	son las seis y cinco
it's quarter to five	*it's five past six*
son las siete menos diez	son las ocho y diez
it's ten to seven	*it's ten past eight*
son las nueve y cuarto	son las diez
it's quarter past nine	*it's ten o'clock*
son las once y veinte	son las doce menos veinte
it's twenty past eleven	*it's twenty to twelve*

This is another way of telling the time:

¿Qué hora es?
What time is it?

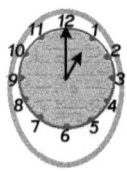  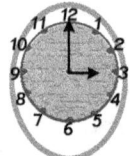

la una — las dos — las tres
one o'clock — *two o'clock* — *three o'clock*

11.1 New words

menos	minus, to	*son*	you [uds]/they are	*y*	and, past

11.2 Watch out for your pronunciation

→ Repeat after the Spanish speaker: *ga, go, gu, gue, gui, ge, gi.*

→ Compare: *ga/ja, ge/gue/je, gi/gui/ji, go/jo, gu/ju.*

→ Let's practise the letter 'g': *garaje, amigo, agua, segundo, gracias, Inglaterra, vegetariano, congelador, espaguetis, siguiente.*

→ Notice that the 'u' is silent when it comes after a 'g' and is followed by 'e' or 'i' as in 'gue' and 'gui'.

→ Let's now revise the letter 'j': *José, dejar, equipaje, jerez, jueves, junto, hijo, jardín, mujer.*

→ Joining words together: When people tell you the time, it tends to sound fast. Notice that it is these numbers in particular that are tricky to understand, because they get joined to *las*: *las seis y media, las siete y cuarto, las ocho menos diez, las once menos cinco.*

→ Be careful with *las dos/las doce*, and *las seis/las siete*. They can be easily confused.

→ Difficult words: Listen to these words and practise saying them: *las cuatro y cuarto, las doce menos diez, las cinco menos veinticinco, las nueve y veinte, las doce y cinco, las dos y diez.*

11.3 Important notes

→ *Es la una* but *son las dos, son las tres*, etc. The reason why we say <u>es</u> *la una* (and not *son*) is because *una* is singular. All the other hours are plural and, therefore, go with *son*: *son las cuatro, son las siete*, etc.

→ Notice that the answer to *¿qué hora es?* can be either, for instance, *son las dos y media* or *las dos y media*. As we have seen in the previous dialogues, Spanish speakers tend to drop unnecessary words, so you are more likely to hear *las dos y media* than *son las dos y media* when asking the time. But they are both correct.

→ When writing the time down, you should put 2:35 instead of 2.35 (i.e. use a colon instead of a dot).

→ Useful expressions: *¿qué hora es?* (what time is it?), *de la mañana* (in the morning), *de la tarde* (in the afternoon, in the evening), *de la noche* (in the evening, at night).

11.4 Tip of the day

Not all study days are equally fruitful. Sometimes you'll have the feeling that you're not learning anything. Occasionally you'll even feel that you're forgetting more than you're learning. Don't worry, this is normal, so just keep going.

11.5 You may wonder...

Do **y** *and* **menos** *often mean 'past' and 'to'?* No. *Y* and *menos* only mean 'past' and 'to' in a telling the time context.

*When asked ¿***a qué hora vamos a ir?** *can you answer* **las cinco** *instead of* **a las cinco?** No. Generally, when a question starts with *a*, its answer has to start with *a* too.

How do you say 'an hour and a half' and 'two and a half hours'? Una hora y media and dos horas y media.

When do you use **de la mañana, de la tarde** *and* **de la noche?** *De la mañana* is used from 12.01am till noon. *De la tarde* is used from noon till about 8.00pm, and *de la noche* from about 8.00 till midnight. *De la tarde* and *de la noche* are quite flexible terms and people often use them depending on the sun. In summer you often hear *las nueve de la tarde* and in winter *las siete de la noche*.

Do you ever use the 24 hour clock in Spanish? Yes, very frequently. Unlike English, Spanish seldom uses *am* and *pm*. Instead, you can say either *las cuatro y media de la tarde* or *las dieciséis treinta*, for instance, although the first one is much more common in non-business communications.

11.6 Spanish words with something in common

- → *Cuatro* (four) and *cuarto* (quarter).

- → *La una* (one o'clock) and *una* (one, a).

- → *Medio* (half, [masculine]) and *media* (half, [feminine]).

- → *Más* (more) and *menos* (less, minus, to).

- → *Soy* (I am), *eres* (you [tú] are), *es* (he/she/it is, you [ud] are), *son* (you [uds]/they are). See page 237

11.7 Building up new sentences

Son las cuatro y veinte de la tarde.
It's twenty past four in the afternoon.
Vienen a las siete de la mañana.
They're coming at seven in the morning.
Vienen mañana por la mañana a las ocho y media.
They're coming tomorrow morning at half past eight.
Vamos a cenar a las nueve.
We're going to have dinner at nine.
Abren a las nueve y media de la mañana.
They open at nine thirty (or half past nine) in the morning.
Cierran a las doce y media de la noche.
They close at half past twelve at night (or half past midnight)
Van a ir a la una de la tarde.
They're going to go at one in the afternoon (at 1.00pm)

11.8 Exercises

(See solutions on p. 210)

Exercise 1: Say these sentences in Spanish:

a. It's 3.30pm.   b. It's 1.15am.
c. It's 10.05pm. d. It's 11.10am.
e. It's 3.45pm.   f. It's 2.10pm.
g. It's 4.35pm.   h. It's 11.20pm.
i. It's 12.45pm. j. It's 6.40pm.

Exercise 2: Which time has been said in each case?

a.	12:15	2:15	10:15
b.	2:40	6:20	3:20
c.	4:35	4:25	3:35
d.	4:50	10:05	5:10
e.	6:55	6:05	5:55
f.	5:11	11:05	11:55
g.	2:30	12:30	10:30
h.	1:50	10:00	1:10
i.	6:50	7:10	6:10
j.	8:20	7:40	8:40

Exercise 3: Match the Spanish sentences with their English translations:

a.	La una y diez	Half past five
b.	Las dos y cuarto	Twenty to eleven
c.	Las dos menos veinticinco	Quarter to seven
d.	Las tres y cinco	Ten to seven
e.	Las tres y veinte	Quarter past two
f.	Las cinco y media	Ten past one
g.	Las siete menos diez	Five to twelve
h.	Las siete menos cuarto	Twenty-five to two
i.	Las once menos veinte	Twenty past three
j.	Las doce menos cinco	Five past three

11.8 Exercises

Exercise 4: Write down the following times using *de la mañana*, *de la tarde* and *de la noche*, for example: 14 : 20 = *son las dos y veinte de la tarde*.

a. 1:35 ....

b. 17:45 ....

c. 24:00 ....

d. 11:15 ....

e. 2:20 ....

f. 3:10 ....

g. 15:25 ....

h. 18:05 ....

i. 6:55 ....

j. 22:30 ....

Lesson 12. Ordering tapas

Note: Some of the words in this lesson - like octopus - might not be everyday words in English, but they are in Spanish and are used when you are having tapas in Spain.

Diálogo

Camarero:	¿Qué vais a tomar?
Silvia:	Una ración de croquetas de jamón y queso y un pincho de tortilla.
Felipe:	Yo voy a pedir canapés de atún y huevos duros rellenos de bonito.
Pablo:	Yo quiero banderillas, aceitunas y una ración de albóndigas caseras.
Laura:	Y yo pulpo a la gallega, gambas en gabardina y setas al jerez.
Camarero:	Vamos a ver. No me quedan ni banderillas ni croquetas.
Silvia:	Entonces una de patatas bravas.
Pablo:	¿Qué otras tapas tienes?
Camarero:	Tengo anchoas, calamares fritos, chorizos, buñuelos de bacalao, callos a la madrileña, almejas con setas, berenjenas fritas, jamón serrano ...
Pablo:	¿Tienes calamares a la romana?
Camarero:	Hoy no me quedan.
Pablo:	Entonces una de riñones al jerez.
Silvia:	¡A mí no me gustan los riñones!
Camarero:	Las patatas alioli y los caracoles al ajillo están muy buenos.
Felipe:	¡A mí no me gustan los caracoles!
Pablo:	¡Qué pena! ¿Y las morcillas de arroz?
Camarero:	Tampoco tengo morcillas.
Silvia:	¿Te gustan las empanadillas de cerdo?
Pablo:	No, prefiero los mejillones al vapor con limón. ¿Os gustan los mejillones?
Felipe:	Sí, mucho.
Camarero:	Vale. ¿Y para beber?
Silvia:	Cuatro cañas.

Dialogue

Waiter:	What are you going to have?
Sylvia:	A portion of ham and cheese croquettes, and a small portion of Spanish potato omelette.
Philip:	I'm going to order tuna canapés and hard boiled eggs (lit: hard eggs) stuffed with tuna.
Paul:	I want banderillas[1], olives and a portion of homemade meatballs.
Laura:	And I (want) Galician-style octopus, prawns in batter, and mushrooms in sherry.
Waiter:	Let's see. I don't have any banderillas or croquettes left.
Sylvia:	Then one portion of spicy potatoes (lit: Then one of spicy potatoes).
Paul:	What other tapas do you have?
Waiter:	I have anchovies, fried squid, spicy sausages, cod fritters, Madrid-style tripe, clams with mushrooms, fried aubergines, Spanish cured ham ...
Paul:	Do you have batter-fried squid?
Waiter:	Today I don't have any left.
Paul:	Then one (portion) of kidneys in sherry.
Sylvia:	I don't like kidneys!
Waiter:	The potatoes in garlic mayonnaise and the garlic snails are very good.
Philip:	I don't like snails!
Paul:	What a pity! And rice blood sausages?
Waiter:	I don't have blood sausages either.
Sylvia:	Do you like pork pasties?
Paul:	No, I prefer steamed mussels with lemon. Do you like mussels?
Philip:	Yes, very much (lit: Yes, much).
Waiter:	OK. And to drink?
Sylvia:	Four small beers.

---

[1] *Banderillas*: pickled onions, gherkins, peppers, etc., on cocktail sticks.

12. Ordering tapas

12.1 New words

aceituna (f)	olive	jamón (m)	ham
albóndiga (f)	meatball	jamón serrano (m)	Spanish cured ham
a la gallega	Galician-style	Laura	Laura
a la madrileña	Madrid-style	me gustan	I like
a la romana	batter-fried	mejillón (m)	mussel
alioli (m)	garlic mayonnaise	morcilla (f)	blood sausage
a mí	to me	mucho	much, a lot
al ajillo	with garlic	muy	very
al vapor	steamed	ni ... ni	not ... or, neither ... nor
almeja (f)	clam		
anchoa (f)	anchovy	os gustan	you [vosotros] like
atún (m)	tuna	otras	other, others (f/pl)
bacalao (m)	cod	Pablo	Paul
banderilla (f)	banderilla	patatas bravas (f/pl)	spicy potatoes
berenjena (f)	aubergine	pedir	to ask for, to order
bonito (m)	tuna	pincho (m)	snack, small portion
buenos	good (m/pl)	prefiero	I prefer
buñuelo (m)	fritter	pulpo (m)	octopus
calamar (m)	squid	qué pena	what a pity
callos (m/pl)	tripe	queso (m)	cheese
canapé (m)	canapé	ración (f)	portion
caracol (m)	snail	rellenos	stuffed (m/pl)
caseras	homemade (f/pl)	riñón (m)	kidney
cerdo (m)	pork	seta (f)	mushroom
chorizo (m)	spicy sausage	Silvia	Sylvia
croqueta (f)	croquette	tampoco	not ... either, neither
duros	hard (m/pl)	tapa (f)	tapa, small dish, snack
empanadilla (f)	pasty		
en gabardina	in batter	te gustan	you [tú] like
Felipe	Philip	tienes	you [tú] have
fritos	fried (m/pl)	tortilla (f)	Spanish potato omelette
gamba (f)	prawn		
hoy	today	vais	you [vosotros] go
huevo (m)	egg		

12.2 Watch out for your pronunciation

→ Repeat after the Spanish speaker: *lla, lle, lli, llo, llu; ya, ye, yi, yo, yu*.

12.3 Important notes

- → Let's practise the 'll': *tortilla, rellenos, banderillas, gallega, callos, morcillas, empanadillas.*

- → Let's also practise the 'y': *playa, yo, desayuno, mayonesa.* Notice that the *y* at the end of a word sounds just like the 'i': *hay, hoy, estoy, soy, voy.*

- → Let's now revise the letter 'j'. Pay particular attention to the difference in sound between the English and the Spanish 'j': *jamón, jerez, almejas, berenjenas, ajillo, mejillones.*

- → Difficult words: Listen to the following words and practise saying them: *ración, croquetas, huevos, aceitunas, albóndigas, bravas, anchoas, chorizos, buñuelos, romana, riñones, vapor.*

12.3 Important notes

- → Compare the sentence *¿qué vais a tomar?* (what are you going to have?) in this dialogue with *¿qué van a tomar?* (what are you going to have?) on p. 40. *Vais* refers to *vosotros* which is the colloquial plural form of 'you'. *Van* refers to *ustedes* which is the formal plural form of 'you'. Compare also *¿tienes calamares?* (do you have squid?) in this dialogue, with *¿tiene una mesa para cinco?* (do you have a table for five?) on p. 28. *Tienes* refers to *tú*, which is the colloquial singular form of *you*. *Tiene* refers to *usted* which is the formal singular form of *you*.

- → This may sound a bit confusing at the moment, but you will soon get used to it. Do not worry about it just now. Roughly speaking, if you are talking to people who are your age or with whom you have something in common, you use the *tú* and *vosotros* forms. On more formal occasions, you use the *usted* and *ustedes* forms.

- → *Me gustan* (I like), *te gustan* (you [tú] like), *os gustan* (you [vosotros] like). If you think of *me gustan las patatas* (I like potatoes) as meaning 'potatoes please me'; *te gustan las patatas* (you like potatoes) as meaning 'potatoes please you' (you = tú); and *os gustan las patatas* (you like potatoes) as meaning 'potatoes please you' (you = vosotros), I think it

12. Ordering tapas

makes it easier to understand how these words are used. We will see more about it on p. 127, and in many of the dialogues.

→ **The double negative:** To say 'I don't have any banderillas or croquettes left' in Spanish, you have to say something in the lines of 'I don't have no banderillas nor croquettes left': *no me quedan ni banderillas ni croquetas*. The double negative has to be used.

→ **Other useful expressions:** *a mí no me gustan ...* (I don't like ...), *¡qué pena!* (what a pity!)

12.4 Tip of the day

When a word comes with *el* or *la* always learn this too, rather than the noun on its own. It's no effort when you first come across the new word, but it's nightmarish when you have dozens to re-learn.

12.5 You may wonder...

What is a **tapa?** *Tapas* are small dishes or snacks.

How do you say 'garlic'? *El ajo.*

What is the difference between **atún** *and* **bonito?** Not much, really. They are both 'tuna'.

What is the difference between **setas** *and* **champiñones?** *Champiñones* are the round white mushrooms you often find at the supermarket. *Setas* are all the other varieties, often darker, flatter and with more flavour.

Could Silvia say in the dialogue above **entonces una <u>ración</u> de patatas ...?** She could, but as we have seen, in Spanish you tend to drop words that sound redundant, like *ración* in this case.

12.6 Spanish words with something in common

When you say **a mí no me gustan los riñones** *(I don't like kidneys), why say* **a mí?** *A mí* is there to emphasise the fact that it is me who does not like them, and not you or him.

Does **a mí no me gustan los caracoles** *mean* **I don't like snails** *in general or* **I don't like the snails?** It means both.

Does the word **muy** *ever change form?* No. Compare these sentences: *el pescado está muy bueno* (the fish is very good), *la empanadilla está muy buena* (the pasty is very good), *los mejillones están muy buenos* (the mussels are very good), *las gambas están muy buenas* (the prawns are very good).

In the New words section, why are there some **las** *and* **los** *words, like* **las patatas bravas***, and not just* **el** *and* **la** *words?* I have given you the *las* or *los* form (instead of the *el* or *la* forms) of a word when it is more common to use that word in the plural. In previous lessons we have seen: *las vacaciones* (the holidays), *las instrucciones* (the instructions), *los espaguetis* (the spaghetti).

12.6 Spanish words with something in common

- ➡ *Voy* (I go), *va* (he/she/it goes, you [ud] go), *vamos* (we go), *vais* (you [vosotros] go), *van* (you [uds]/they go). For more information, go to p. 235.
- ➡ *La tortilla* (the Spanish potato omelette) and *la tortilla francesa* (the French omelette).
- ➡ *La aceituna* (the olive) and *el aceite* (the oil).
- ➡ *Otra* (another - feminine singular) and *otras* (other, others - feminine plural). By now we can guess how to say 'another' (masculine singular): *otro*; and 'other' (masculine plural): *otros*.
- ➡ *Fritas* (fried - feminine plural) and *fritos* (fried - masculine plural).
- ➡ *Bien* (well) and *bueno* (good).
- ➡ *Muy* (very) and *mucho* (a lot, much).
- ➡ *También* (also, too) and *tampoco* (not ... either, neither).

12.7 Building up new sentences

¿Qué vais a beber?
What are you going to drink?

Quiero pinchos de queso
I want cheese snacks.

¿Os gustan las setas al jerez?
Do you like mushrooms in sherry.

No me gustan los pimientos rellenos
I don't like stuffed peppers.

¿Te gustan los champiñones al ajillo?
Do you like garlic mushrooms?

Hoy no me quedan aceitunas rellenas.
Today I don't have any stuffed olives left.

No tengo ni toallas ni mantas.
I have neither towels nor blankets.

¿Qué otros pescados tienes?
What other fish do you have?

A mí no me gustan mucho las almejas
I don't like clams very much.

Los zumos del supermercado están muy buenos.
The supermarket juices are very good.

Tampoco tenemos leche.
We don't have milk either.

Prefiero la sopa de mariscos.
I prefer shellfish soup.

12.8 Exercises

(See solutions on p. 211)

Exercise 1: Say these sentences in Spanish:

1. Do you like apples? (you = tú)
2. I, myself, don't like pasties.
3. I don't have any hard boiled eggs left.
4. What other vegetables do you have? (you = tú)
5. I want four anchovies and three olives.
6. We're going to order two small beers and a small portion of Spanish potato omelette.
7. Do you like fried aubergines? (you = vosotros)
8. We have Spanish cured ham and cheese.
9. The squid is very good.
10. We don't have mussels either.

Exercise 2: Which phrase is the answer to each question you hear?

1. Sí, me gustan mucho.
2. Dos descafeinados y un batido.
3. Tengo plátanos y fresas.
4. Las once menos cuarto.
5. A las cinco y media.
6. El jueves.
7. En la nevera.
8. Con mi prima Clara.
9. Sí, hay dos.
10. Margarita.

12. Ordering tapas

Exercise 3: According to the dialogue on p. 86, is each statement true or false?

1. Voy a tomar un pincho de tortilla.	T	F
2. Voy a pedir pimientos rellenos de bonito.	T	F
3. No me quedan croquetas de jamón y queso.	T	F
4. Tengo anchoas, chorizos, pinchos de queso ...	T	F
5. Quiero una ración de patatas fritas.	T	F
6. Tengo calamares a la romana.	T	F
7. Las patatas alioli no están buenas.	T	F
8. No tenemos morcillas de arroz.	T	F
9. Prefiero las empanadillas.	T	F
10. Quieren beber cerveza.	T	F

Exercise 4: What would you put before each of the words below: *el, la, los* or *las*?

1. ..... jamón
2. ..... canapés
3. ..... atún
4. ..... ración
5. ..... calamares
6. ..... riñones
7. ..... caracoles
8. ..... mejillones
9. ..... limón
10. ..... jerez

Lesson 13.   Transport

Diálogo 1

Gerardo:	¿Me puede dar cuatro billetes de ida y vuelta a Barcelona?
Empleado:	¿Quiere asientos de fumador o no fumador?
Gerardo:	De no fumador. Somos dos adultos y dos niños. ¿Hacen descuento a los niños?
Empleado:	Sí, hacemos un descuento del veinte por ciento.
Gerardo:	¿Cuándo sale el próximo tren?
Empleado:	A las once y veinte. Tienen que esperar media hora.
Gerardo:	¿Y cuánto dura el viaje?
Empleado:	Una hora y treinta y cinco minutos.

Diálogo 2

Yolanda:	Dos billetes, por favor.
Empleada:	Aquí tiene. Son dos euros y veinte céntimos.
Yolanda:	¿Me puede dar un plano del metro?
Empleada:	Sí, claro.
Yolanda:	¿Qué línea tengo que coger para ir a Sol?
Empleada:	Tiene que coger la línea 4 y hacer transbordo en Goya.
Yolanda:	¿Cuándo sale el último metro para Sol?
Empleada:	A la una y media.

Diálogo 3

Bárbara:	¿Cuánto cuesta el metrobús?
Empleado:	Cinco euros y veinte céntimos.
Bárbara:	¿Me puede dar uno? ... ¿Qué autobús tengo que coger para ir a Callao?
Empleado:	El 1 o el 44. La parada está aquí mismo.
Bárbara:	¿Dónde tenemos que bajarnos?
Empleado:	Frente a los grandes almacenes.

Dialogue 1

Gerard:	Can you give me four return tickets to Barcelona?
Clerk:	Do you want smoking or non smoking seats? (lit: Do you want seats of smoker of non-smoker?)
Gerard:	Non-smoker. We are two adults and two children. Do you give a discount to children? (lit: Do you make discount to the children?)
Clerk:	Yes, we give a twenty per cent discount (lit: yes, we make a discount of the twenty per cent).
Gerard:	When does the next train leave?
Clerk:	At twenty past eleven. You have to wait half an hour.
Gerard:	And how long does the journey last? (lit: And how much lasts the journey?)
Clerk:	One hour and thirty-five minutes.

Dialogue 2

Yolanda:	Two tickets, please.
Clerk:	Here you are. It's two euros and twenty cents (lit: They are two euros ...).
Yolanda:	Can you give me a map of the metro?
Clerk:	Yes, of course.
Yolanda:	Which line do I have to take to go to Sol?
Clerk:	You have to take line 4 and change in Goya (lit: ... and make change in Goya).
Yolanda:	When does the last train to Sol leave?
Clerk:	At half past one.

Dialogue 3

Barbara:	How much does the 'metrobús' (the 10-journey ticket) cost?
Clerk:	Five euros and twenty cents.
Barbara:	Can you give me one? ... Which bus do I have to take to go to Callao?
Clerk:	Number 1 or number 44 (lit: the 1 or the 44). The bus stop is right here.
Barbara:	Where do we have to get off?
Clerk:	Opposite the department store.

13. Transport

13.1 New words

adulto (m)	adult	ida y vuelta (f)	round trip
aquí mismo	right here	línea (f)	line
asiento (m)	seat	metro (m)	underground, metro
autobús (m)	bus	metrobús (m)	10-journey ticket
bajarnos	(us) to get off	niños (m/pl)	children
Barcelona	Barcelona	no fumador (m)	non-smoker
billete (m)	ticket	parada (f)	stop, bus stop
coger	to take, to catch	plano (m)	street map
cuánto cuesta	how much is	por ciento	per cent
descuento (m)	discount	próximo	next
dura	it lasts	quiere	he/she/it/ wants, you [ud] want
empleada (f)	employee (f)		
empleado (m)	employee (m)	sale	he/she/it leaves, you [ud] leave
esperar	to wait		
frente a	in front of, opposite	somos	we are
		tengo que	I have to
fumador (m)	smoker	tiene que	he/she/it has to, you [ud] have to
Gerardo	Gerard		
grandes almacenes (m/pl)	department store	tienen que	you [uds] have to, they have to
hacemos	we make/do	transbordo (m)	change (train, etc.)
hacen	you [uds]/they make/do	tren (m)	train
		último	last
hacer	to make/do	viaje (m)	trip, journey
ida (f)	outward journey	vuelta (f)	return

13.2 Watch out for your pronunciation

→ Repeat after the Spanish speaker: *ca, que, qui, co, cu; ce, ci.*

→ Let's practise the letter 'c': *aparcar, azúcar, cuatro, Barcelona, descuento, hacemos, ciento, cuándo, once, caracoles, cuesta, cinco, céntimos, claro, coger, almacenes.*

13.3 Important notes

- And let's also practise the 'qu': *que, queda, pequeña, quédese, Enrique, croquetas, queso, aquí, equipaje, quiere, Joaquín.*

- Notice that the only vowels that can come after 'qu' are 'e' and 'i'. Notice also that the 'u' in these cases (in 'que' and 'qui') is silent. Remember that the 'u' is also silent in 'gue' and 'gui', as we saw on p. 81

- Difficult words: Listen to these words and practise saying them: *billetes, asientos, próximo, hacen, viaje, transbordo, Goya, último, autobús, bajarnos.*

13.3 Important notes

- Notice the difference between *¿cuánto cuesta ...?* (how much is ...?) and *¿cuánto cuestan...?* (how much are ... ?). *¿Cuánto cuesta?* is used to ask the price of one thing, like *la sandía*: *¿cuánto cuesta la sandía?* (how much is the watermelon?). *¿Cuánto cuestan?* is used to ask the price of two or more things, like *las sandías*: *¿cuánto cuestan las sandías?* (how much are the watermelons?).

- *El último metro* and *el próximo autobús*: we have seen that describing words generally follow the noun they describe. This general rule has some exceptions, like *último* and *próximo*, which usually precede the noun they describe.

- *Por favor* and *gracias*. As you can tell from the dialogues, both *por favor* and *gracias* are used less often in Spanish than in English. You make up for them by using a friendly sounding intonation.

- Other useful expressions: *un billete de ida y vuelta* (a return ticket), *de no fumador* (non smoking), *veinte por ciento* (twenty per cent), *hacer transbordo en* (to change trains in), *aquí mismo* (right here), *frente a* (in front of, opposite).

13.4 Tip of the day

> If you're starting to get mixed up and you've forgotten many of the words you've learnt in this book, revise the last few lessons for a couple of days before you learn anything new.

13.5 You may wonder...

Where is Barcelona? Barcelona is the capital of Catalonia, which is situated in the north-east of Spain. To see where it is on the map, go to p. 230.

***What are* Sol, Goya *and* Callao?** They are all metro stations in Madrid.

***In the dialogue, could you say* ¿me puede dar un metrobús, por favor?** *instead of* ¿me puede dar uno, por favor?*?* Yes, you could, but *metrobús* has been said immediately before, so it is an unnecessary word and can be dropped.

***In the dialogue, is there another way of saying* el 1?** Yes, you could say *el autobús número 1*.

***In the dialogue, could you answer just* la línea 4 ... *instead of* tiene que coger la línea 4 ...?** Yes, you could. Like in English, there are often several ways of giving an answer. Spanish speakers tend to use short ones, but adding the odd word makes the speaker sound more friendly, like in this example.

How do you say 'the department stores'? *Los grandes almacenes*, which is the same as for *the department store* (i.e. the singular). In context it should not be a problem to know whether someone means one or several department stores.

How do you say 'buses'? *Los autobuses*. Unlike other nouns ending in 's', *el autobús* takes 'es' in the plural. Remember *el lavaplatos/los lavaplatos, el microondas/los microondas* where only *el* and *los* change.

Does* metro *also mean 'metre'? Yes, it does. Here are two examples: *dos metros* (two metres), *diez metros* (ten metres).

Am I ever going to understand the dialogues in this book without looking at the English translation? Yes, you are. Here are some things you can do to achieve that: when you start a new lesson, always listen to the dialogue first, with the book closed, before reading it in either English or Spanish; learn any new vocabulary well before you go on to the next lesson; make sure you understand every line in the dialogues you have seen so far; listen to the old dialogues frequently; read the dialogues along with the Spanish speakers to get used to the speed.

13.6 Spanish words with something in common

→ *Soy* (I am), *eres* (you [tú] are), *es* (he/she/it is; you [ud] are), *somos* (we are), *sois* (you [vos] are), *son* (you [uds]/they are).

→ *Hacer* (to make, to do), *hacemos* (we make/do), *hacen* (you [uds]/they make/do). For more information, see the verb table on p. 235

→ *Tengo que* (I have to), *tiene que* (he/she/it has to, you [ud] have to), *tenemos que* (we have to), *tienen que* (you [uds]/they have to).

→ *Quiero* (I want), *quiere* (he/she/it wants, you [ud] want), *quieren* (you [uds]/they want).

→ *Aquí mismo* (right here) and *ahora mismo* (right away).

13.7 Building up new sentences

¿Me puede hacer un favor?
Can you do me a favour?
Quiero cinco billetes de ida y vuelta a Segovia.
I want five return tickets to Segovia.
Hacemos un descuento del diez por ciento.
We give a ten per cent discount.
¿Me puede dar un asiento de fumador?
Can you give me a smoking seat?
¿Qué tren tenemos que coger para ir a Barcelona?
Which train do we have to take to go to Barcelona?
¿Cuándo sale el próximo autobús para la playa?
When does the next bus to the beach leave?
¿Cuánto cuesta el billete de ida?
How much is the single ticket?
¿Dónde tengo que bajarme?
Where do I have to get off?
El garaje está frente a los apartamentos.
The garage is opposite the apartments.

13.8 Exercises

(See solutions on p. 212)

Exercise 1: Say these sentences in Spanish:
1. I want a return ticket to Barcelona.
2. How many apples are there in the fridge?
3. We are Barbara's sisters.
4. We give a fifteen per cent discount.
5. When does the next train to the beach leave?
6. They have to wait twenty minutes.
7. Can you give me two, please? (you = ud)
8. Which bus do we have to take to go to the hotel?
9. How much is the milk?
10. I don't like buses.

13.8 Exercises

Exercise 2: Which of the two sentences is being said?

1. Quieren dos billetes de ida y vuelta.
   Quiero dos billetes de ida y vuelta.

2. Somos los primos de Ana
   Somos las primas de Ana.

3. Tengo que ir al hotel en autobús
   Tienen que ir al hotel en autobús.

4. ¿Me puede dar seis asientos de fumador?
   ¿Me puede dar siete asientos de no fumador?

5. ¿Qué tren tengo que coger?
   ¿Qué tren tienen que coger?

6. ¿Cuánto cuesta el billete?
   ¿Cuánto cuestan los billetes?

7. ¿Te gustan las patatas fritas?
   ¿Os gustan las patatas fritas?

8. Son las cuatro y cuarto
   Son las cuatro menos cuarto

9. La prima de mi madre se llama Juana
   El primo de mi padre se llama Juan.

10. ¿Me puede traer otra cerveza?
    ¿Nos puede traer otra cerveza?

13. Transport

Exercise 3: Complete each sentence with one of the missing words:

> Missing words: cuestan, mejillones, vuelta, quieren,
> cuesta, quiere, hay, ciento, coger, café

1. Quieren dos billetes de ida y ....
2. ¿Cuántas manzanas .... en la nevera?
3. Hacemos un descuento del doce por ....
4. ¿Qué autobús tengo que .... para ir al apartamento?
5. ¿Cuánto .... el zumo de naranja?
6. ¿Cuánto .... las galletas?
7. No me quedan ....
8. No me queda ....
9. Los abuelos .... ir a la playa.
10. El abuelo .... ir a la playa.

Exercise 4: How would you translate these sentences into Spanish?

1. They want a kilo of clams.
1. *Translation:* ....

2. I want sixteen tuna pasties.
2. *Translation:* ....

3. He wants ten meatballs.
3. *Translation:* ....

4. We are Frank's friends.
4. *Translation:* ....

5. I'm Louis's father.
5. *Translation:* ....

13.8 Exercises

6. Are you Mary's mother?

6. *Translation:* ....

7. He's Joseph's uncle.

7. *Translation:* ....

8. Are you sisters? (colloquial you)

8. *Translation:* ....

9. They're Paul's sons.

9. *Translation:* ....

10. She's going to be my aunt.

10. *Translation:* ....

Revising: Revising is the secret when it comes to really learning a foreign language. That is why, from now on, we are going to revise an old lesson as soon as we finish a new one. These are some of the things you can do when revising: cover up the Spanish dialogue and try to come up with the Spanish sentences by following the English translation; repeat all the exercises, even if you made no mistakes the first time around; read the Pronunciation notes, the Important Notes, the You May Wonder sections and the Spanish Words With Something In Common sections to make sure that everything is clear; build new sentences using everything you have learnt so far.

Revise Lesson 1.

Lesson 14. Shops and eating places

Diálogo 1

Cristina: ¿Hay muchas tiendas en tu calle?
Emilio: Sí, hay una agencia de viajes, una tienda de regalos, una tienda de muebles, una farmacia y una librería. ¿Y en tu calle?
Cristina: También hay varias. Tenemos una pastelería, una tienda de deportes, una zapatería y una tienda de bocadillos.
Isabel: En mi calle hay una frutería, una carnicería, una panadería y una verdulería, y cerca hay un centro comercial con muchas tiendas de ropa que están abiertas todo el día.

Diálogo 2

Gabriel: Perdona, ¿dónde está el supermercado?
Elena: En la próxima calle, a la izquierda.
Gabriel: ¿A qué hora abren por la mañana?
Elena: A las ocho y media.
Gabriel: ¿Cierran a mediodía?
Elena: Sí, de dos a cinco.
Gabriel: ¿Y a qué hora cierran por la tarde?
Elena: No sé, creo que a las nueve.

Diálogo 3

Diana: Perdona, ¿dónde puedo encontrar una panadería?
Pilar: En la plaza, entre el autoservicio y la pescadería.
Diana: ¿Y una pizzería?
Pilar: En esta calle, frente a la peluquería.
Diana: ¿Y sabes dónde hay un mercado?
Pilar: No, creo que no hay ninguno por aquí.

Dialogue 1

Christine:	Are there many shops in your street?
Emilio:	Yes, there is a travel agency, a gift shop, a furniture shop, a chemist's and a bookshop. And in your street?
Christine:	There are several too. We have a pastry shop, a sports shop, a shoe shop and a sandwich shop.
Elizabeth:	In my street there is fruit shop, a butcher's, a bakery and a vegetable shop, and nearby there is a shopping centre with many clothes shops that are open all day.

Dialogue 2

Gabriel:	Excuse me, where is the supermarket?
Helen:	On the next street, on the left.
Gabriel:	At what time do they open in the morning?
Helen:	At half past eight.
Gabriel:	Do they close at lunchtime?
Helen:	Yes, from two till five.
Gabriel:	And at what time do they close in the evening?
Helen:	I don't know, I think at nine.

Dialogue 3

Diana:	Excuse me, where can I find a bakery?
Pilar:	In the square, between the self-service restaurant and the fishmonger's.
Diana:	And a pizzeria?
Pilar:	On this street, opposite the hairdresser's.
Diana:	And do you know where there's a market?
Pilar:	No, I think there aren't any around here.

14. Shops and eating places

14.1 New words

a la izquierda	on the left	junto al	next to
a mediodía	at lunchtime	librería (f)	bookshop
abiertas	open (f/pl)	mercado (m)	market
agencia (f)	agency	muchas	many (f/pl)
agencia (f) de viajes	travel agency	muebles (m/pl)	furniture
autoservicio (m)	self-service restaurant	ninguno	none
		panadería (f)	bakery
		pastelería (f)	pastry shop
bocadillo (m)	sandwich	peluquería (f)	(the) hairdresser's
calle (f)	street	perdona	excuse me, I'm sorry
carnicería (f)	(the) butcher's		
centro (m)	centre	pescadería (f)	(the) fishmonger's
centro comercial (m)	shopping centre	pizzería (f)	pizzeria
creo	I believe/think	plaza (f)	(the) square
Cristina	Christine	por aquí	around here, this way
deporte (m)	sport		
Elena	Helen	próxima	next (f)
Emilio	Emile	regalo (m)	present, gift
entre	between, among	ropa (f)	clothes
esta	this (f)	sabes	you [tú] know
farmacia (f)	chemist's, pharmacy	sé	I know
		tienda (f)	shop, store
frutería (f)	fruit shop	varias	several (f/pl)
Gabriel	Gabriel	verdulería (f)	vegetable shop
Isabel	Elizabeth	zapatería (f)	shoe shop
izquierda (f)	(the) left		

14.2 Watch out for your pronunciation

→ Repeat after the Spanish speaker: *za, ce, ci, zo, zu; ca, que, qui, co, cu; cha, che, chi, cho, chu*. Notice the spelling for each of the sounds.

→ Let's practise the letter 'z': *cerveza, terraza, manzana, zanahoria, zapatería, plaza, zona, chorizo, zumo.*

14.3 Important notes

→ Notice that the English 'z' sound in words like 'zone', 'Elizabeth' or 'size' does not exist in Spanish.

→ Let's also practise the 'ch': *chorizo, derecha, leche, ocho, lechuga, champiñón, noche, anchoas.*

→ And now let's revise the letter 'c': *carnicería, cerca, centro, agencia, farmacia, cierran, calle, comercial, cuesta.* Go to p. 98 if you want to go over the 'c' sound again.

→ In the south of Spain and in Central and South America people tend to pronounce *za, ce, ci, zo, zu* the same way as *sa, se, si, so, su*.

→ Difficult words: Listen to the following words and practise saying them: *varias, pastelería, verdulería, ropa, izquierda, autoservicio, mediodía, Gabriel, peluquería.*

14.3 Important notes

→ *Mi* (my), *mis* (my), *tu* (your [you=tú]), *tus* (your [you=tú]): *Mi* and *tu* are used with the singular (both masculine and feminine), and *mis* and *tus* with the plural (both masculine and feminine). Here are some examples of how to use these words: *Jorge es mi hermano* (George is my brother), *Ana es mi hermana* (Anne is my sister), *Jorge y José son mis hermanos* (George and Joseph are my brothers), *Ana y Clara son mis hermanas* (Anne and Clare are my sisters), *Jorge es tu hermano* (George is your brother), *Ana es tu hermana* (Anne is your sister), *Jorge y José son tus hermanos* (George and Joseph are your brothers), *Ana y Clara son tus hermanas* (Anne and Clare are your sisters).

→ Double negative: We have already seen *no me quedan ni banderillas ni croquetas* (I don't have any banderillas or croquettes left) on p. 86. In the current lesson we had: *creo que no hay ninguno por aquí* (I think there aren't any around here; literally: I think that there aren't none around here). Once again, we have to use the double negative.

14. Shops and eating places

→ Other useful expressions: *todo el día* (all day), *a la izquierda* (on the left), *a mediodía* (at lunchtime), *por la tarde* (in the afternoon), *creo que ...* (I think that ...), *por aquí* (around here; this way).

14.4 Tip of the day

Learning useful expressions is essential. People say them all the time, that's why we've included so many of them in this book.

14.5 You may wonder...

How do you say 'there are two fruit shops'? *Hay dos fruterías.* As we have seen, the word *hay* means both *there is* and *there are*.

How do you say 'opposite the market'? *Frente al mercado.* Notice the word *al* before *mercado*.

How do you say 'there aren't any markets'? *No hay ningún mercado.* Once more, we have to use the double negative. Also, notice that *ninguno* (none) becomes *ningún* (no, not any) when <u>followed</u> by the noun it refers to, just like *uno* and *un* (to revise this, go to p. 21). Compare these examples: *no hay ninguno* (there aren't any) and *no hay ningún mercado* (there are no markets or there aren't any markets).

How do you say 'closed'? *Cerrado, cerrada, cerrados, cerradas.* Here are some examples of how to use them: *el mercado está cerrado* (the market is closed), *la tienda está cerrada* (the shop is closed), *los mercados están cerrados* (the markets are closed), *las tiendas están cerradas* (the shops are closed).

How do you say 'the library' in Spanish? *La biblioteca.*

14.6 Spanish words with something in common

How important is it to learn when to write an accent on a word? It is good to get used to writing the accents, especially if you are aiming to learn Spanish to an advanced level. Accents are there to help you stress words right. If you know when to write an accent, the odds are that you will also stress that word properly.

14.6 Spanish words with something in common

- *Muchas* (many - feminine plural) and *mucho* (much, a lot of - masculine singular). By now we can guess *mucha* (much, a lot of - feminine singular) and *muchos* (many - masculine plural). Here are some examples of how to use them: *tengo mucho vino* (I have a lot of wine), *tengo mucha cerveza* (I have a lot of beer), *tengo muchos billetes* (I have many tickets), *tengo muchas aceitunas* (I have many olives).

- *Esta* (this - feminine), *ésta* (this one - feminine) and *está* (he/she/it is, you [ud] are).

- *Sé* (I know), *sabe* (he/she/it knows, you [ud] know) and *sabes* (you [tú] know). For more information, go to p. 236

- *La fruta* (the fruit) and *la frutería* (the fruit shop).

- *La carne* (the meat) and *la carnicería* (the butcher's).

- *Las verduras* (the vegetables) and *la verdulería* (the vegetable shop).

- *El pescado* (the fish) and *la pescadería* (the fishmonger's).

14. Shops and eating places

14.7 Building up new sentences

¿Hay muchos niños en la piscina?
Are there many children in the swimming pool?

Tenemos mucha leche en la nevera.
We have a lot of milk in the fridge.

También hay varios platos vegetarianos.
There are also several vegetarian dishes.

Cerca hay unos grandes almacenes que están abiertos toda la tarde.
Nearby there is a department store which is open all afternoon and evening.

No sé, creo que vienen mañana.
I don't know, I think they're coming tomorrow.

La zapatería está entre la farmacia y la carnicería.
The shoe shop is between the chemist's and the butcher's.

Creo que no van a cenar aquí esta noche.
I don't think they're having dinner here tonight.

No hay ninguna mesa en el salón.
There aren't any tables in the sitting room.

¿Hay alguna sandía en la frutería?
Are there any watermelons in the fruit shop?

¿Hay algún pepino en la verdulería?
Are there any cucumbers in the vegetable shop?

No, no hay ninguno.
No, there aren't any.

Mi apartamento está frente al centro comercial.
My flat is opposite the shopping centre.

14.8 Exercises

(See solutions on p. 213)

Exercise 1: Say these sentences in Spanish:

1. Are there many gifts in the shop?
2. On this street, on the left.
3. I don't know, I think we're going today.
4. The bottles are between the fruit and the fish.
5. Where is there a sports shop?
6. There aren't any cars in the garage.
7. There aren't any chemist's on my street.
8. My friends are at the butcher's.
9. Your (male) cousins want to go to the bookshop.
10. How much are the sandwiches?

Exercise 2: Which phrase is the answer to each question you hear?

1. Sí, hay cinco.
2. En la próxima calle, a la derecha.
3. No sé, creo que vienen mañana.
4. No, no hay ninguna.
5. Es mi tío.
6. A las cinco y veinticinco.
7. Cinco euros y veinte céntimos.
8. Mucho.
9. Un descafeinado y un café con leche.
10. Las seis y media.

14. Shops and eating places

Exercise 3: Match the Spanish sentences with their English translations:

1. Mi sobrino está en esta tienda.	*My niece is in this shop.*
2. Mi sobrina está en esta tienda.	*Your nephew is in this shop.*
3. Mis sobrinos están en esta tienda.	*Your nieces are in this shop.*
4. Mis sobrinas están en esta tienda.	*My nephews are in this shop.*
5. Tu sobrino está en esta tienda.	*Your nephews are in this shop.*
6. Tu sobrina está en esta tienda.	*His niece is in this shop.*
7. Tus sobrinos están en esta tienda.	*Your niece is in this shop.*
8. Tus sobrinas están en esta tienda.	*His nephew is in this shop.*
9. Su sobrino está en esta tienda.	*My nephew is in this shop.*
10. Su sobrina está en esta tienda.	*My nieces are in this shop.*

Exercise 4: What would you put before each of the words below: *el* or *la*?

1. ..... calle
2. ..... viaje
3. ..... día
4. ..... billete
5. ..... tren
6. ..... autobús
7. ..... metrobús
8. ..... ración
9. ..... carne
10. ..... información

Revise Lesson 2.

Lesson 15. At the chemist's

Diálogo 1

Farmacéutica: Buenas tardes, ¿en qué puedo ayudarla?
Luisa: Necesito un calmante. ¿Puedo comprarlo sin receta?
Farmacéutica: Sí, puedo darle éste sin receta. ¿Alguna cosa más?
Luisa: ¿Me puede recomendar algo para la fiebre?
Farmacéutica: Sí, tengo estas pastillas. Son buenas.
Luisa: Vale. Quiero también una caja de tiritas, una venda, aspirinas y un chupete. Ah, y también quiero llevarme unos kleenex, compresas y vitaminas.

Diálogo 2

Mónica: Buenos días, ¿tiene biberones?
Farmacéutica: Sí, tenemos varios donde elegir. ¿Cuál prefiere?
Mónica: Éste.
Farmacéutica: ¿Desea alguna otra cosa?
Mónica: Sí, voy a llevarme champú, suavizante, un cepillo, jabón, pasta de dientes y un desodorante.
Farmacéutica: No vendemos cepillos.
Mónica: Bueno, entonces un peine.
Farmacéutica: Lo siento, tampoco vendemos peines.
Mónica: Vale. ¿Me puede decir cuánto es todo?

Diálogo 3

Nuria: Hola, ¿tiene líquidos para lentillas?
Farmacéutica: Sí, tengo varios. ¿Cuál quiere?
Nuria: Éste de aquí. ¿Me puede dar también un protector solar, una crema hidratante para la cara y una caja de tampones?
Farmacéutica: Sí, ¿qué más?
Farmacéutica: Necesito también unos potitos, pañales y papel higiénico. Eso es todo.

Dialogue 1

Pharmacist:	Good afternoon, how can I help you? (lit: in what can I help you?)
Louise:	I need a painkiller. Can I buy it without prescription?
Pharmacist:	Yes, I can give you this one without a prescription. Anything else?
Louise:	Can you recommend something for a temperature?
Pharmacist:	Yes, I have these tablets. They're good.
Louise:	OK. I also want a box of plasters, a bandage, aspirins and a dummy. Oh, and I also want to take some tissues, sanitary towels and vitamins (lit: I also want to take with me ...).

Dialogue 2

Monica:	Good morning, do you have feeding bottles?
Pharmacist:	Yes, we have several to choose from (lit: we have several where to choose). Which one do you prefer?
Monica:	This one.
Pharmacist:	Do you want anything else? (lit: do you wish anything else?)
Monica:	Yes, I'm going to take shampoo, conditioner, a hairbrush, soap, toothpaste and a deodorant.
Pharmacist:	We don't sell hairbrushes.
Monica:	Well, a comb then.
Pharmacist:	I'm sorry, we don't sell combs either (lit: neither we sell combs).
Monica:	OK. Can you tell me how much everything is?

Dialogue 3

Nuria:	Hi, do you have contact lens solutions?
Pharmacist:	Yes, I have several. Which one do you want?
Nuria:	This one here. Can you also give me a suntan lotion, a moisturising face cream and a box of tampons?
Pharmacist:	Yes, what else?
Nuria:	I also need some jars of baby food, nappies and toilet tissue. That's all.

15. At the chemist's

15.1 New words

aspirina (f)	aspirin	éste	this one, this
ayudar	to help	farmacéutica (f)	pharmacist
ayudarla	to help you [ud/f[1]], to help her	fiebre (f)	temperature, fever
		jabón (m)	soap
biberón (m)	feeding bottle	kleenex (m)	tissue, paper handkerchief
protector solar (m)	sun block		
buenas	good (f/pl)	lentilla (f)	contact lens
bueno	good	líquido (m)	solution, liquid
caja (f)	box, till	llevarme	to take (with me)
calmante (m)	painkiller	Luisa	Louise
cara (f)	face	pañal (m)	nappy
cepillo (m)	hairbrush	papel (m)	paper
champú (m)	shampoo	papel	
chupete (m)	(baby's) dummy	higiénico (m)	toilet tissue
comprar	to buy	pasta (f) de dientes	toothpaste
comprarlo	to buy it	pastilla (f)	tablet, pill
compresa (f)	sanitary towel	peine (m)	comb
crema (f)	cream	potito (m)	jar of baby food
crema hidratante (f)	moisturising cream	prefiere	he/she/it prefers, you [ud] prefer
		receta (f)	prescription
cuál	which, which one	recomendar	to recommend
darle	to give him/her/it	suavizante (m)	conditioner
desea	he/she/it wishes, you [ud] wish	tampón (m)	tampon
		tirita (f)	plaster
desodorante (m)	deodorant	unos	some
diente (m)	tooth	venda (f)	bandage
donde	where	vendemos	we sell
elegir	to choose	vitamina (f)	vitamin
estas	these (f/pl)		

15.2 Watch out for your pronunciation

→ Repeat after the Spanish speaker: *sa, se, si, so, su.*

→ Let's practise the letter 's': *buenas tardes, necesito, sin, pastillas, suavizante, desodorante, lo siento, cervezas, plazas, zumos, recetas.*

---

[1] ud/f = usted, female

15.3 Important notes

→ The Spanish 's' is always strong, as in 'suntan' or 'hairdresser', and never soft and z-like, as in 'choose' or 'lens'. Also, the sound 'sh' does not exist in Castilian Spanish. Finally, remember that the English 'z' sound does not exist in Spanish either, as we saw on p. 109

→ Important: Spanish words are never spelt with a 'ss'. Compare 'passport' and *pasaporte*.

→ Difficult words: Listen to these words and practise saying them: *ayudarla, recomendar, fiebre, vitaminas, biberones, cepillo, líquidos, protector, hidratante, pañales, higiénico*.

15.3 Important notes

→ *Ayudarla* (to help you [ud/f], to help her), *comprarlo* (to buy it), *darle* (to give him/her/it/you [ud]), *llevarme* (to take with me). The small words *la, lo, le, me* can be used in the following ways: 1. Attached to the end of an infinitive: *¿puedo ayudarla?* (can I help you?), *voy a comprarlo* (I'm going to buy it), *quiero darle dos* (I want to give him two), *voy a llevarme ésta* (I'm going to take this one with me). 2. Before other verb forms: *la ayudo* (I help you), *lo compro* (I buy it), *le doy* (I give him), *me lo llevo* (I take it with me).

→ *Cuál* (which one, which) refers to both masculine and feminine nouns. At the chemist's, for instance, if you are shown a number of *cremas* (las cremas, the creams) or *cepillos* (los cepillos, the hairbrushes) you will be asked *¿cuál prefiere?* in both cases.

→ Have you noticed how many words look similar in English and Spanish? So far, we have seen: *aspirinas, champú, desodorante, recomendar, vitaminas, agencia, centro, adulto, principal, garaje*, etc.; and there are many more still to come.

→ Other useful expressions: *¿en qué puedo ayudarla?* (how can I help you?), *donde elegir* (to choose from), *éste de aquí* (this one here).

15. At the chemist's

15.4 Tip of the day

> The only way to learn to speak Spanish is by practising speaking. By that I mean that just listening to the audio recordings - even if you learn the dialogues by heart - can't compare to saying your own sentences out loud.

15.5 You may wonder...

In dialogue 1, could you say ¿me puede recomendar alguna cosa para la fiebre? *(can you recommend something for a temperature?)?* Yes, that is perfectly correct.

In dialogue 1, why do you say first quiero también una caja ... *(I want also a box ...) and then* y también quiero llevarme unos kleenex *(and I also want to take some tissues)? Can* también *go both before and after* quiero? Yes. In fact, you could also say *también quiero una caja* (I also want a box) and *y quiero llevarme también unos kleenex* (I want to also take some tissues). The word *también* can go in many places.

How do you say 'a tissue'? Un kleenex. Notice that the word *kleenex* is the same in singular and plural.

How do you say 'I don't sell combs'? No vendo peines.

How do you say 'the (male) pharmacist'? El farmacéutico.

15.6 Spanish words with something in common

→ *Estas* (these - feminine) and *esta* (this - feminine). Compare: *estas cremas* (these creams) and *esta crema* (this cream).

→ *Estos* (these - masculine) and *este* (this - masculine). Compare: *estos chupetes* (these dummies) and *este chupete* (this dummy).

15.7 Building up new sentences

→ *Prefiero* (I prefer) and *prefiere* (he/she/it prefers, you [ud] prefer).

→ *Recomendar* (to recommend), *recomiendo* (I recommend) and *recomienda* (he/she/it recommends, you [ud] recommend).

→ *La farmacia* (the chemist's) and *la farmacéutica* (the pharmacist).

→ *El biberón* (the feeding bottle) and *beber* (to drink).

15.7 Building up new sentences

¿Puedo comprarlo en el supermercado?
Can I buy it at the supermarket?
¿Puedo darle un kilo de calamares?
Can I give you a kilo of squid?
Estos chupetes son muy buenos.
These dummies are very good.
Estas tiritas no son buenas.
These plasters aren't good.
Tenemos varias cajas donde elegir.
We have several boxes to choose from.
Voy a llevarme tres protectores solares.
I'm going to take three sun blocks with me.
También quiero comprar papel higiénico.
I also want to buy toilet tissue.
No vendo cremas para la cara.
I don't sell facial creams.
¿Cuál es tu coche?
Which one is your car?
Esta tarde vamos a ver estas tiendas.
This afternoon we're going to see these shops.
Esta carnicería está cerrada.
This butcher's is closed.
La panadería está más cerca que la pastelería.
The bakery is closer than the pastry shop.

15. *At the chemist's*

15.8 Exercises

(See solutions on p. 215)

Exercise 1: Say these sentences in Spanish:

1. Can I buy kiwis at the market?
2. Can you [ud] give me two kilos of tomatoes?
3. These cucumbers aren't good.
4. I don't like these creams.
5. I have several flats to choose from.
6. I also want to take a box of aspirins with me.
7. I prefer grey tables.
8. Do you like these hairbrushes?
9. This shoe shop is closed.
10. There aren't any hairdressers' on my street.

Exercise 2: Which of the two words is being said?

1. esta	estas	2. este	esta
3. estos	estas	4. prefiero	prefiere
5. recomiendo	recomienda	6. recomendar	recomienda
7. mucho	mucha	8. muchos	muchas
9. mucho	muchos	10. mucha	muchas

Exercise 3: Complete each sentence with one of the missing words:

Missing words: están, son, esta, es, estas, mucho, está, este, mucha, estos

1. .... pañales no son buenos.
2. .... lentillas son muy buenas.
3. .... suavizante no me gusta.
4. ¿Cuánto cuesta .... crema?
5. La tienda .... cerrada.
6. Los grandes almacenes .... abiertos.
7. Los cepillos .... grandes.
8. El peine .... pequeño.
9. Tenemos .... donde elegir.
10. Tienen .... pasta de dientes.

15.8 Exercises

Exercise 4: Translate these sentences into Spanish:

1. I'm at the chemist's with my friend Gabriel.
1. *Translation:* ....

2. Are you married? (you = tú)
2. *Translation:* ....

3. It's closed till Monday.
3. *Translation:* ....

4. They're on holiday with the children.
4. *Translation:* ....

5. I'm your [you=tú] brother's friend.
5. *Translation:* ....

6. Are you Joanna, my (female) cousin's friend?
6. *Translation:* ....

7. It's late.
7. *Translation:* ....

8. We are Christine's parents.
8. *Translation:* ....

9. Are you cousins?
9. *Translation:* ....

10. They're friends.
10. *Translation:* ....

Revise Lesson 3.

Lesson 16. On holiday

Diálogo 1

Olga:	Hola, ¿estáis de vacaciones?
Paco:	Sí. Vamos a estar aquí dos semanas. Hoy queremos ir a la playa.
Sonia:	Nosotras queremos ir al lago y a las montañas, pero primero tenemos que comprar una guía.
Olga:	¿Qué vais a hacer en la playa?
Paco:	Vamos a tomar el sol todo el día. Nos vamos a llevar la colchoneta, la sombrilla y la cámara.
Ramón:	Por la tarde quiero dormir la siesta. Esta noche hay una fiesta en la discoteca del hotel.
Olga:	A mí me gusta mucho bailar. ¿Por qué no vamos, Sonia?
Sonia:	¿Por qué no? Ahora vamos a ir a comprar un polo y un helado. ¿Queréis venir?

Diálogo 2

Jaime:	Por favor, ¿nos puedes sacar una foto?
Fernando:	Sí, ¡cómo no!
Lucía:	Muchas gracias. ¿Sabes dónde podemos alquilar una tumbona y una sombrilla?
Jaime:	Sí, ese señor las alquila. ¿Cuánto tiempo lleváis aquí?
Fernando:	Dos días. Ésta es la primera vez que venimos a bañarnos. Mañana queremos hacer esquí acuático.
Lucía:	Yo quiero hacer submarinismo.
Jaime:	Yo prefiero la piscina. En la playa hay demasiados mosquitos y hace mucho calor.

Diálogo 3

Patricia:	Hola, ¿me puedes revelar este carrete para mañana?
Dependiente:	Mañana cerramos. Te lo podemos revelar para el lunes.
Patricia:	Vale, para el lunes entonces. ¿Tienes flotadores?
Dependiente:	No, pero ¿por qué no preguntas en la tienda de al lado?
Patricia:	¿Tengo que pagar hoy las fotos?
Dependiente:	No es necesario. Puedes pagar el lunes.

Dialogue 1

Olga:	Hello, are you on holiday?
Paco:	Yes. We're going to be here for two weeks (lit: We're going to be here two weeks). Today we want to go to the beach.
Sonia:	We want to go to the lake and to the mountains, but first we have to buy a guide.
Olga:	What are you going to do on the beach?
Paco:	We're going to sunbathe all day. We're going to take the air bed, the beach umbrella and the camera.
Ramon:	I, myself, want to have a nap in the afternoon (lit: In the afternoon I want to sleep the siesta). Tonight there is a party at the hotel club.
Olga:	I like dancing very much. Why don't we go, Sonia?
Sonia:	Why not? Now we're going to buy an ice lolly and an ice cream. Do you want to come?

Dialogue 2

Jaime:	Excuse me, can you take our picture? (lit: ... us a picture?)
Ferdinand:	Yes, of course!
Lucia:	Thank you very much. Do you know where we can hire a sun lounger and a beach umbrella?
Jaime:	Yes, that man hires them out. How long have you been here for? (lit: How much time do you take here?)
Ferdinand:	Two days. This is the first time we've come to bathe (lit: ... time that we come to bathe ourselves). Tomorrow we want to water-ski (lit: ... to do water-skiing).
Lucia:	I want to go scuba diving (lit: **I** want to do scuba diving).
Jaime:	I prefer the swimming pool. There are too many mosquitoes on the beach and it's very hot (lit: ... and it makes much heat).

Dialogue 3

Patricia:	Hi, can you develop this film for me for tomorrow?
Shop assistant:	We are closed tomorrow. We can develop it for you for Monday.
Patricia:	OK, for Monday then. Do you have rubber rings?
Shop assistant:	No, but why don't you ask in the shop next door?
Patricia:	Do I have to pay for the photos today?
Shop assistant:	It's not necessary. You can pay on Monday.

16. On holiday

16.1 New words

alquila	he/she/it hires (out), you [ud] hire (out)	hacer submarinismo	to go scuba diving
alquilar	to hire, to hire out	helado (m)	ice cream
bailar	to dance	Jaime	Jaime
bañarnos	(us) to bathe	lado (m)	side
calor (m)	heat	lago (m)	lake
cámara (f)	camera	lleváis	you [vos] take
carrete (m)	film (for a camera)	me gusta mucho ...	I like ... very much
cerramos	we close	montaña (f)	mountain
colchoneta (f)	air bed	mosquito (m)	mosquito
cuánto tiempo	how long	necesario	necessary
de al lado	next, next door	nosotras	we (all females)
de vacaciones	on holiday, on vacation	pagar	to pay
		Patricia	Patricia
		pero	but
demasiados	too many	polo (m)	ice lolly
dependiente (m)	shop assistant	por qué	why
discoteca (f)	(night)club, disco	pregunta	he/she/it/you ask(s)
dormir	to sleep	primera	first (f)
dormir la siesta	to have a nap	puedes	you [tú] can
ese	that	queréis	you [vos] want
esquí acuático (m)	water-skiing	queremos	we want
esta noche	tonight	revelar	to develop
estáis	you [vos[1]] are	sacar	to take out
estar	to be	semana (f)	week
Fernando	Ferdinand	siesta (f)	nap
fiesta (f)	party	sombrilla (f)	beach umbrella
flotador (m)	rubber ring	submarinismo (m)	scuba diving
foto (f)	photograph, picture	tiempo (m)	time
guía (f)	guide, guidebook	tomar el sol	to sunbathe
hace	he/she/it/you make(s)	tumbona (f)	sun lounger
hace mucho calor	it's very hot	venimos	we come
hacer esquí acuático	to water-ski	venir	to come
		vez (f)	time, occasion

16.2 Watch out for your pronunciation

→ Let's practise the letters 'b', 'd', 'p' and 't'. Notice that in Spanish they sound softer when they are in the middle of the word than when they are

---

[1] vos = vosotros

16.3 Important notes

→ at the beginning. Examples: *bailar, sabes; dos, helado; pero, comprar; tenemos, carrete.*

→ These four letters sound very similar in English and Spanish, but they are slightly stronger in English. Listen to: *botella, desodorante, aspirina, mosquito.* Now say in English: *bottle, deodorant, aspirin, mosquito.*

→ Difficult words: Listen to these words and practise saying them: *lago, montañas, guía, colchoneta, fiesta, helado, queréis, alquilar, hacer, esquí, submarinismo, flotadores, necesario.*

16.3 Important notes

→ *Me gusta* and *me gustan*. Notice the difference between *me gusta el zumo* and *me gustan los zumos*. When you like one thing you use the word *gusta* (*me gusta el zumo*, I like the juice), and when you like two or more things you use the word *gustan* (*me gustan los zumos*, I like juices). The same applies to *te gusta, te gustan, os gusta, os gustan*, etc.

→ *Me gusta* is also used with verbs. See, for instance: *me gusta limpiar* (I like cleaning).

→ Negative sentences: We have seen how the word *no* goes before the verb: *no me quedan ...* (I do not have any ... left), *no sé* (I do not know). The following sentence in the dialogue above is no exception: *no es necesario* (it is not necessary). Notice that, unlike in English, the word *no* goes before *es* (it is).

→ *Hace calor* (it's hot) but *son las tres* (it's three o'clock). When it comes to common words, like *hace* in Spanish and *it is* in English, you will find that they do not always translate the way you expect. That is why it is more effective to learn words in context rather than in lists with fixed translations.

→ Other useful expressions: *tomar el sol* (to sunbathe), *dormir la siesta* (to have a nap), *¿por qué no?* (why not?), *¿cuánto tiempo?* (how long?), *hacer esquí acuático* (to water-ski), *hacer submarinismo* (to go scuba diving), *hace mucho calor* (it's very hot).

16. On holiday

16.4 Tip of the day

> Almost every Spanish word you learn you're bound to forget at some point. It's only by using them again and again that they'll stick.

16.5 You may wonder...

***In dialogue 1, why do you say* nosotras queremos ir al lago *and not just* queremos ir al lago?** *Nosotras* is there to emphasise that it is *us* who wants to go, and not Paco and Ramon who want to do something different. Related to this is the second translation of *yo quiero hacer submarinismo* (I, myself, want to go scuba diving), where *yo* is translated as 'I, myself' for emphasis.

***Could you use* tomar *instead of* llevar *in* nos vamos a llevar la colchoneta?** No. Although both verbs can translate as 'to take', *tomar* means 'to seize, consume, drink or eat', whereas *llevar* means 'to carry, bring or wear'.

How do you say 'there are too many beach umbrellas'? Hay demasiadas sombrillas. Notice that *demasiado* changes to *demasiada, demasiados* and *demasiadas* like all other describing words ending in 'o'.

Is* foto *a feminine word? Yes, it is. It is short for *la fotografía*.

How do you say 'to want'? *Querer.* For more information, go to p. 236

***What is the plural of* la vez?** *Las veces.* Notice that in the plural the 'z' becomes a 'c'. That is just because the spelling 'ze' is rarely used in Spanish.

16.6 Spanish words with something in common

→ *Alquilo* (I hire (out)), *alquilas* (you [tú] hire (out)), *alquila* (he/she/it hires (out), you [ud] hire (out)), *alquilamos* (we hire (out)), *alquiláis* (you [vos] hire (out)), *alquilan* (you [uds]/they hire (out)), *alquilar* (to hire (out)).[2]

16.6 Spanish words with something in common

→ *Cierro* (I close), *cierras* (you [tú] close), *cierra* (he/she/it closes, you [ud] close), *cerramos* (we close), *cerráis* (you [vos] close), *cierran* (you [uds]/they close), *cerrar* (to close), and *cerrado* (closed).

→ *Estoy* (I am), *estás* (you [tú] are), *está* (he/she/it is, you [ud] are), *estamos* (we are), *estáis* (you [vos] are), *están* (you [uds]/they are), *estar* (to be).

→ *Puedo* (I can), *puedes* (you [tú] can), *puede* (he/she/it can, you [ud] can), *podemos* (we can), *podéis* (you [vos] can), *pueden* (you [uds]/they can), *poder* (can).

→ *Quiero* (I want), *quieres* (you [tú] want), *quiere* (he/she/it wants, you [ud] want), *queremos* (we want), *queréis* (you [vos] want), *quieren* (you [uds]/they want), *querer* (to want).

→ *Vengo* (I come), *vienes* (you [tú] come), *viene* (he/she/it comes, you [ud] come), *venimos* (we come), *venís* (you [vos] come), *vienen* (you [uds]/they come), *venir* (to come).

→ *Este* (this - masculine) and *ese* (that - masculine).

→ *Primera* (first - feminine) and *primero* (first - masculine).

→ *¿Cuánto tiempo lleváis aquí?* (how long have you been here for?), *voy a llevarme* (I'm going to take with me).

→ *El polo* (the ice lolly) and *el pollo* (the chicken).

→ *Demasiados* (too many - masculine) and *demasiado* (too much - masculine).

---

[2]Remember that you can find more information on p. 234

16.7 Building up new sentences

Estoy de vacaciones.
I'm on holiday.
Voy a estar aquí tres semanas.
I'm going to be here for three weeks.
¿Me puedes sacar una foto?
Can you take my picture?
¿Cuánto tiempo lleváis de vacaciones?
How long have you been on holiday for?
Esta es la segunda vez que vienen.
This is the second time they come.
Hay demasiados vasos en el salón.
There are too many glasses in the sitting room.
Hoy no hace mucho calor.
Today it's not very hot.
Hace demasiado calor.
It's too hot.
¿Por qué no preguntas en el hotel de al lado?
Why don't you ask at the hotel next door?

16.8 Exercises

(See solutions on p. 216)

Exercise 1: Say these sentences in Spanish:

1. They're on holiday.
2. We're going to be here for four days.
3. We want to hire a beach umbrella.
4. Why don't we go to the sports shop?
5. How long have you [vos] been in the hotel for?
6. There are too many sun loungers at the swimming pool.
7. Today it's too hot.
8. First we have to have dinner.
9. Do you (tú) like sunbathing?
10. Do you (tú) like ice creams?

16.8 Exercises

Exercise 2: Which of the two words is being said?

1. estás	están	2. estáis	están
3. estás	estar	4. están	estar
5. estáis	estás	6. quiere	quieren
7. quiere	quiero	8. quieren	quiero
9. quieren	queréis	10. polo	pollo

Exercise 3: Match the questions with the appropriate answers:

1. ¿Cuánto tiempo vais a estar aquí?	*No, prefiero las verduras.*
2. ¿Tenemos que pagar ahora?	*Un euro.*
3. ¿Hay algún pepino en la nevera?	*A la una.*
4. ¿Hay alguna tumbona en la piscina?	*Lo siento, no me quedan.*
5. ¿Qué vais a hacer mañana?	*Tres días.*
6. ¿Te gustan los trenes?	*Sí, hay una.*
7. ¿Te gusta la fruta?	*Sí, hay uno.*
8. ¿Tiene chupetes?	*Vamos a ir al lago.*
9. ¿Cuánto cuestan las vendas?	*No, pueden pagar más tarde.*
10. ¿A qué hora vienen?	*No, prefiero los autobuses.*

Exercise 4: What would you put before each of the words below: *el, la, los* or *las*?

1. .... vacaciones
2. .... sol
3. .... fotos
4. .... calor
5. .... carretes
6. .... flotador
7. .... calmantes
8. .... fiebre
9. .... chupetes
10. .... biberón

Revise Lesson 4.

Lesson 17. At the supermarket 2

Diálogo 1

Sra Álvarez: Buenos días, ¿me puede poner cien gramos de salami, una docena de salchichas y medio kilo de carne picada?
Dependiente: Lo siento, no me queda salami. ¿Quiere salchichón?
Sra Álvarez: No, gracias. Me voy a llevar sólo las salchichas y la carne picada.

Diálogo 2

Sra Álvarez: Buenos días, ¿qué fruta tienes hoy?
Dependienta: Tengo ciruelas, cerezas, albaricoques, melocotones, piñas, peras y pomelos.
Sra Álvarez: ¿No tienes mandarinas?
Dependienta: No, no me quedan, pero vienen mañana.
Sra Álvarez: Vale. ¿Y qué verduras tienes?
Dependienta: Berenjenas, judías verdes, coliflores ...
Sra Álvarez: Dame una coliflor mediana y tres cuartos de kilo de judías verdes.
Dependienta: Te voy a poner un poco de perejil. Es gratis.

Diálogo 3

Sra Álvarez: Buenos días, ¿dónde tienen los guisantes congelados?
Dependienta: Los congelados están en el siguiente pasillo.
Sra Álvarez: (*Junto a los congelados*) Buenos días, ¿dónde tienen los botes de mermelada?
Dependienta: Aquí mismo.
Sra Álvarez: ¿Y las bolsas de patatas fritas?
Dependienta: Junto al pan y los bollos, detrás de las chocolatinas y los cereales.
Sra Álvarez: ¿Y los yogures?
Dependienta: Allí, junto a la margarina y la mantequilla.

DIALOGUE 1

Mrs Álvarez:	Good morning, can you give me a hundred grams of salami, a dozen sausages and half a kilo of mince? (lit: a dozen of sausages and half kilo of minced meat).
Shop assistant:	I'm sorry, I don't have any salami left. Do you want salami-type sausage?
Mrs Álvarez:	No, thanks. I'm going to take only the sausages and the mince.

DIALOGUE 2

Mrs Álvarez:	Good morning, what fruit do you have today?
Shop assistant:	I have plums, cherries, apricots, peaches, pineapples, pears and grapefruit.
Mrs Álvarez:	Don't you have tangerines?
Shop assistant:	No, I don't have any left, but they're coming tomorrow (lit: but they come tomorrow).
Mrs Álvarez:	OK. And what vegetables do you have?
Shop assistant:	Aubergines, French beans, cauliflowers ...
Mrs Álvarez:	Give me a medium cauliflower and three quarters of a kilo of French beans.
Shop assistant:	I'm going to give you a bit of parsley. It's free.

DIALOGUE 3

Mrs Álvarez:	Good morning, where do you have frozen peas?
Shop assistant:	The frozen food is in the next aisle (lit: The frozens are in the next aisle).
Mrs Álvarez:	(*Next to the frozen food*) Good morning, where do you have the jam jars? (lit: where do you have the jars of jam?)
Shop assistant:	Right here.
Mrs Álvarez:	And bags of crisps? (lit: And the bags of fried potatoes?)
Shop assistant:	Next to the bread and buns, behind the chocolate bars and cereals.
Mrs Álvarez:	And the yoghurts?
Shop assistant:	Over there, next to the margarine and the butter.

17. At the supermarket 2

17.1 New words

albaricoque (m)	apricot	mandarina (f)	tangerine
allí	there, over there	mantequilla (f)	butter
bollo (m)	bun	margarina (f)	margarine
bolsa (f)	bag	mediana	medium(-sized) (f)
bote (m)	jar	melocotón (m)	peach
carne picada (f)	mince	mermelada (f)	jam, marmalade
cereal (m)	cereal	pan (m)	bread
cereza (f)	cherry	patatas fritas (f/pl)	crisps, french fries
chocolatina (f)	chocolate bar	pera (f)	pear
ciruela (f)	plum	perejil (m)	parsley
coliflor (f)	cauliflower	piña (f)	pineapple
congelados	frozen	pomelo (m)	grapefruit
congelados (m/pl)	frozen food	salami (m)	salami
dame[1]	give me (command)	salchicha (f)	sausage
detrás de	behind	salchichón (m)	salami-type sausage
docena (f)	dozen		
gramo (m)	gram	tres cuartos	three quarters
gratis	free	un poco de	a bit of, some
guisante (m)	pea	yogur (m)	yoghurt
judías verdes (f/pl)	French beans		

17.2 Watch out for your pronunciation

→ Repeat after the Spanish speaker: *fa, fe, fi, fo, fu; va, ve, vi, vo, vu.*

→ Let's practise the letter 'f': *coliflor, fiesta, flotador, foto, fiebre, prefiere, farmacia.*

→ Important: Spanish words are never spelt with a 'ph'. Compare: 'the photo' and *la foto.*

→ Let's also practise the letter 'v': *individual, reserva, televisión, servicios, vegetariano, divorciado, Silvia, vitaminas.*

---

[1] *Dame = da + me* (give me).

17.3 Important notes

→ Difficult words: Listen to these words and practise saying them: *albaricoques, allí, cereales, cerezas, chocolatinas, congelados, docena, guisantes, mantequilla, mermelada, perejil, salchichas, yogur.*

17.3 Important notes

→ *Me voy a llevar* and *voy a llevarme* both mean *I'm going to take* or *I'm going to take with me*. As we saw on p. 119, the word *me* can go either before the verb *voy* or after the infinitive *llevar*. Here's another example: on p. 124, you could say *vamos a llevarnos* instead of *nos vamos a llevar*, and it would mean exactly the same thing.

→ *Dame una coliflor* (give me a cauliflower) is not as polite as *¿me puedes dar una coliflor?*, but is something you hear very often. When said with a friendly intonation, it is not considered rude.

→ *El siguiente pasillo*. As we know, describing words generally follow the noun they describe. The word *siguiente* is an exception in that it can go either before or after the noun it describes.

→ *Un poco de* (a bit of, some), when followed by a feminine noun, does not change to *poca*. Compare: *el vino/un poco de vino* (the wine/a bit of wine) and *la mantequilla/un poco de mantequilla* (the butter/a bit of butter).

→ Other useful expressions: *una docena de* (a dozen of), *tres cuartos de kilo de* (three quarters of a kilo of), *es gratis* (it's free), *detrás de* (behind).

17.4 Tip of the day

Try to set yourself specific targets, like 'I want to complete a new lesson every four days' or 'I am going to review a lesson every two days'.

17.5 You may wonder...

How do you say 'behind the bread'? Detrás del pan.

In the dialogues, why do the speakers sometimes say **tienes** *and others* **tienen**? *Tienes* (you [tú] have) is colloquial. It is the form you use with people you are in first name terms with. *Tienen* (you [uds] have) is formal. It is the form you use with people you are not in first name terms with. For more details, go back to p. 23.

Do you have another word for 'jam'? No. *Mermelada* means both *marmalade* and *jam*.

How do you say 'the sausages are free'? Las salchichas son gratis. Notice that the word *gratis* does not change, even with a feminine plural noun.

17.6 Spanish words with something in common

→ *Doce* (twelve) and *la docena* (the dozen).

→ *Medio* (half - masculine), *media* (half - feminine), and *mediana* (medium[-sized], feminine).

→ *El congelador* (the freezer) and *los congelados* (the frozen food). Try saying: *los congelados están en el congelador* (the frozen food is in the freezer).

→ *El pan* (the bread) and *la panadería* (the bakery).

→ *La chocolatina* (the chocolate bar) and *el chocolate* (the chocolate).

→ *Allí* (there, over there) and *aquí* (here).

17.7 Building up new sentences

¿Me puede poner una docena de huevos?
Can you give me a dozen eggs?

Me voy a llevar sólo una coliflor mediana.
I'm only going to take a medium cauliflower.

¿No tienes carne picada?
Don't you have mince?

Dame tres cuartos de kilo de albaricoques.
Give me three quarters of a kilo of apricots.

¿Me puede dar un poco de agua?
Can you give me a bit of water?

Los cereales son gratis.
The cereals are free.

La carne está congelada y el pescado también.
The meat is frozen and the fish too.

Los botes de aceitunas están detrás de las latas.
The olive jars are behind the tins.

A mí no me gustan los yogures de melocotón.
I don't like peach yoghurts.

Sólo quiero un café solo.
I only want a black coffee.

Me quedan dos melones medianos.
I have two medium(-sized) melons left.

¿Te gusta la mermelada de fresa?
Do you like strawberry jam?

17.8 Exercises

(See solutions on p. 217)

Exercise 1: Say these sentences in Spanish:
1. Can you [ud] give me a dozen mussels?
2. I'm going to take half a kilo of sausages.
3. Give me three quarters of a kilo of mince.
4. Can you (ud) give me a bit of rice?
5. The peas are frozen.
6. The bottles of oil are behind the bread.
7. Do you (tú) like pineapple yoghurts?
8. I have four rooms with bathroom left.
9. Why do they want to go today?
10. How much is the salami?

Exercise 2: Which of the two sentences is being said?
1. Quiero una docena.
   Quiero doce.
2. Tenemos una hora y media.
   Tenemos dos horas y media.
3. ¿Dónde está el congelador?
   ¿Dónde están los congelados?
4. No me gusta el chocolate.
   No me gustan las chocolatinas.
5. Quieren un poco de té.
   Quiere un poco de café.
6. Es gratis.
   Son gratis.
7. Cerramos a las dos.
   Cierran a las dos.
8. Prefiero los pomelos.
   Prefiere los pomelos.
9. Les recomiendo las judías verdes.
   Nos recomienda las judías verdes.
10. Esta casa está en Inglaterra.
    Estas casas están en Inglaterra.

17.8 Exercises

Exercise 3: According to the dialogue on p. 132, is each phrase true or false?

1. Es por la mañana.	T	F
2. La señora Álvarez quiere cien gramos de carne picada.	T	F
3. El dependiente no tiene salami.	T	F
4. La señora Álvarez no va a comprar salchichón.	T	F
5. Las mandarinas vienen mañana.	T	F
6. La señora Álvarez no quiere berenjenas.	T	F
7. El perejil cuesta mucho.	T	F
8. En el supermercado no hay congelados.	T	F
9. Las bolsas de patatas fritas están junto a los bollos.	T	F
10. No hay ni mantequilla ni margarina en el supermercado.	T	F

Exercise 4: Write down the plurals of these words (using *los* or *las*):

1. albaricoque   ....

2. bote   ....

3. cereal   ....

4. coliflor   ....

5. melocotón   ....

6. yogur   ....

7. salchichón   ....

8. vez   ....

9. jardín   ....

10. guisante   ....   Revise Lesson 5.

Lesson 18. Days, months and dates

Diálogo 1

Alicia:	¿Qué día es hoy?
Gonzalo:	Miércoles, veinticinco de noviembre. ¿Por qué?
Alicia:	Mañana por la tarde viene mi madre.
Gonzalo:	¿Cuántos días se va a quedar?
Alicia:	Hasta el domingo. El lunes que viene tiene que estar en Sevilla.
Gonzalo:	El martes viene Joaquín y se queda hasta el viernes. El miércoles vamos a cenar con sus padres y el jueves vamos a casa de su hermana.
Alicia:	El sábado tenemos que ir con mi madre a comprar el regalo de Jaime.

Diálogo 2

Carolina:	¿Qué día es tu cumpleaños?
Dolores:	El treinta y uno de enero.
Arancha:	Mi cumpleaños es el veintisiete de febrero.
Begoña:	Y el mío el dieciséis de marzo, este mes. Y el de Carolina es el nueve de abril.
Dolores:	El cumpleaños de mi padre es el diecinueve de mayo y el de mi madre el veintitrés de junio.
Arancha:	El doce de julio es el cumpleaños de mi novio y el uno de agosto es el de la novia de Pablo.
Carolina:	No, es el trece de septiembre.
Dolores:	El trece de octubre es el cumpleaños de mi hermano y el quince de diciembre el de mi hermana.

Diálogo 3

Abuela:	¿Qué vais a hacer esta semana?
Estefanía:	Esta tarde vamos a ir al cine y mañana por la mañana vamos a ir de compras.
Federico:	Mañana por la tarde tenemos una fiesta en casa de Arancha y el viernes por la noche vamos a ir a la discoteca nueva.
Estefanía:	Hoy por la noche viene el tío Gonzalo. Este año va a pasar las Navidades con nosotros. Y este fin de semana vamos a ir con él a ver a la abuela Alicia.

Dialogue 1

Alice:	What day is it today?
Gonzalo:	Wednesday, the twenty-fifth of November. Why? (lit: Wednesday, twenty-five of November)
Alice:	My mother's coming tomorrow evening (lit: Tomorrow in the evening comes my mother).
Gonzalo:	How long is she going to stay for? (lit: How many days is she going to stay?)
Alice:	Until Sunday. Next Monday she has to be in Seville (lit: The Monday that comes she has to ...)
Gonzalo:	Joachim comes on Tuesday and he's staying until Friday. On Wednesday we're going for dinner with his parents and on Thursday we're going to his sister's (lit: ... and the Thursday we go to house of his sister).
Alice:	On Saturday we have to go with my mother to buy Jaime's present (lit: to buy the present of Jamie).

Dialogue 2

Caroline:	What day is your birthday?
Dolores:	On the thirty-first of January.
Arancha:	My birthday is the twenty-seventh of February.
Begoña:	And mine is 16 March, this month. And Caroline's is 9 April.
Dolores:	My father's birthday is 19 May and my mother's is 23 June (lit: The birthday of my father is the nineteen of May and that of my mother 23 of June).
Arancha:	12 July is my boyfriend's birthday and 1 August is Paul's girlfriend's birthday.
Caroline:	No, it's 13 September.
Dolores:	My brother's birthday is 13 October and my sister's is 15 December.

Dialogue 3

Grandmother:	What are you going to do this week?
Stephanie:	This afternoon we're going to go to the cinema and tomorrow morning we're going shopping (lit: we go to go shopping).
Frederick:	Tomorrow evening we have a party at Arancha's and on Friday night we're going to the new nightclub (lit: .. a party in house of Arancha and ...).
Stephanie:	Uncle Gonzalo is coming tonight. This year he's going to spend Christmas with us. And this weekend we're going to go with him to see Grandmother Alice.

18. Days, months and dates

18.1 New words

abril	April	marzo	March
agosto	August	mayo	May
Alicia	Alice	mes (m)	month
año (m)	year	miércoles	Wednesday
Carolina	Caroline	mío	mine
cine (m)	cinema	Navidades (f/pl)	Christmas, Christmas season
compra (f)	shopping, purchase		
cuántos	how many	nosotros	we
cuántos días	how long, how many days	noviembre	November
		nueva	new
cumpleaños (m)	birthday	octubre	October
diciembre	December	pasar	to spend, to pass
domingo	Sunday	qué día es hoy	what day is it today
enero	January	que viene	next
Estefanía	Stephanie	quedarse	to stay
febrero	February	sábado	Saturday
Federico	Frederick	se queda	he/she/it/ stays, you [ud] stay
fin (m)	end		
fin de semana (m)	weekend	septiembre	September
ir de compras	to go shopping	Sevilla	Seville
jueves	Thursday	sus	his, her, its, your[1], their
julio	July		
junio	June	viene	he/she/it/ comes, you [ud] come
lunes	Monday		
martes	Tuesday	viernes	Friday

18.2 Watch out for your pronunciation

→ Repeat after the Spanish speaker: *ña, ñe, ñi, ño, ñu; na, ne, ni, no, nu*. Notice the difference between the 'n' and the 'ñ'.

→ Let's practise the letter 'ñ': *baño, señor, caña, pequeño, enseño, mañana, niños, champiñones, montaña, piña, cumpleaños*.

→ Now let's also practise the letter 'n': *Arancha, cine, enero, fin, lunes, Navidades, noviembre, nueva, tiene*.

---

[1] For more details about *su*, go to p. 145

18.3 Important notes

→ Difficult words: Listen to these words and practise saying them: *abril, agosto, diciembre, febrero, julio, marzo, mayo, miércoles, noviembre, nueva, nueve, octubre, septiembre, viene, viernes.*

18.3 Important notes

→ *El lunes* and *los lunes.* Notice that some of the days of the week have the same singular and plural: *el martes/los martes, el miércoles/los miércoles, el jueves/los jueves, el viernes/los viernes.*
However: *el sábado/los sábados, el domingo/los domingos.*

→ *Me queda* and *se queda.* Although they look similar, they actually have quite different meanings. Compare: *me queda uno* (I have one left) with *Juan se queda hasta el domingo* (John's staying till Sunday). Just as a curiosity, this is how you say 'I'm staying till Sunday': *Me quedo hasta el domingo*, and 'he has one left': *le queda uno.* We will not go into this any further in this book.

→ Notice the difference between *viene* (he/she/it comes or is coming, you [ud] come or are coming) and *que viene* (next). Compare: *Bernardo viene el viernes* (Bernard's coming on Friday) with *el viernes que viene* (next Friday). Try saying this sentence: *Bernardo viene el viernes que viene* (Bernard is coming next Friday).

→ *Mío* (mine - masculine). By now, we can guess the other three forms of 'mine'. Here are some examples: *la bolsa es mía* (the bag is mine), *el bollo es mío* (the bun is mine), *las bolsas son mías* (the bags are mine), *los bollos son míos* (the buns are mine). Notice that *mío, mía, míos, mías* have to agree with *el, la, los, las respectively.*

→ *En casa de Arancha* (at Arancha's). You could also say *en la casa de Arancha*, but it is more colloquial to say *en casa de* (without *la*). 'At home' is *en casa.* Here is one example: *estamos en casa* (we're at home).

→ *Usted*, *ustedes*, *yo* and *tú* are both masculine and feminine.

→ Other useful expressions: *¿qué día es hoy?* (what day is it today?), *¿cuántos días ...?* (how long?), *ir de compras* (to go shipping), *el viernes* *por la noche* (on Friday night), *pasar las Navidades* (to spend Christmas), *el fin de semana* (the weekend).

18.4 Tip of the day

> Why don't you occasionally go back to the 'Watch out for your pronunciation' sections of the lessons you've already done, to make sure you're pronouncing all the letters correctly?

18.5 You may wonder...

Can you write the months and the days with a capital letter? No. The spelling rules in Spanish dictate that they must all be written in lower case.

How do you say 'this Wednesday' and 'next Wednesday morning'? Este miércoles and el miércoles que viene por la mañana.

Can you say **el próximo lunes** *instead of* **el lunes que viene**? Yes, both are correct, and they both mean next Monday.

In Dialogue 1, why have you translated **vamos a cenar con sus padres** *as 'we're going for dinner with his parents', when in previous lessons* **vamos a cenar** *was translated as 'we're going to have dinner'?* I have given you a different translation to show you that, as long as the right message is conveyed, you can choose different ways of wording your translation.

In Dialogue 2, could you say ... **y el cumpleaños de mi madre es el veintitrés de junio?** Yes, but it sounds clumsy to repeat the word *cumpleaños* if you can avoid it.

What is the plural of **el cumpleaños** *(the birthday)? Los cumpleaños.* Notice that it is like *los lavaplatos* (the dishwashers) and *los microondas* (the microwaves), where the singular and plural have the same spelling, and unlike *el autobús/los autobuses* (the bus/the buses).

How do you say 'Merry Christmas and a Happy New Year'? *Feliz Navidad y Próspero Año Nuevo.*

What is the difference between **la Navidad** ***and*** **las Navidades?** Apart from the fact that *la Navidad* is singular and *las Navidades* plural, not much, really. They both tend to refer to 'the Christmas season'. 'Christmas', as in 25 December, is *el día de Navidad*.

18.6 Spanish words with something in common

→ *Cuánto* (how much - masculine), *cuánta* (how much - feminine), *cuántos* (how many - masculine) and *cuántas* (how many - feminine). Compare: *¿cuánto café quieres?* (how much coffee do you want?), *¿cuánta leche quieres?* (how much milk do you want?), *¿cuántos pimientos quieres?* (how many peppers do you want?), *¿cuántas galletas quieres?* (how many biscuits do you want?).

→ *Su* (his/her/its/your [of ud or uds]/their - singular) and *sus* (his/her/its/your [of ud or uds]/their - plural). Compare: *esta es su toalla* (this is his/her/its/your/their towel) with *estas son sus toallas* (these are his/her/its/your/their towels).

→ *Nosotras* (we - feminine) and *nosotros* (we - masculine). *Nosotras* is used when 'we' are all females, and *nosotros* is used when one of us, or more, is a male. The same goes for *vosotras* (you - feminine plural) and *vosotros* (you - masculine plural).

→ *Vienen* (you [uds]/they come) and *viene* (he/she/it comes, you [ud] come).

→ *La compra* (the shopping) and *comprar* (to shop, buy).

18. Days, months and dates

18.7 Building up new sentences

El viernes por la noche vienen sus primos.
His cousins are coming on Friday night.

¿Cuántos días vais a estar aquí?
How long are you going to be here for?

El año que viene voy a pasar las Navidades aquí.
Next year I'm going to spend Christmas here.

Su sobrino se queda hasta el sábado.
Her nephew is staying till Saturday.

¿Qué día es el cumpleaños de tu tía?
When's your aunt's birthday?

Este pasaporte es mío.
This passport is mine.

Esta caja es mía.
This box is mine.

Alicia tiene una maleta nueva.
Alice has a new suitcase.

¿Dónde van a estar este fin de semana?
Where are they going to be this weekend?

¿Cuántos años tienes?
How old are you?

Queremos ir con vosotros.
We want to go with you.

Hoy es martes, treinta de marzo.
Today is Tuesday, 30 March.

18.8 Exercises

See solutions on p. 218

Exercise 1: Say these sentences in Spanish:

1. On Wednesday afternoon we're going to the cinema.
2. Next month they're going to buy a TV.
3. Her mother prefers to go by car.
4. What day is their son's birthday?
5. This computer is mine.
6. This jug is mine.
7. On Friday night we have to see John.
8. Tomorrow morning they're coming to clean.
9. Today is Thursday, 15 January.
10. The grandparents are going to spend Christmas with us.

Exercise 2: Which phrase is the answer to each question you hear?

1. Sí, me gusta mucho.
2. No, no nos gustan.
3. No, tenemos muchas cosas en la nevera.
4. Martes.
5. Sí, nos gusta mucho.
6. No, no me quedan.
7. No, no me gustan.
8. Hasta el sábado.
9. Cuarenta.
10. Vamos a ir de compras.

18. Days, months and dates

Exercise 3: Complete each sentence using the following missing words:

> Missing words and phrases: viene, tengo que, vienen, tengo, tiene que, tiene, tenemos, tienen que, tenemos que, tienen

1. (Yo) .... ir con mi hermano a ver a mi padre.
2. (Ella) .... ir con su hermano a ver a su padre.
3. (Nosotros) .... ir con vosotros.
4. (Ellos) .... ir con nosotros.
5. (Yo) .... veinticuatro años.
6. (Ella) .... una casa en la playa.
7. (Nosotros) .... dos colchonetas.
8. (Ellos) .... cuatro regalos.
9. (Él) .... mañana.
10. (Ellos) .... el lunes que viene.

Exercise 4: Finish each new sentence using the describing word from the examples given:

Example: el bote es mío ⇒ la toalla ... ⇒ la toalla es mía

1. El coche es nuevo ⇒ La nevera ....
2. Las lentillas son nuevas ⇒ Los cepillos ....
3. El billete es mío ⇒ La manta ....
4. Patricia es pequeña ⇒ Emilio ....
5. Los botes son pequeños ⇒ Las camas ....
6. El peine es grande ⇒ La plaza ....
7. Los calamares son grandes ⇒ Las almejas ....
8. Mi tía está soltera ⇒ Mi tío ....
9. Mis primos están solteros ⇒ Mis primas ....
10. Mi abuela está viuda ⇒ Mi abuelo ....

Revise Lesson 6.

Lesson 19. Asking for directions

Diálogo 1

Julián:	¿Me puedes decir cómo se va a la estación de autobuses?
Víctor:	Sí, coge la segunda calle a la derecha, luego la primera a la izquierda y al fondo está la estación.
Julián:	¿Está muy lejos?
Víctor:	No, está bastante cerca.

Diálogo 2

Daniel:	¿Cómo se va al restaurante El Mar?
Gregorio:	¿En qué calle está?
Daniel:	En la avenida de Extremadura número cuarenta y cinco.
Gregorio:	Entonces tienes que seguir por aquí hasta llegar al cruce y luego girar a la izquierda y seguir todo recto. La avenida de Extremadura es la cuarta calle a la derecha.
Daniel:	¿Está cerca?
Gregorio:	A cinco minutos a pie.
Daniel:	Vale, gracias.

Diálogo 3

Guillermo:	¿Puedes indicarme dónde estamos en el plano?
Encarna:	Sí, estamos aquí, en el centro, junto a la estación de tren.
Guillermo:	Más despacio, por favor.
Encarna:	Uy, perdona.
Guillermo:	¿Sabes dónde está la calle Bolivia?
Encarna:	Sí, detrás de este edificio.
Guillermo:	¿Y la oficina de Correos?
Encarna:	Al final de esta calle, en la esquina.
Guillermo:	¿Está cerca de la estación de metro?
Encarna:	Sí, está al otro lado de la plaza.

Dialogue 1

Julian:	Can you tell how you get to the bus station? (lit: Can you tell me how one goes to ...)
Victor:	Yes, take the second street on the right, then the first on the left and at the end is the station.
Julian:	Is it very far?
Victor:	No, it's quite close.

Dialogue 2

Daniel:	How do you get to The Sea Restaurant?
Gregory:	Which street is it on?
Daniel:	It's on Extremadura Avenue, number forty-five.
Gregory:	In that case you have to continue along here until you get to the crossing and then turn left and continue straight ahead. Extremadura Avenue is the forth street on the right.
Daniel:	Is it close?
Gregory:	Five minutes by foot.
Daniel:	OK, thanks.

Dialogue 3

William:	Can you show me where we are on the map?
Encarna:	Yes, we're here, in the centre, next to the train station.
William:	Slower, please (lit: More slowly, please).
Encarna:	Oh, sorry.
William:	Do you know where Bolivia Street is?
Encarna:	Yes, behind this building.
William:	And the post office?
Encarna:	At the end of this street, on the corner.
William:	Is it close to the metro station?
Encarna:	Yes, it's on the other side of the square.

19. Asking for directions

19.1 New words

a cinco minutos	five minutes (away)	Extremadura	Extremadura
al final	at the end	final (m)	the end
al otro lado	on the other side	girar	to turn
a pie	by foot, on foot	Gregorio	Gregory
avenida (f)	avenue	indicarme[1]	to show me
bastante	quite	Julián	Julian
Bolivia	Bolivia	lejos	far
coge	take (a command)	llegar	to get to, to arrive
cómo se va a	how do you get to, how does one get to	luego	then, later
		mar (m)	sea
Correos	post office	más despacio	slower
cruce (m)	crossing	me puedes decir	can you [tú] tell me
cuarta	forth (f)	oficina (f)	office
Daniel	Daniel	oficina de Correos (f)	post office
despacio	slowly		
edificio (m)	building	otro	another, another one
esquina (f)	corner	recto	straight
estación (f)	station	restaurante (m)	restaurant
estación de autobuses (f)	bus station	seguir	to continue, to go on
estación de metro (f)	metro station, underground station	tienes que	you [tú] have to
		todo recto	straight ahead
		Víctor	Victor
estación de tren (f)	train station		

19.2 Watch out for your pronunciation

→ Repeat after the Spanish speaker: *ma, me, mi, mo, mu; na, ne, ni, no, nu*.

→ Let's practise the letter 'm': *me, cómo, primera, Extremadura, muy, estamos, más, metro*.

→ And let's revise the letter 'n': *estación, segunda, fondo, bastante, indicarme, tren, oficina, final*.

---

[1] *Indicarme = indicar + me* (to show me)

19.3 Important notes

→ Difficult word. Listen to these words and practise saying them: *coge, restaurante, avenida, seguir, cruce, girar, recto, despacio, Bolivia, edificio, Correos, esquina.*

19.3 Important notes

→ *Se va, se escribe, se paga, se sirve* and *se deja* are all impersonal forms. Their literal translation is 'one goes', 'one writes', 'one pays', 'one serves' and 'one leaves'. Having said that, the word 'one' tends to be avoided quite often in English and other forms are preferred. Let's see some real translations then: *¿cómo se va a la plaza?* (how do you get to the square?, *se escribe con H* (it's written with an H), *se paga aquí* (you pay here), *¿dónde se sirve el desayuno?* (where is breakfast served?), *la basura se deja en los cubos* (the rubbish should be left in the bins).

→ Giving addresses: This is how you say where you live: *Vivo en la calle Boliva número catorce* (I live at 14 Bolivia Street). And this is how you write your address on an envelope: *Calle Bolivia, nº 14* or *C/ Bolivia, 14.* The house number comes after the street name.

→ Double letters in Spanish: Here is an interesting spelling rule: the only double consonants that you get in Spanish are *cc, ll, nn, rr.* You don't see other double letters. Compare the following Spanish spellings with those in English: *la oficina*/the office, *el mensaje*/the message, *recomendar*/to recommend, *la botella*/the bottle. This rule does not apply to foreign words borrowed into Spanish, like *la pizzería.*

→ *Lejos* (far away) and *cerca* (close). Notice that these two words do not change. Compare: *el edificio está lejos* (the building is far away), *las casas están lejos* (the houses are far away), *la calle está cerca* (the street is close), *los restaurantes están cerca* (the restaurants are close).

→ Other useful expressions: *la estación de autobuses* (the bus station), *la estación de tren* (the train station), *bastante cerca* (quite close), *todo recto* (straight ahead), *a pie* (on foot), *más despacio* (slower), *al final de* (at the end of), *al otro lado de* (on the other side of).

19. Asking for directions

19.4 Tip of the day

> Try to use a separate dictionary as little as possible. Dictionaries can be quite frustrating, especially when you're still getting used to the new language. Instead, use the glossary at the end of this book if you need to check the translation of any of the words that come up in the dialogues.

19.5 You may wonder...

Where are **Extremadura** *and* **Bolivia***?* Extremadura is in Spain, and Bolivia in South America. To find out exactly where they are, have a look at the maps on pp. 230 and 231

In the dialogue, could you say **¿puedes decirme?** *instead of* **¿me puedes decir?***?* Yes, and it would mean the same thing: 'can you tell me?'. To revise this word order, go to p. 135 and see the examples: *me voy a llevar* and *voy a llevarme* (I'm going to take with me).

How do you say 'it's ten minutes away by car'? Está a diez minutos en coche.

19.6 Spanish words with something in common

→ *Coger* (to take) and *coge* (take - a command given to you [tú]).

→ *Cuatro* (four) and *cuarta* (forth - feminine).

→ *Correos* (the post office) and *el correo* (the mail, the post).

→ *El final* (the end) and *el fin* (the end). *El final* generally refers to the end of concrete things like: a film, party, book, list, queue, street or match. *El fin*, however, tends to be more abstract. It's used in phrases like: the end of an era, the end of the world, to put an end to, to come to an end, etc.

19.7 Building up new sentences

¿Tienes un restaurante en la calle Goya número sesenta y cuatro?
Do you have a restaurant at 64 Goya Street?

Vivo en la avenida de Bolivia número cuarenta.
I live at 40 Bolivia Avenue.

La oficina de Correos está en el siguiente cruce.
The post office is at the next crossing.

La plaza de Inglaterra está demasiado lejos de mi casa.
England Square is too far from my house.

¿Qué estación de metro está más cerca del hotel?
Which underground station is closer to the hotel?

Las oficinas están a quince minutos en coche de tu calle.
The offices are fifteen minutes away by car from your street.

¿Cómo se va a la calle Segovia?
How do you go to Segovia Street?

Me gusta bastante este plano.
I quite like this map.

¿En qué calle está la pastelería de tu amigo?
On which street is your friend's pastry shop?

Tienes que seguir por esta calle hasta llegar a la primera plaza.
You have to continue along this street until you get to the first square.

Perdona, ¿sabes dónde estamos?
Excuse me, do you know where we are?

19.8 Exercises

(See solutions on p. 220)

Exercise 1: Say these sentences in Spanish:

1. Do you have a small map?
2. You have to buy a train ticket.
3. I live at 11 Segovia Street.
4. How do you get to the post office?
5. The bus station is very close to my house.
6. I quite like this restaurant.
7. Today is Friday, 13 May.
8. The underground station is too far from here.
9. Which stop is closer?
10. We have to continue straight ahead.

Exercise 2: Fill in the missing words when you hear them?

1. .... recto
2. .... pie
3. .... despacio
4. al final ....
5. al otro .... de
6. el .... de semana
7. tres .... de kilo de
8. no .... necesario
9. todo .... día
10. .... la izquierda

19.8 Exercises

Exercise 3: Match the Spanish sentences with their English translations:

1. Hay demasiados restaurantes en esta plaza.
2. Hay demasiadas tiendas en esta calle.
3. Hace demasiado calor en la terraza.
4. El viaje dura demasiado.
5. Tenemos demasiado que hacer.
6. Hay demasiadas oficinas en este edificio.
7. Tienes demasiada leche en la nevera.
8. Los grandes almacenes son demasiado pequeños.
9. Tenemos demasiadas maletas en el coche.
10. Me quedan demasiados botes de mermelada.

We have too much to do.
There are too many offices in this building.
I have too many jam jars left.
There are too many shops on this street.
It's too hot in the balcony.
The trip is too long.
We have too many suitcases in the car.
There are too many restaurants in this square.
You have too much milk in the fridge.
The department store is too small.

Exercise 4: What would you put before each of the words below: *el* or *la*?

1. ..... final
2. ..... pie
3. ..... estación
4. ..... mar
5. ..... restaurante
6. ..... cumpleaños
7. ..... mes
8. ..... yogur
9. ..... perejil
10. ..... viaje

Revise Lesson 7.

Lesson 20.   101 to 1000, and more

101	ciento uno	512	quinientos doce
110	ciento diez	600	seiscientos
167	ciento sesenta y siete	602	seiscientos dos
200	doscientos	700	setecientos
258	doscientos cincuenta y ocho	772	setecientos setenta y dos
300	trescientos	800	ochocientos
328	trescientos veintiocho	843	ochocientos cuarenta y tres
400	cuatrocientos	900	novecientos
482	cuatrocientos ochenta y dos	915	novecientos quince
500	quinientos	1000	mil

first	*primero*	sixth	*sexto*
second	*segundo*	seventh	*séptimo*
third	*tercero*	eighth	*octavo*
forth	*cuarto*	ninth	*noveno*
fifth	*quinto*	tenth	*décimo*

20.1   Watch out for your pronunciation

→ Let's practise the letter 'u'. Repeat after the Spanish speaker: *segundo, cuarto, uno, nueve, cincuenta, puede, tumbona, yogur, jueves, octubre*.

→ Make sure you say the 'u' clear as in 'pool', and not as in 'but', 'grateful' or 'secure'.

→ The silent 'u'. Remember that the 'u' is silent in the spellings *gue, gui, que, qui*. Practise saying: *espaguetis, guía, queréis, quinto, quince, mosquito, peluquería, queso, pequeña, siguiente, seguir, guisante*.

→ Now practise reading the following numbers at the same speed as the Spanish speaker: *ciento cuarenta y siete* (147), *doscientos veinticuatro* (224), *trescientos cincuenta y ocho* (358), *cuatrocientos cincuenta y*

20.2 Important notes

nueve (459), *quinientos noventa y seis* (596), *seiscientos setenta y siete* (677), *setecientos ochenta y seis* (786), *ochocientos treinta y dos* (832), *novecientos setenta y tres* (973).

→ Difficult words: Listen to these numbers and practise saying them: *doscientos, trescientos, cuatrocientos, quinientos, seiscientos, setecientos, ochocientos, novecientos, mil.*

20.2 Important notes

→ Here are examples of some numbers from 101 to 1000, to give you an idea of how to build up the names for these numbers: *doscientos treinta y cuatro* (234), *trescientos cuarenta y seis* (346), *quinientos dos* (502), *setecientos catorce* (714), *ochocientos treinta* (830).

→ Notice that the word *y* (and) goes between the last two figures (*doscientos treinta y cuatro*, 234), unlike in English where it goes between the first two (two hundred and thirty-four). If one of the last two figures is a '0', the word *y* is not used, for example: *quinientos dos* (502), *ochocientos treinta* (830). Also, if the last two figures form a one-word number (*once, quince, dieciocho, veinticinco*, etc.), the word *y* is not used either, for example: *setecientos catorce* (714).

→ Feminine numbers. As we saw on p. 75, all Spanish numbers ending in *uno* also have a feminine form. Here are some more feminine versions of numbers: *doscientas, trescientas, cuatrocientas, quinientas, seiscientas, setecientas, ochocientas, novecientas* (i.e. 200 to 900); *primera, segunda, tercera, cuarta, quinta, sexta, séptima, octava, novena, décima* (i.e. 1st to 10th).

→ *Veintiún* to *noventa y un*. Just like the number *uno* becomes *un* before a masculine noun (*un coche*/one car), all other numbers ending in *uno* change in the same way. Here are some examples: *me quedan treinta y un melocotones* (I have 31 peaches left), *tenemos doscientos veintiún albaricoques* (we have 221 apricots), *quieren trescientos cuarenta y un tomates* (they want 341 tomatoes), *¿me puedes dar novecientos un bollos?* (can you give me 901 buns?).

20. 101 to 1000, and more

→ You write 1st, 2nd, 3rd, etc., in Spanish using a little 'o': $1^{\underline{o}}$, $2^{\underline{o}}$, $3^{\underline{o}}$, $4^{\underline{o}}$, $5^{\underline{o}}$, $6^{\underline{o}}$, $7^{\underline{o}}$, $8^{\underline{o}}$, $9^{\underline{o}}$, $10^{\underline{o}}$. As you might expect, feminine numbers have their own abbreviation too, using a little 'a': $1^{\underline{a}}$, $2^{\underline{a}}$, $3^{\underline{a}}$, $4^{\underline{a}}$, $5^{\underline{a}}$, $6^{\underline{a}}$, $7^{\underline{a}}$, $8^{\underline{a}}$, $9^{\underline{a}}$, $10^{\underline{a}}$.

→ Now compare the following numbers: *cinco/quince/cincuenta/quinientos* (5/15/50/500); *seis/sesenta/seiscientos* (6/60/600); *siete/setenta/setecientos* (7/70/700); *nueve/noventa/novecientos* (9/90/900). Notice, in particular, how the vowels differ between similar numbers.

→ Finally, this is how you use the number *mil* (1000): *tengo mil euros* (I have a thousand euros), *hay mil manzanas en el supermercado* (there are one thousand apples in the supermarket). Notice that in Spanish *mil* comes on its own, whereas in English you say *a thousand* or *one thousand*.

20.3 Tip of the day

Patience always pays off when studying a language.

20.4 You may wonder...

Is the word* cien *only used when saying 'a hundred'? That is correct. To say 101 through to 199, you have to use the word *ciento* instead. Here are some examples: *ciento ocho* (108), *ciento veinticuatro* (124), *ciento noventa y siete* (197).

What if I miss the* y *or put it in the wrong place? People will most likely guess what you are trying to say, but you risk being misunderstood.

How do you say 'eleventh, twelfth', etc.? After 'tenth' (*décimo*), Spanish speakers tend to use *once* (eleven), *doce* (twelve), *trece* (thirteen), etc.

20.5 Spanish words with something in common

→ *Doscientos, trescientos ... novecientos.* Notice that these numbers are formed by adding other numbers together, e.g. *dos-cientos, tres-cientos, cuatro-cientos*, etc., which literally mean *two hundreds*, *three hundreds*, *four hundreds*, etc.

→ *Tres/tercero, cuatro/cuarto, cinco/quinto, seis/sexto, siete/séptimo, ocho/octavo, nueve/noveno.* Notice the similarities between these numbers. It will make it easier for you to remember and recognise them.

20.6 Building up new sentences

Tienen cuatrocientos treinta y cuatro euros.
They have 434 euros.
Cuesta quinientos doce euros.
It costs 512 euros.
Cuestan seiscientos dieciocho euros.
They cost 618 euros.
¿Me puedes dar setecientos cuatro euros?
Can you give me 704 euros?
Me quedan ochocientos setenta y siete euros.
I have 877 euros left.
Quiero novecientos cincuenta y tres euros.
I want 953 euros.
Vivo en la primera calle a la derecha.
I live on the first street on the right.
Tiene que estar en la segunda calle a la izquierda.
It has to be on the second street on the left.
La zapatería está en la tercera calle a la izquierda.
The shoe shop is on the third street on the left.
La oficina de Correos está en la cuarta calle a la derecha.
The post office is on the fourth street on the right.
Los grandes almacenes están en la Quinta Avenida.
The department store is on Fifth Avenue.

20.7 Exercises

(See solutions on p. 221)

Exercise 1: Read these numbers out loud in Spanish:

a. 147   b. 251   c. 313   d. 460   e. 511
f. 628   g. 706   h. 895   i. 919   j. 1000

Exercise 2: Here is an extra speaking exercise. Read these numbers out loud in Spanish:

a. 1º   b. 2º   c. 3ª   d. 4ª   e. 5º
f. 6ª   g. 7º   h. 8ª   i. 9º   j. 10ª

Exercise 3: Which of the two numbers is being said?

a. 676   776   b. 554   445
c. 898   989   d. 383   838
e. 202   212   f. 916   917
g. 166   177   h. 413   414
i. 754   645   j. 115   105

Exercise 4: Match the Spanish words with the correct figures:

a. setecientos cuarenta y cinco	664
b. setecientos cincuenta y cuatro	754
c. seiscientos cuarenta y cinco	674
d. seiscientos cincuenta y cuatro	745
e. setecientos sesenta y cuatro	646
f. setecientos setenta y cuatro	747
g. seiscientos setenta y cuatro	764
h. seiscientos sesenta y cuatro	645
i. setecientos cuarenta y siete	774
j. seiscientos cuarenta y seis	654

20.7 Exercises

Exercise 5: Write down the numbers you hear:

a. .... b. .... c. .... d. .... e. ....

f. .... g. .... h. .... i. .... j. ....

Revise Lesson 8.

Lesson 21. At the tourist office

Diálogo

Miguel:	Buenos días, ¿me puede recomendar un hotel barato?
Empleada:	Sí, el hotel Alicante cuesta veintidós euros por noche y el Torrevieja veintiséis.
Miguel:	¿Están cerca del centro?
Empleada:	El hotel Torrevieja está ahí, entre la catedral y el Museo de Arte Moderno, y el Alicante está junto al monasterio.
Miguel:	¿Me puede reservar una habitación en el hotel Alicante?
Empleada:	¿Para cuántas noches?
Miguel:	Para tres. ... ¿Tiene folletos sobre la zona?
Empleada:	Sí, tenemos muchos. ¿Qué sitios desea visitar?
Miguel:	¿Cuáles son los sitios de interés?
Empleada:	La iglesia de la Virgen, el Palacio Real, el Monumento a la Victoria y el parque público.
Miguel:	¿Hay algún castillo cerca?
Empleada:	Sí, a veinte kilómetros hay un pueblo con un castillo y a treinta kilómetros hay un lugar muy interesante con un parador y muchos edificios históricos.
Miguel:	¿Cuánto cuesta la entrada al castillo?
Empleada:	La entrada es gratuita, pero sólo abren de nueve a una.
Miguel:	¿Y a qué hora abren los museos en general?
Empleada:	En general de nueve de la mañana a siete de la tarde, pero muchos cierran los lunes.
Miguel:	Otra cosa. ¿Me puede dar el horario de los barcos que van a la isla?
Empleada:	Sí, aquí tiene. Hay una excursión a la isla todos los días que empieza a las diez de la mañana.
Miguel:	¿Tiene un mapa de la isla?
Empleada:	No, no me queda ninguno. Pero tengo una guía con mapas de toda la región.
Miguel:	¿Está en inglés?
Empleada:	No, sólo en español. Si prefiere, hay otra oficina de turismo en la calle Argentina. Allí le pueden dar los mapas que necesita.
Miguel:	Vale, muchas gracias. Hasta luego.

Dialogue

Michael:	Good morning, can you recommend a cheap hotel?
Employee:	Yes, the Alicante Hotel costs twenty-two euros per night and the Torrevieja twenty-six.
Michael:	Are they near the centre?
Employee:	The Torrevieja Hotel is there, between the cathedral and the Modern Art Museum, and the Alicante is next to the monastery.
Michael:	Can you book a room for me at the Alicante Hotel?
Employee:	For how many nights?
Michael:	For three ... Do have brochures about the area?
Employee:	Yes, we have many. Which places do you wish to visit?
Michael:	Which are the places of interest?
Employee:	The church of the Virgin, the Royal Palace, the Monument to Victory and the public park.
Michael:	Is there a castle nearby?
Employee:	Yes, twenty kilometres away there's a small town with a castle and thirty kilometres away there's a very interesting place with a state-owned hotel and many historical buildings.
Michael:	How much does a ticket for the castle cost?
Employee:	The ticket is free, but they only open from nine till one.
Michael:	And when are the museums open in general? (lit: and at what time do the museums open in general?)
Employee:	In general from nine in the morning till seven in the evening, but many close on Mondays.
Michael:	Another thing. Can you give me the timetable for the boats that go to the island?
Employee:	Yes, here you are (lit: Yes, here you have). There is an excursion to the island every day that starts at ten in the morning.
Michael:	Do you have a map of the island?
Employee:	No, I don't have any left. But I have a guide with maps of the whole region.
Michael:	Is it in English?
Employee:	No, only in Spanish. If you prefer, there is another tourist office in Argentina Street. There they can give you the maps that you need.
Michael:	OK, thank you very much. See you later.

21. At the tourist office

21.1 New words

ahí	there, over there	mapa (m)	map
Alicante	Alicante	Miguel	Michael
Argentina	Argentina	moderno	modern
arte (m)	art	monasterio (m)	monastery
barato	cheap	monumento (m)	monument
barco (m)	boat, ship	muchos	many
castillo (m)	castle	museo (m)	museum
catedral (f)	cathedral	necesita	he/she/it needs, you [ud] need
cuáles	which		
empieza	he/she/it starts, you [ud] start	oficina (f) de turismo	tourist office
en general	in general	palacio (m)	palace
entrada (f)	(entrance) ticket	parador (m)	state-owned hotel
español (m)	Spanish language	parque (m)	park
excursión (f)	excursion	público	public
folleto (m)	brochure	pueblo (m)	small town, village
gratuita	free (f)	real	royal
históricos	historical	región (f)	region
horario (m)	timetable	reservar	to book, to reserve
iglesia (f)	church	sitio (m)	place
inglés (m)	English language	turismo (m)	tourism
interés (m)	interest	victoria (f)	victory
interesante	interesting	virgen (f)	virgin
isla (f)	island	visitar	to visit
lugar (m)	place		

21.2 Watch out for your pronunciation

→ Repeat after the Spanish speaker: *la, le, li, lo, lu; lla, lle, lli, llo, llu.*

→ Let's practise the letter 'l': *Alicante, español, iglesia, lugar, pueblo, lunes, inglés, lejos, luego, polo.*

→ Now let's revise the 'll': *pollo, folletos, castillo, allí, llave, botella, cebolla, toalla, galleta, pasillo, ella.*

21.3 Important notes

→ Notice that the Spanish and the English 'l' do not sound exactly the same. Compare the 'l' in these pairs of words: *hotel/hotel, catedral/cathedral, en general/in general, isla/island, Miguel/Michael, palacio/palace, público/public, real/real.*

→ Difficult words: Listen to these words and practise saying them: *monasterio, sitios, visitar, excursión, virgen, monumento, victoria, parque, interesante, parador, museos, horario, empieza, región, turismo, Argentina.*

21.3 Important notes

→ Word order: Spanish speakers tend to put the information that is most important first in a sentence. Observe these sentences from the dialogue: *¿hay algún castillo cerca? a veinte kilómetros hay un pueblo con un castillo* (is there a castle nearby? twenty kilometres away there is a small town with a castle). Here, the most important information is the distance. In *hay una excursión a la isla todos los días ...* (there is an excursion to the island every day ...), the employee is highlighting the fact that there is an excursion at all, and then that it takes place every day. If you revise the previous dialogues, you will find more examples of information-related word order.

→ The word *que* often means 'that'. In the dialogue, we have seen: *los barcos que van a la isla* (the boats that go to the island), *una excursión ... que empieza* (an excursion ... that starts), *los mapas que necesita* (the maps that you need). Do not confuse *que* (that) with the question word *qué* (what, which). Compare: *¿qué sitios desea visitar?* (which places do you wish to visit?) with *los sitios que desea visitar* (the places that you wish to visit). Notice that the word 'that' is often dropped in English (the maps you need), but *que* has to always be there in Spanish.

→ *El/la* and 'the' are not always used the same way in both languages, as we saw on p. 32. Sometimes you would not use 'the' in English but would use *el* or *la* in Spanish. Other times you use 'the' but not *el* or *la*, although this is much less common. Compare these sentences: *el restaurante está en la avenida de Extremadura* (the restaurant is in

21. At the tourist office

Extremadura Avenue), *me gustan los mejillones* (I like mussels), *tiene que coger la línea 4* (you have to take line 4), *el desayuno se sirve de siete a nueve* (breakfast is served from seven till nine); but *¿pago aquí o en caja?* (do I pay here or at the till? on p. 56).

→ *Aquí* (here), *ahí* (there, over there), *allí* (there, over there). When pointing at something 'there', you can use either *allí* or *ahí*. When pointing at two different things 'there', you use *ahí* for the closest one and *allí* to refer to the furthest of the two. The reason why two different words are used is to emphasise that you are talking about two different places. Here is an example: *una está ahí y la otra allí* (one is there and the other one over there).

→ Other useful expressions: *por noche* (per night), *a veinte kilómetros* (twenty kilometres away), *en general* (in general), *otra cosa* (another thing), *todos los días* (every day), *si prefiere* (if you prefer).

21.4 Tip of the day

> The more you know about the Spanish-speaking world and its cultures, the easier you'll find it to understand the language. That's because languages reflect the way people live, their history, economy, religion, climate, humour, politics, and everything that surrounds them.

21.5 You may wonder...

*In the dialogue, can you translate ¿***hay algún castillo cerca?** *as 'are there any castles nearby?'* Yes, that is correct.

Is **mapa** *(map) a masculine word?* It is. Remember that not all words ending in 'a' are feminine.

What is the difference between **mapa** *and* **plano?** *Un plano* is a city map, whereas *un mapa* shows roads, paths, rivers, etc., rather than streets.

21.6 Spanish words with something in common

What is the difference between **lugar** *and* **sitio?** In the dialogue above, they both mean the same thing. You could say *¿cuáles son los lugares de interés?* (which are the places of interest?) and *hay un sitio muy interesante* (there is a very interesting place) instead.

Do you ever write **Juan es español** *(John is Spanish) or* **Tomás es inglés** *(Thomas is English) with a capital letter on* **español** *or* **inglés?** No, never.

How do the describing words **inglés, español** *and* **real** *(English, Spanish, royal) change in the feminine and in the plural?* The feminine singulars are: *inglesa, española, real*. The masculine plurals are: *ingleses, españoles, reales*. The feminine plurals are: *inglesas, españolas, reales*.

How can I master words like **a, en, de, por, para,** *etc?* With a lot of practise. Rules can help, but it is mostly usage that will make you familiar with when to use them.

21.6 Spanish words with something in common

→ *Necesito* (I need), *necesitas* (you [tú] need), *necesita* (he/she/it needs, you [ud] need), *necesitamos* (we need), *necesitáis* (you [vos] need), *necesitan* (you [uds]/they need), *necesitar* (to need). For more information, go to p. 234

→ *Cuál* (which or which one - singular, masculine and feminine) and *cuáles* (which or which ones - plural, masculine and feminine).

→ *Gratuita* (feminine) and *gratis* (masculine and feminine, singular and plural) both mean 'free'. *Gratis*, however, is more colloquial and more common than *gratuita*.

→ *El horario* (the timetable) and *la hora* (the time).

→ *Interesante* (interesting) and *de interés* (of interest).

21.7 Building up new sentences

¿Nos puede recomendar algún museo interesante?
Can you recommend any interesting museums (to us)?

¿Está muy lejos de la catedral?
Is it very far from the cathedral?

¿Me puede reservar una mesa en el restaurante del parador?
Can you book a table for me at the state-owned hotel restaurant?

¿Cuáles son los parques públicos más interesantes de la región?
Which are the most interesting public parks in the region?

El castillo de la isla creo que no es interesante.
I don't think the castle on the island is interesting.

El pueblo de mis abuelos está a dos kilómetros de la estación de tren.
My grandparents' village is two kilometres away from the train station.

Vivo en un lugar que está cerca de la playa.
I live in a place that's close to the beach.

Tampoco tengo el horario de los autobuses.
I don't have the timetable for the buses either.

Queremos hacer una excursión a una de las islas.
We want to make an excursion to one of the islands.

Vienen todos los días a ver a su abuela.
They come every day to see their grandmother.

Mis primas son inglesas y mis amigos son españoles.
My cousins are English and my friends are Spanish.

En esta tienda tienen los planos que necesito.
In this shop they have the maps I need.

21.8 Exercises

(See solutions on p. 222)

Exercise 1: Say these sentences in Spanish:
1. The beds are very cheap.
2. My house is far from the church.
3. I don't like going to the island by boat.
4. Which are the most interesting excursions?
5. I don't think we've got entrance tickets.
6. In general, do you like museums?
7. I don't know if it's close to the centre.
8. Can you give me two brochures in English?
9. Which small town is the castle in?
10. Can you tell me how you get to the cathedral?

Exercise 2: Which of the two words is being said?

1. ahí	allí	2. aquí	ahí
3. barato	barata	4. español	española
5. gratuito	gratuita	6. inglés	inglesa
7. interesante	interesantes	8. moderno	moderna
9. necesito	necesita	10. público	pública

Exercise 3: According to the dialogue on p. 164, is each of these statements true or false?

1. Miguel quiere una habitación en un hotel barato.	T	F
2. El hotel Alicante cuesta menos que el Torrevieja.	T	F
3. El hotel Torrevieja está al lado del monasterio.	T	F
4. No nos quedan folletos sobre la zona.	T	F
5. El Palacio Real es interesante.	T	F
6. Hay un castillo a menos de treinta kilómetros.	T	F
7. La entrada al castillo cuesta bastante.	T	F
8. El castillo abre por la tarde.	T	F
9. Muchos museos abren a las nueve.	T	F
10. Los lunes no hay excursión a la isla.	T	F

21. At the tourist office

Exercise 4: Translate these sentences into Spanish:

1. I like having dinner in this restaurant.
1. *Translation:* ....

2. Can you recommend a good hotel (to me)?
2. *Translation:* ....

3. The pears are cheaper than the strawberries.
3. *Translation:* ....

4. The cinema is one kilometre away from my house.
4. *Translation:* ....

5. The church is far from the village.
5. *Translation:* ....

6. How much does it cost to send an email message?
6. *Translation:* ....

7. How much do the dishwashers cost?
7. *Translation:* ....

8. Every day we go shopping in the supermarket.
8. *Translation:* ....

9. My uncle is not English, but he's called Smith.
9. *Translation:* ....

10. Where are the tangerines from?
10. *Translation:* ....

Revise Lesson 9.

Lesson 22. Clothes and shoes

Diálogo

Dependienta:	Buenas tardes, ¿te atienden?
Marina:	No, todavía no. ¿Me puedes enseñar los pantalones del escaparate? ¿Los tienes en rojo?
Dependienta:	Sí, los tenemos en varios colores: blanco, amarillo, rojo, marrón, azul y negro.
Marina:	Vale, entonces, ¿me puedo probar los azules?
Dependienta:	¿Qué talla usas?
Marina:	La cuarenta. También quiero probarme esta falda, este bañador y este bikini.
Dependienta:	Vale. El probador está aquí mismo.
Marina:	¿Cuánto cuesta el vestido rosa?
Dependienta:	Cuarenta y seis euros, pero sólo me queda la talla treinta y ocho. Éste otro está de oferta, tiene un descuento del veinte por ciento.
Marina:	No me gusta mucho el color. ¿Lo tienes en verde?
Dependienta:	Creo que no. Voy a ver ... No, no lo tengo. ¿Quieres ver alguna camisa o camiseta?
Marina:	Tengo ya muchas. Prefiero ver las chaquetas y los sombreros.
Dependienta:	Los sombreros están en la segunda planta con los bolsos, las gorras, las corbatas y los abrigos.
Marina:	¿Tenéis zapatos y zapatillas?
Dependienta:	Sí, están aquí, detrás de las blusas y los jerseys.
Marina:	... ¿Puedo probarme éstos?
Dependienta:	¿Qué número calzas?
Marina:	El treinta y siete. ¿Me puedes traer también estas zapatillas en el treinta y ocho?
Dependienta:	Ahora mismo te traigo todo.
Marina:	(*Unos minutos más tarde*) El bañador no me queda bien. Me voy a llevar los pantalones, el bikini naranja y estos zapatos.
Dependienta:	¿Vas a pagar en efectivo o con tarjeta?
Marina:	Con tarjeta. ¿Aceptáis Visa?
Dependienta:	Sí, claro. .. . Firma aquí, por favor. ... Aquí tienes el recibo.
Marina:	Muchas gracias. Por cierto, ¿cuándo empiezan las rebajas?
Dependienta:	El jueves de la semana que viene.

Dialogue

Shop assistant:	Good afternoon, are you being served? (lit: do they serve you?)
Marina:	No, not yet. Can you show me the trousers in the shop window? Do you have them in red?
Shop assistant:	Yes, we have them in several colours: white, yellow, red, brown, blue and black.
Marina:	OK, then, can I try the blue ones on?
Shop assistant:	What size do you take? (lit: What size do you use?)
Marina:	A 40. I also want to try on this skirt, this swimming costume and this bikini.
Shop assistant:	OK. The changing room is right here.
Marina:	How much does the pink dress cost?
Shop assistant:	46 euros, but I only have size 38s left. This other one is on offer, it has a 20% discount (lit: it has a discount of the 20%).
Marina:	I don't like the colour very much. Do you have it in green?
Shop assistant:	I don't think so (lit: I believe that no). I'm going to check ... (lit: I go to see ...). No, I don't have it. Do you want to see any shirts or T-shirts?
Marina:	I have plenty already. I'd prefer to see the jackets and the hats (lit: I prefer to see ...).
Shop assistant:	The hats are on the second floor with the handbags, caps, ties and coats.
Marina:	Do you have shoes and trainers?
Shop assistant:	Yes, they're here, behind the blouses and the jumpers.
Marina:	... Can I try these on?
Shop assistant:	What shoe size do you take? (lit: What number do you wear?)
Marina:	A 37. Can you also bring me these trainers in a 38?
Shop assistant:	I'll bring you everything right away (lit: Right away I bring you everything).
Marina:	(*A few minutes later*) The swimming costume doesn't fit me. I'm going to take the trousers, the orange bikini and these shoes.
Shop assistant:	Are you going to pay cash or by card?
Marina:	By card. Do you accept Visa?
Shop assistant:	Yes, of course. ... Sign here, please. ... Here is the receipt (lit: Here you have the receipt).
Marina:	Thank you very much. By the way, when do the sales start?
Shop assistant:	Next week on Thursday (lit: The Th. of the week that comes).

22. Clothes and shoes

22.1 New words

abrigo (m)	coat	los	them, the (m/pl)
aceptáis	you [vos] accept	marrón	brown
amarillo	yellow	negro	black
atienden	you [uds]/they serve	no me queda bien	it doesn't fit/suit me
azul	blue	número (m)	(shoe) size, number
bañador (m)	swimming costume	o	or
bikini (m)	bikini	oferta (f)	offer
blanco	white	pantalones (m/pl)	trousers
blusa (f)	blouse	planta (f)	floor, plant
bolso (m)	handbag	por cierto	by the way
calzas	you [tú] wear	probador (m)	changing room
camisa (f)	shirt	probar	to try, to try on
camiseta (f)	T-shirt	probarme	to try on (me)
chaqueta (f)	jacket	quieres	you [tú] want
color (m)	colour	rebajas (f/pl)	sales
con tarjeta	by card	recibo (m)	receipt
corbata (f)	tie	rojo	red
empiezan	you [uds]/they start	rosa	pink
en efectivo	cash	sombrero (m)	hat
enseñar	to show	talla (f)	(clothes) size
escaparate (m)	shop window	tarjeta (f)	card
está de oferta	it's on offer	todavía	yet, still
éste otro	this other one	traigo	I bring
estos	these	usas	you [tú] use
éstos	these ones	verde	green
falda (f)	skirt	vestido (m)	dress
firma	sign (a command)	Visa	Visa
gorra (f)	cap	ya	already
jersey (m)	jumper	zapatilla (f)	trainer, sports shoe
lo	it	zapato (m)	shoe

22.2 Watch out for your pronunciation

→ Let's practise the letter 'x': *mixta, ex, próximo, kleenex, Extremadura, sexto, excursión.*

→ It has to be said that Spanish speakers often pronounce the 'x' like an 's'. Listen to these words in the recordings: *mixta, próximo, Extremadura, sexto, excursión.*

22.3 Important notes

→ Difficult words: Listen to these words and practise saying them: *aceptáis, atienden, chaqueta, empiezan, gorras, jersey, marrón, rebajas, tarjeta, todavía, zapatillas*.

22.3 Important notes

→ Colours. Like all other describing words, colours have either two forms or four. Here are some colours with two forms: *naranja/naranjas, rosa/rosas, marrón/marrones, verde/verdes, azul/azules, gris/grises*. Some of the colours with four forms are: *blanco/blanca/blancos/blancas, amarillo/amarilla/amarillos/amarillas, rojo/roja/rojos/rojas, negro/negra/negros/negras*.

→ Notice that *rosa* and *naranja* are both masculine and feminine, even though they end in 'a'. Look at these examples: *el vestido naranja es mío* (the orange dress is mine), *la camisa naranja es mía* (the orange shirt is mine), *el sombrero rosa no es mío* (the pink hat isn't mine), *la gorra rosa no es mía* (the pink cap isn't mine).

→ *Los*. Compare: *¿me puedes enseñar los pantalones del escaparate?* (can you show me the trousers in the shop window?) with *¿los tienes en rojo?* (do you have them in red?). Notice that in the first sentence *los* means *the*, and in the second one it means *them*. Here is a useful rule: *los* (the) goes before a masculine plural noun, whereas *los* (them) goes before a verb.

→ *Aceptáis* means 'you [vos] accept'. Here is the vosotros form of some other verbs you know: *cenar/cenáis* (you have dinner), *limpiar/limpiáis* (you clean), *comprar/compráis* (you buy), *alquilar/alquiláis* (you hire), *pagar/pagáis* (you pay). To find out more, see the tables on p. 233.

→ Other useful expressions: *todavía no* (not yet), *éste otro* (this other one), *está de oferta* (it's on offer), *no me queda bien* (it doesn't fit me), *pagar en efectivo* (to pay cash), *pagar con tarjeta* (to pay by card), *por cierto* (by the way).

22.4 Tip of the day

> Practise using words in context, rather than on their own. Lists of words will only stick in your mind for a day or two, and then they'll vanish, whereas phrases will stay.

22.5 You may wonder...

In the dialogue above, could you say ¿Cuál es tu talla? (what's your size?)? Yes, that is correct.

How do you say 'I don't like ties very much'? No me gustan mucho las corbatas. Notice that *mucho* does not change, as it goes with the verb *gustan* rather than with the plural noun *las corbatas*.

Does tengo ya muchas *mean 'I have plenty already' or 'I have many already'?* It means both things. Once again, to let you see that translations can be worded in different ways, I have chosen a new English word (plenty) rather than using the translation you already know (many).

What is the difference between todavía *and* ya? *Todavía* means *yet* or *still*, and *ya* means *already*.

In the dialogue above, what does el *refer to in ...* estas zapatillas en el treinta y ocho *(... these trainers in a thirty-eight)?* It refers to *el número* (the size). The reason why the word *número* has been dropped is because, in context, it is obvious that it is the shoe size we are talking about.

22.6 Spanish words with something in common

→ *Quiero* (I want), *quieres* (you [tú] want), *quiere* (he/she/it wants, you [ud] want), *queremos* (we want), *queréis* (you [vos] want) and *quieren* (you [uds]/they want). For more information, go to p. 236

→ *Probar* (to try on) and *el probador* (the changing room).

22.7 Building up new sentences

→ *No me queda bien* (it doesn't fit/suit me) and *no me queda agua* (I don't have any water left).

→ *La camisa* (the shirt) and *la camiseta* (the T-shirt).

→ *Los zapatos* (the shoes), *las zapatillas* (the trainers) and *la zapatería* (the shoe shop).

→ *Firma* (sign - a command given to you [tú]) and *firme* (sign - a command given to you [ud]).

22.7   Building up new sentences

Todavía no tenemos chaquetas para la boda.
We still don't have jackets for the wedding.

Prefiero los pantalones marrones y las zapatillas negras.
I prefer the brown trousers and the black trainers.

Ésta otra no está de oferta.
This other one is not on offer.

Ya tiene un bikini verde.
She already has a green bikini.

¿En qué planta están los abrigos de señora?
Which floor are the women's coats on?

¿Puedo probarme estos zapatos en el treinta y nueve?
Can I try on these shoes in a thirty-nine?

¿Puedo pagar con tarjeta?
Can I pay by card?

¿De qué color es tu vestido?
What colour is your dress?

22.8 Exercises

(See solutions on p. 223)

Exercise 1: Say these sentences in Spanish:
   1. They still don't have a car.
   2. I don't like white coats very much.
   3. How much is the yellow cap in the shop window?
   4. I don't think they're going to buy new towels this year.
   5. The handbags are on the fifth floor.
   6. I don't know if the T-shirts are on offer.
   7. By the way, when is your brother coming?
   8. I prefer to pay cash.
   9. Can you tell me which floor the jumpers are on?
   10. The black trousers don't fit me.

Exercise 2: Which of the two sentences is being said?
   1. No me gustan mucho estas camisas.
      No me gusta mucho esta camisa.
   2. Prefiero los rojos.
      Prefiere las rojas.
   3. ¿Cuánto cuestan estas camisas?
      ¿Cuánto cuesta esta camisa?
   4. Todos los lunes visitan a su abuela.
      Todos los lunes visitas a tu abuela.
   5. No sé dónde está tu corbata negra.
      No sé dónde están tus corbatas negras.
   6. La camisa blanca está de oferta.
      Las camisas blancas están de oferta.
   7. Los abrigos están en la cuarta planta.
      Los abrigos están en la quinta planta.
   8. ¿Puedo probarme estos vestidos?
      ¿Puedo probarme este vestido?
   9. El pueblo de mi padre está a seis kilómetros.
      El pueblo de mi madre está a siete kilómetros.
   10. Mis amigos son ingleses.
       Mis amigas son inglesas.

22.8 Exercises

Exercise 3: Complete the sentences using the correct form of the words in brackets:

1. Tenemos dos billetes .... (blue)
2. ¿Cuántos autobuses .... hay en la parada? (red)
3. No me queda arroz .... (white)
4. ¿Tiene chupetes .... ? (yellow)
5. No vendemos biberones .... (pink)
6. ¿No tienes flotadores ....? (black)
7. En la estación hay dos trenes .... (grey)
8. Quiero comprar tres bikinis .... (white)
9. Me gustan mucho estos pantalones .... (green)
10. El helado de fresa es .... (pink)

Exercise 4: Translate these sentences into Spanish:

1. We don't want to have dinner yet.
1. *Translation:* ....
2. I don't like white swimming costumes very much.
2. *Translation:* ....
3. How much are the trousers in the shop window?
3. *Translation:* ....
4. I don't know her name.
4. *Translation:* ....
5. The white T-shirts are on offer.
5. *Translation:* ....
6. They already have too many caps.
6. *Translation:* ....
7. Which floor are the shoes on?
7. *Translation:* ....
8. Can I pay by Visa?
8. *Translation:* ....
9. The department store is close to the beach.
9. *Translation:* ....
10. These islands are very interesting.
10. *Translation:* ....

Revise Lesson 10.

Lesson 23. Renting a car

Diálogo

Mercedes: Buenos días, ¿te puedo ayudar en algo?
Alejandro: Sí, quiero alquilar un coche automático con aire acondicionado.
Mercedes: Lo siento, no alquilamos coches automáticos, pero tenemos todos estos modelos.
Alejandro: ¿Cuánto cuesta el monovolumen?
Mercedes: Por semana, cuatrocientos cincuenta euros y tres días, doscientos cincuenta.
Alejandro: Es demasiado caro. Vamos a ver. ¿Cuánto cuesta la categoría B?
Mercedes: Aquí tienes las tarifas de todas las categorías. Los precios incluyen: kilometraje ilimitado, seguro a todo riesgo y el IVA.
Alejandro: ¿Podemos devolver el coche en el aeropuerto?
Mercedes: Sí. Por cierto, aquí tengo un folleto con la oferta especial de este mes.
Alejandro: Mmm, no está mal. Tiene un maletero grande. Otra cosa, ¿dónde puedo alquilar una moto?
Mercedes: En nuestra tienda de la carretera de Murcia. Está a quinientos metros, pero a esta hora hay mucho tráfico. Es mejor ir por la tarde.
Alejandro: ¿Hay algún aparcamiento por allí?
Mercedes: Sí, detrás del supermercado hay uno y junto al parque hay otro.
Alejandro: Vale. Voy a alquilar el modelo de la oferta especial por una semana.
Mercedes: Muy bien, ¿puedo ver tu carné de conducir? ... Vale, gracias, ¿me puedes dar tu tarjeta de crédito?
Alejandro: Aquí tienes. ¿Me puedes dar cambio para el parquímetro?
Mercedes: Por supuesto. Aquí tienes los papeles con el número de la matrícula y el seguro, y aquí tienes el cambio. Te voy a dar también un plano de la ciudad, por si acaso.
Alejandro: ¿Me puedes decir dónde está la gasolinera más cercana?
Mercedes: A trescientos metros de aquí. Al otro lado de la autovía. Este modelo consume gasolina sin plomo.

Dialogue

Mercedes:	Good morning, can I help you with anything?
Alexander:	Yes, I want to rent an automatic car with air conditioning.
Mercedes:	I'm sorry, we don't rent out automatic cars, but we have all these models.
Alexander:	How much does the people carrier cost?
Mercedes:	Per week, 450 euros, and three days, 250.
Alexander:	It's too expensive. Let's see. How much does the category B cost?
Mercedes:	Here are the tariffs for all categories (lit: Here you have the tariffs of all the categories). Prices include: unlimited mileage, comprehensive insurance and VAT.
Alexander:	Can we return the car at the airport?
Mercedes:	Yes. By the way, here is a brochure with this month's special offer (lit: ... here I have a brochure with the special offer of ...).
Alexander:	Mmm, it's not bad. It's got a large boot. Another thing, where can I rent a motorbike?
Mercedes:	In our shop on Murcia Road. It's 500 metres away, but at this hour there's a lot of traffic. It's better to go in the afternoon.
Alexander:	Is there a car park around there?
Mercedes:	Yes, there's one behind the supermarket, and there's another next to the park.
Alexander:	OK. I'm going to rent the special offer model for a week.
Mercedes:	Very well, can I see your driving licence? ... OK, thanks, can I have your credit card? (lit: can you give me your credit card?)
Alexander:	Here you are. Can you give me change for the parking meter?
Mercedes:	Of course. Here are the papers with the registration number and the insurance, and here is your change (lit: and here you have the change). I'm also going to give you a city map, just in case.
Alexander:	Can you tell me where the closest petrol station is?
Mercedes:	Three hundred metres away from here. On the other side of the dual carriageway. This model takes unleaded petrol.

23. Renting a car

23.1 New words

aeropuerto (m)	airport
a esta hora	at this hour, at this time of day
Alejandro	Alexander
alquilamos	we rent (out)
aparcamiento (m)	car park
automático	automatic
autovía (f)	dual carriageway
carné (m)	identity card, membership card
carné de conducir (m)	driving licence
caro	expensive
carretera (f)	road
categoría (f)	category
cercana	close, near (f)
ciudad (f)	city, town
conducir	to drive
consume	he/she/it/you take(s), he/she/it/you consume(s)
demasiado	too
devolver	to return, to give back
especial	special
gasolina (f)	petrol
gasolinera (f)	petrol station, gas station
ilimitado	unlimited
incluyen	you [uds] include, they include
IVA (m)	VAT
kilometraje (m)	mileage
mal	bad
maletero (m)	(car) boot
matrícula (f)	number plate, licence plate
mejor	better
metro (m)	metre
modelo (m)	model
monovolumen (m)	people carrier
moto (f)	motorbike
muy bien	very well
no está mal	it's not bad
nuestra	our (f)
número de matrícula (m)	registration no.
parquímetro (m)	parking meter
plomo (m)	lead (the metal)
por allí	around there
por semana	per week
por si acaso	just in case
por supuesto	of course
precio (m)	price
riesgo (m)	risk
seguro (m)	insurance
seguro (m) a todo riesgo	comprehensive insurance
sin plomo	unleaded
tarifa (f)	tariff
tarjeta (f) de crédito	credit card
tráfico (m)	traffic

23.2 Watch out for your pronunciation

→ Let's revise some words that you may be pronouncing wrong. Repeat after the Spanish speaker: *aeropuerto, automático, categoría, especial, modelos, tráfico, colores, jerseys, Argentina, verde, catedral, general, excursión, televisión, interesante, histórico, parque, región, rosa.*

23.3 Important notes

→ Here are some of the mistakes which are commonly made: dropping the 'o' in *aer<u>o</u>puerto, model<u>o</u>s* and *tráfic<u>o</u>*. Dropping the 'i' in *excurs<u>i</u>ón, telev<u>i</u>sión* and *reg<u>i</u>ón*. Pronouncing the 'au' in *<u>au</u>tomático* as an 'o' instead of 'a - u'. Dropping the last 'a' in *categorí<u>a</u>*. Dropping the last 'e' in *verd<u>e</u>, interesant<u>e</u>, color<u>e</u>s* and *parqu<u>e</u>*. Pronouncing the 'j' and the 'g' as an English 'j' in *Ar<u>g</u>entina, <u>j</u>ersey, <u>g</u>eneral* and *re<u>g</u>ión*. Pronouncing the 'v' as an English 'v' in *<u>v</u>erde* and *tele<u>v</u>isión*. Pronouncing the 'c' like 'sh' in *espe<u>c</u>ial*. Forgetting that the 'h' is silent in *<u>h</u>istórico*. Forgetting that the 'u' is silent in *parq<u>u</u>e*. Pronouncing the 's' in *ro<u>s</u>a* as an English 'z'. Not rolling the 'r' enough in *<u>r</u>osa*. Stressing the wrong vowel in words like *especi<u>a</u>l, col<u>o</u>res, catedr<u>a</u>l, gener<u>a</u>l, excursi<u>ó</u>n* and *televisi<u>ó</u>n*. We will see more about this on p. 195

→ To avoid these mistakes, the trick is to read the dialogues along with the Spanish speakers over and over.

→ Above all, it is very important that you get the following letters right: the five vowels (*a, e, i, o, u*), the 'j' (which should sound like a very strong English 'h'), the silent 'h', the 's' (which is never said like an English 'z'), and the silent 'u' in *que, qui, gue, gui*.

→ Difficult words: Listen to these words and practise saying them: *Alejandro, alquilamos, autovía, ciudad, devolver, incluyen, kilometraje, matrícula, mejor, parquímetro, riesgo*.

23.3 Important notes

→ *Por* and *para*. Here are the two basic rules of when to use one or the other: *por* is followed by a cause or reason, whereas *para* is followed by an aim or consequence. Compare: *me gusta por el color* (I like it because of the colour) with *una mesa para cinco* (a table for five, i.e. the aim being to sit five people at the table). *Por* is also used for periods of time. In the dialogue above we've seen *por semana, cuatrocientos cincuenta euros* (per week, 450 euros).

→ *Por* also means 'through' or 'along': *tenemos que seguir por esta calle* (we have to continue along this street).

→ *Para* also comes before deadlines or points in time: *la sandía es para mañana* (the watermelon is for tomorrow); and destinations: *el autobús para Barcelona* (the bus to Barcelona).

→ Finally, we have seen *por* in many fixed expressions: *por favor* (excuse me, please), *por la mañana* (in the morning), *por ciento* (per cent), *por cierto* (by the way), etc.

→ Words ending in *-dad* are feminine. Here are two examples: *la Navidad* (Christmas) and *la ciudad* (the city, the town).

→ Other useful expressions: *por semana* (per week), *seguro a todo riesgo* (comprehensive insurance), *no está mal* (it's not bad), *a esta hora* (at this hour, at this time of day), *es mejor* (it's better), *por allí* (around there), *muy bien* (very well), *por supuesto* (of course), *por si acaso* (just in case).

23.4 Tip of the day

Use the words you've learned so far to help you learn new words. The 'Spanish Words With Something In Common' section is there to highlight words that can be learned by association.

23.5 You may wonder...

How do you say 'we have all these motorbikes'? *Tenemos todas estas motos.*

How do you say 'the shop is too expensive' and 'the shops are too expensive'? *La tienda es demasiado cara* and *las tiendas son demasiado caras*. Notice that *demasiado* does not change, but *caro* does.

How do you say 'our car', 'our cars' and 'our shops'? *Nuestro coche, nuestros coches* and *nuestras tiendas*. The four forms of 'our' agree with the thing or things we own, and not with *us*, males or females.

23.6 Spanish words with something in common

Is* moto *a masculine word? No, it is a feminine word despite ending in 'o'. *La moto* is short for *la motocicleta* (the motorbike), just like *la foto* is short for *la fotografía* (the photograph).

Does* alquilar *mean 'to hire' or 'to hire out'? It means both things. In fact, it also means: 'to rent, to rent out' and 'to let'.

What is the difference between* la ciudad *and* el pueblo*? A *ciudad* is a city or town, and a *pueblo* is a small town or a village. More specifically, *un pueblo pequeño* is a village, *un pueblo grande* is a small town or simply a town, and a large town is *una ciudad*.

23.6 Spanish words with something in common

→ *Por allí* (around there) and *por aquí* (around here).

→ *Más cercana* (closest - feminine) and *más cerca* (closer).

→ *La gasolina* (the petrol) and *la gasolinera* (the petrol station).

→ *El aparcamiento* (the car park), *el parquímetro* (the parking meter) and *aparcar* (to park).

→ *El kilómetro* (the kilometre) and *el kilometraje* (the mileage).

→ *El maletero* (the boot [of the car]) and *la maleta* (the suitcase).

→ *El aeropuerto* (the airport) and *el aire* (the air).

23.7 Building up new sentences

Quiero alquilar un apartamento en el playa por dos semanas.
I want to rent an apartment on the beach for two weeks.

Los coches automáticos son demasiado caros.
The automatic cars are too expensive.

¿Puedo devolver el abrigo si no me queda bien?
Can I return the coat if it doesn't fit me?

Por cierto, ¿tenéis alguna oferta especial este mes?
By the way, do you have any special offers this month?

Estamos en nuestra casa de Alicante con nuestros hijos.
We are at our house in Alicante with our children.

A esta hora hace mucho calor en la calle.
At this time of day it's very hot in the street.

Es mejor ir en metro cuando hay tráfico.
It's better to go on the underground when there's traffic.

Todavía no tengo carné de conducir.
I still don't have a driving licence.

Hoy no puedo pagar con tarjeta de crédito.
Today I can't pay by credit card.

¿Nos puedes dar cambio para el aparcamiento?
Can you give us change for the car park?

Por supuesto que no vamos a ir.
Of course we're not going.

¿Cómo se llama la ciudad más cercana?
What's the closest city called?

23.8 Exercises

(See solutions on p. 224)

Exercise 1: Say these sentences in Spanish:

1. We want to hire this model for a week.
2. The ties in this shop are too expensive.
3. When do I have to return the car?
4. By the way, what's your (tú) name?
5. Our children aren't going to spend Christmas in a hotel.
6. It's better to wait an hour.
7. I still don't know what time they're coming.
8. I think I have three credit cards.
9. Can you [tú] give me change for a coffee?
10. How much is this month's special offer?

Exercise 2: Which phrase is the answer to each question you hear?

1. No, no tengo ninguna.
2. Las cuatro y veinte.
3. Roja.
4. Sí, tengo uno.
5. A las siete y media.
6. Sí, me gustan mucho.
7. Sí, tenemos dos.
8. No, no nos gustan mucho.
9. Tres euros y veinte céntimos.
10. El viernes que viene.

Exercise 3: Match the English with the Spanish expressions:

1. no está mal	cash
2. por allí	it's not bad
3. por supuesto	not yet
4. por si acaso	on foot
5. todavía no	straight ahead
6. no me queda bien	around there
7. en efectivo	just in case
8. por cierto	of course
9. todo recto	by the way
10. a pie	it doesn't fit me

23. Renting a car

Exercise 4: Translate these sentences into Spanish:

1. They want to hire a small car.
1. *Translation:* ....

2. The jumpers in this shop are too expensive.
2. *Translation:* ....

3. The brown shoes don't fit me.
3. *Translation:* ....

4. Today we're going to have dinner with our English (f) friends.
4. *Translation:* ....

5. Can you [ud] give me a map of the city?
5. *Translation:* ....

6. It's better to buy fruit at the fruit shop.
6. *Translation:* ....

7. They still don't have the children's presents.
7. *Translation:* ....

8. I'd prefer to see an interesting museum.
8. *Translation:* ....

9. The blankets are on offer today.
9. *Translation:* ....

10. Which floor are the microwaves on?
10. *Translation:* ....

Revise Lesson 11.

Lesson 24. At the bank

Diálogo 1

Almudena: Buenos días, quiero cambiar ciento cincuenta libras a euros y cien dólares a euros también. ¿A cuánto está el cambio?

Empleado: Hoy la libra esterlina vale 1, 42 (uno coma cuarenta y dos) euros y el dólar americano 0, 89 (cero coma ochenta y nueve).

Almudena: ¿Cobran comisión?

Empleado: Sí, cobramos un 1, 5% (un uno coma cinco por ciento).

Almudena: Vale. También quiero cobrar este cheque de viaje.

Empleado: ¿Puedo ver su carné de identidad o su pasaporte?

Almudena: Aquí tiene. ¿Me puede dar siete billetes de diez euros, cinco de veinte y el resto en billetes de cinco? Ah, y también quiero varias monedas de un euro.

Empleado: En seguida se lo doy. ... Firme aquí, por favor.

Almudena: ¿Me puede decir si hay algún cajero automático cerca de la playa?

Empleado: Sí, hay uno en la calle Venezuela.

Almudena: ¿Y hay algún banco en el aeropuerto?

Empleado: Sí, tenemos una sucursal cerca de las salidas internacionales.

Diálogo 2

Borja: Buenas tardes, ¿me puede dar dos sellos de un euro y un sello para una postal? Ah, y quiero mandar esta carta por correo certificado a Irlanda.

Empleada: Son cinco euros y sesenta y cinco céntimos.

Borja: Por cierto, ¿me puede decir dónde hay un buzón?

Empleada: Tenemos uno aquí, a la entrada, y hay otro en la plaza.

Borja: Vale, me voy a llevar también dos sobres, un paquete de tabaco, una caja de cerillas y un encendedor. ¿Puedo pagar con tarjeta? Casi no me queda dinero.

Empleada: No, lo siento, no aceptamos tarjetas.

Borja: Entonces, ahora vuelvo. Tengo que sacar dinero.

DIALOGUE 1

Almudena:	Good morning, I want to change one hundred and fifty pounds into euros and one hundred dollars into euros too. What's the exchange rate? (lit: At how much is the exchange?)
Clerk:	Today the pound sterling is worth 1.42 euros, and the American dollar 0.89.
Almudena:	Do you charge commission?
Clerk:	Yes, we charge 1.5%.
Almudena:	OK. I also want to cash in this traveller's cheque.
Clerk:	May I see your identity card or your passport?
Almudena:	Here you are. Can you give me seven ten euro notes, five twenties, and the rest in five euro notes? Oh, and I also want several one euro coins.
Clerk:	I'll give it to you at once (lit: At once I give it to you). ... Sign here, please.
Almudena:	Can you tell me if there is a cash dispenser near the beach?
Clerk:	Yes, there is one in Venezuela Street.
Almudena:	And is there a bank at the airport?
Clerk:	Yes, we have a branch close to the international departures.

DIALOGUE 2

Borja:	Good afternoon, can you give me two one euro stamps and a stamp for a postcard? Oh, and I want to send this letter by registered mail to Ireland.
Clerk:	It's five euros and sixty-five cents.
Borja:	By the way, can you tell me where there is a letterbox?
Clerk:	We have one here, at the entrance, and there is another one in the square.
Borja:	OK, I'm also going to take two envelopes, a packet of cigarettes, a box of matches and a lighter. Can I pay by card? I have almost no money left.
Clerk:	No, I'm sorry, we don't accept cards.
Borja:	Then, I'll be right back (lit: Then, now I return). I have to get some money out.

24. At the bank

24.1 New words

a cuánto está	how much is
a la entrada	at the entrance
aceptamos	we accept
americano	American
banco (m)	bank
billete (m)	note, ticket
buzón (m)	letterbox, mailbox
cajero automático (m)	cash dispenser
cambiar	to change
cambio (m)	exchange, change
carné de identidad (m)	identity card
carta (f)	letter
casi	almost
casi no	hardly
cerilla (f)	match
cheque (m)	cheque
cheque de viaje (m)	traveller's cheque
cobramos	we charge
cobran	you [uds]/they charge
cobrar	to charge, to cash in
coma (f)	comma
comisión (f)	commission
correo certificado (m)	registered mail
dinero (m)	money
dólar (m)	dollar
doy	I give
encendedor (m)	lighter
en seguida	right away
Irlanda	Ireland
internacional	international
libra esterlina (f)	pound sterling
libra (f)	pound
moneda (f)	coin
paquete (m)	packet, parcel
postal (f)	postcard
resto (m)	rest
salida (f)	departure, exit
sello (m)	stamp
sobre (m)	envelope
sucursal (f)	branch
tabaco (m)	tobacco cigarettes
vale	it is worth, it costs
Venezuela	Venezuela
vuelvo	I return

24.2 Watch out for your pronunciation

→ Let's revise other Spanish words that you may be pronouncing wrong. Repeat after the Spanish speaker: *americano, banco, cheque, comisión, dólar, Irlanda, internacional, esterlina, tabaco, Venezuela, avenida, Bolivia, estación, oficina, restaurante, abril, agosto, diciembre, cereal, docena, montaña, aspirinas, vitaminas, recomendar.*

→ Here are some of the mistakes that are commonly made: pronouncing the 'i' as in 'Ireland' in I̲rlanda and vi̲taminas. Pronouncing the 's' or 'c' like 'sh' in comi̲sión, interna̲cional, esta̲ción. Pronouncing the

24.3 Important notes

single 'r' like in English in *americano, dólar, esterlina*. Getting the vowels wrong in *tabaco, restaurante, agosto, montaña*. Pronouncing the Spanish 'z' as an English 'z' in *Venezuela*. Pronouncing the 'a' wrong in *abril*. Pronouncing the 'ea' like in English in *cereal* instead of 'e - a'. Dropping the endings in *avenida, aspirinas, recomendar, cheque, oficina*.

→ For other mistakes which are commonly made, go back to p. 185.

→ Notice that the great majority of infinitives are stressed on the last vowel: *bailar* (to dance), *cambiar* (to change), *cenar* (to have dinner), *cobrar* (to charge), *comprar* (to buy), *estar* (to be), *limpiar* (to clean), *mandar* (to send), *pagar* (to pay); *beber* (to drink), *coger* (to take), *hacer* (to do, to make), *poner* (to put); *conducir* (to drive), *decir* (to say), *dormir* (to sleep), *elegir* (to choose), *venir* (to come).

→ Difficult words: Listen to these words and practise saying them: *aceptamos, buzón, cerillas, encendedor, en seguida, paquete, sellos, sucursal, vuelvo*.

24.3 Important notes

→ *A* and *en*. Here are the basic rules of when to use them: *a* is used with verbs that express movement; *en* is used to say where things or people are. Compare: *mañana vamos a Inglaterra* (we're going to England tomorrow) and *estamos en Inglaterra* (we're in England).

→ *A* is also used with the verb *ir* (to go) to say what people are going to do. *Voy a cenar con ella* (I'm going to have dinner with her), *vamos a limpiar la cocina* (we're going to clean the kitchen), *van a pagar aquí* (they're going to pay here).

→ *A* also comes up in many fixed expressions, for instance: *a nombre de* (in the name of), *de siete a nueve* (from seven till nine), *frente a* (in front of), *a pie* (on foot), *a la izquierda* (on the left), *cambiar libras a euros* (change pounds into euros), etc.

24. At the bank

→ *En* comes up in many fixed expressions too, for instance: *pagar en caja* (to pay at the till), *en lata* (tinned), *hacer transbordo en* (to change trains in), *en general* (in general), *una guía en inglés* (a guide in English), *pagar en efectivo* (to pay cash), etc.

→ Notice that decimals are written as commas. For example, look at how 1.42 is written and said in Spanish: 1, 42 (uno coma cuarenta y dos).

→ I cannot emphasise enough how important it is to go over things again. When you finish this lesson, continue revising lessons 13 through to 24.

→ Other useful expressions: *¿a cuánto está el cambio?* (what's the exchange rate?), *en seguida* (at once), *mandar por correo* (to send by post), *a la entrada* (at the entrance), *un paquete de tabaco* (a paquet of cigarettes), *casi no me queda dinero* (I have almost no money left), *ahora vuelvo* (I'll be right back), *sacar dinero* (to take money out).

24.4 Tip of the day

Make sure you speak loudly and clearly when communicating in Spanish. Often the reason why people can't understand language learners is because they mumble and hesitate, and then say something too quietly.

24.5 You may wonder...

How do you say 'the international arrivals'? Las llegadas internacionales.

How do you say 'I have almost no rooms left'? Casi no me quedan habitaciones. Notice that the word *casi* does not change.

How do you say 'the cigarette' in Spanish? El cigarrillo or el cigarro.

24.6 Spanish words with something in common

- *Cambiar* (to change) and *el cambio* (the change, the exchange).

- *El carné de identidad* (the identity card) and *el carné de conducir* (the driving licence).

- *El sobre* (the envelope) and *sobre* (about).

- *El cajero automático* (the cash dispenser) and *la caja* (the box, the till).

- *Vuelvo* (I return) and *volver* (to return). For more information about verb forms, see the verb tables on p. 233.

- *La salida* (the departure, exit) and *sale* (he/she/it leaves, you [ud] leave).

24.7 Building up new sentences

Quiero cambiar cien euros a libras esterlinas.
I want to change one hundred euros into pounds sterling.
Las zapatillas valen veintisiete euros.
The trainers cost twenty-seven euros.
¿Dónde puedo cobrar este cheque de viaje?
Where can I cash in this traveller's cheque?
No sé dónde está mi carné de conducir.
I don't know where my driving licence is.
Prefiero pagar con billetes de diez euros.
I prefer to pay with ten euro notes.
¿Qué vamos a hacer con el resto?
What are we going to do with the rest?
Tienes que venir en seguida.
You have to return at once.
¿Me puede decir dónde está la salida?
Can you tell me where the exit is?
En este pueblo no hay casi ningún buzón.
In this village there are almost no letter boxes.
Tenemos que sacar dinero antes de ir a cenar.
We have to take money out before going to dinner.

24.8 Exercises

(See solutions on p. 226)

Exercise 1: Say these sentences in Spanish:

1. I want to change fifty pounds sterling into euros.
2. We are going to go at once.
3. Can we cash in traveller's cheques at this branch?
4. Your (you = tú) driving licence is on the kitchen table.
5. I don't know where the rest is.
6. The toilets are next to the international departures.
7. I want to send this parcel by registered mail.
8. I have almost no water left.
9. Where can we take money out?
10. I'm sorry, I don't have any one euro stamps left.

Exercise 2: Which of the words below completes each sentence you hear?

Missing words:	cheques, salidas, sacar, cambiar, correo, carné, casi, cajero, paquetes, entrada

1. Quiero .... doscientas libras esterlinas a euros.
2. Aquí no pueden cobrar .... de viaje.
3. .... no me quedan billetes de cinco euros.
4. ¿Me puede decir dónde están las .... internacionales?
5. Todavía tengo que comprar dos .... de tabaco.
6. ¿Por qué no vamos a .... dinero ahora?
7. ¿Dónde está mi .... de conducir?
8. Creo que hay un .... automático en la otra calle.
9. Hay un buzón a la .... de la estación.
10. ¿Lo quiere mandar por .... certificado?

24.8 Exercises

Exercise 3: According to the dialogue, is each statement true or false?

1. Almudena quiere cambiar 140 libras.	T	F
2. El dólar vale 0,89 euros.	T	F
3. Almudena quiere cobrar dos cheques de viaje.	T	F
4. Almudena quiere seis billetes de diez euros.	T	F
5. No hay ningún cajero automático cerca de la playa.	T	F
6. Hay una sucursal en el aeropuerto.	T	F
7. Borja quiere tres sellos.	T	F
8. La empleada no sabe dónde hay un buzón.	T	F
9. Borja quiere pagar en efectivo.	T	F
10. Borja tiene que sacar dinero.	T	F

Exercise 4: Translate these sentences into Spanish:

1. I don't know where to cash in this traveller's cheque.

1. *Translation:* ....

2. I prefer to take money out at my branch.

2. *Translation:* ....

3. We're going to take the bus at once.

3. *Translation:* ....

4. I have neither stamps nor postcards.

4. *Translation:* ....

5. In this city there are almost no shoe shops.

5. *Translation:* ....

6. Can you [ud] give me two packets of cigarettes?

6. *Translation:* ....

7. The coats in this shop are too expensive.

7. *Translation:* ....

8. By the way, how do you get to the airport?

8. *Translation:* ....

9. It's better to take money out in the morning.

9. *Translation:* ....

10. How much are the lighters?

10. *Translation:* ....

24. At the bank

Revise Lesson 12.

Then revise Lessons 13 through to 24.

Solutions to the exercises

Lesson 1: Numbers: 0 to 30

Exercise 1: Read these numbers out loud in Spanish: a. 10 diez, b. 13 trece, c. 7 siete, d. 30 treinta, e. 8 ocho, f. 15 quince, g. 20 veinte, h. 9 nueve, i. 11 once, j. 16 dieciséis.

Exercise 2: Which of the two numbers is being said?: a. dos (2), b. diez (10), c. doce (12), d. tres (3), e. catorce (14), f. seis (6), g. diecisiete (17), h. quince (15), i. veinte (20), j. veinticuatro (24).

Exercise 3: Match the Spanish words with the figures: a. tres (3), b. veinticinco (25), c. trece (13), d. veintiséis (26), e. catorce (14), f. veintisiete (27), g. once (11), h. veinticuatro (24), i. quince (15), j. veintinueve (29).

Exercise 4: Write down the figures for the numbers you hear: a. 10 (diez), b. 0 (cero), c. 6 (seis), d. 13 (trece), e. 9 (nueve), f. 15 (quince), g. 7 (siete), h. 2 (dos), i. 23 (veintitrés), j. 12 (doce).

Lesson 2: Greetings

Exercise 1: Say these phrases in Spanish: 1. Are you on holiday?, ¿Estás de vacaciones?; 2. Good afternoon, Buenas tardes; 3. Good morning, Buenos días; 4. Hello, how are you?, ¿Hola, qué tal estás?; 5. Me too, Yo también; 6. My name is John, Me llamo Juan; 7. See you soon!, ¡Hasta pronto!; 8. What's your name?, ¿Cómo te llamas?; 9. Where are you from?, ¿De dónde eres?; 10. Which hotel are you in?, ¿En qué hotel estás?

Exercise 2: Which of the two is the answer to each question you hear?: 1. ¿De dónde eres? De Inglaterra (Where are you from? From England); 2. ¿Cómo te llamas? Margarita (What's your name? Margaret); 3. ¿Qué tal estás? Bien, gracias (How are you? Fine, thanks); 4. ¿Estás de vacaciones? Sí (Are you on holiday? Yes); 5. ¿En qué hotel estás? En el Hilton (Which hotel are you in? The Hilton); 6. ¿Dónde estás? En la playa (Where are you?

On the beach); 7. ¿En qué hotel estás? En el Inglaterra (Which hotel are you in? The England); 8. ¿Cómo te llamas? Juan (What's your name? John); 9. ¿De dónde eres? De Inglaterra (Where are you from? From England); 10. ¿Qué tal estás? Bien (How are you? Fine).

Exercise 3: Match the Spanish phrases with their English translations: 1. Hola, ¿qué tal estás?, Hello, how are you?; 2. ¿Eres de Inglaterra?, Are you from England?; 3. Buenos días, María, Good morning, Mary; 4. ¿Qué tal estás?, How are you?; 5. ¿Cómo te llamas?, What's your name?; 6. ¿Dónde estás?, Where are you?; 7. Hasta luego, María, See you later, Mary; 8. Te presento a mi amiga María, This is my friend Mary; 9. Me llamo María, My name is Mary; 10. ¿Estás de vacaciones?, Are you on holiday?

Exercise 4: Write down the words you hear: 1. Hola, Hello; 2. Buenos días, Good morning; 3. Qué, What, which; 4. Entonces, Then; 5. También, Also; 6. Inglaterra, England; 7. Las vacaciones, The holidays; 8. Hasta la vista, See you; 9. Dónde, Where; 10. Me llamo, My name is.

Lesson 3: At the hotel

Exercise 1: Say these sentences in Spanish: 1. ¿Puedo ver el hotel? Can I see the hotel?; 2. ¿Qué tal estás? How are you?; 3. ¿Tienen habitaciones con aire acondicionado? Do you have rooms with air conditioning?; 4. ¿Tienen habitaciones libres? Do you have any rooms free?; 5. ¿Cómo te llamas? What's your name?; 6. Antes de las cuatro. By four o'clock; 7. Hay tres radios en la habitación. There are three radios in the room; 8. Tengo una reserva a nombre de Miller. I have a reservation in the name of Miller; 9. ¿De dónde eres? Where are you from?; 10. Un momento, por favor. One moment, please.

Exercise 2: Which of the two sentences is being said?: 1. ¿Puedo ver el baño?, Can I see the bathroom?; 2. Hay dos ordenadores, There are two computers; 3. Quiero dos habitaciones, I want two rooms; 4. Antes de las doce, By twelve o'clock; 5. Tenemos seis maletas, We have six suitcases; 6. Me puede dar la llave?, Can you give me the key?; 7. Tiene dos habitaciones, You have two rooms; 8. ¿Puedo mandar dos mensajes?, Can I send two messages?; 9. Quiero una radio, I want a radio; 10. Las llaves de María, Mary's keys.

Exercise 3: Match the Spanish sentences with their English translations: 1. ¿Podemos ver su ordenador?, Can we see your (ud) computer?; 2. ¿Puedo ver su ordenador?, Can I see your (ud) computer?; 3. Tenemos un ordenador, We have a computer; 4. Tenemos dos ordenadores, We have two computers; 5. Tengo dos ordenadores, I have two computers; 6. Tengo un ordenador, I have a computer; 7. Tiene dos ordenadores, You (ud) have two computers; 8. Tiene un ordenador, You (ud) have a computer; 9. Tienen un ordenador, You (uds) have a computer; 10. Tienen dos ordenadores, You (uds) have two computers.

Exercise 4: Write down the plurals of these words (using *los* or *las*): 1. el amigo, los amigos (the friends); 2. el hotel, los hoteles (the hotels); 3. la playa, las playas (the beaches); 4. el nombre, los nombres (the names); 5. el pasaporte, los pasaportes (the passports); 6. la cafetería, las cafeterías (the cafeterias); 7. el baño, los baños (the bathrooms); 8. la maleta, las maletas (the suitcases); 9. el desayuno, los desayunos (the breakfasts); 10. la llave, las llaves (the keys).

Lesson 4: At the restaurant

Exercise 1: Say these phrases in Spanish: 1. Buenas tardes, ¿tiene una mesa para tres?, Good afternoon, do you have a table for three? (you = ud); 2. ¿Qué van a tomar?, What are you going to have? (you = uds); 3. Sopa de mariscos y ensalada mixta, Shellfish soup and a mixed salad; 4. Pollo asado con patatas fritas, Roast chicken with chips; 5. ¿Me puede decir dónde está el hotel?, Can you tell me where the hotel is? (you = ud); 6. ¿Tienen sardinas asadas?, Do you have grilled sardines? (you = uds); 7. ¿Me puede traer una botella de agua?, Can you bring me a bottle of water? (you = ud); 8. La cuenta, por favor, The bill, please; 9. ¿Puedo ver la carta?, Can I see the menu?; 10. Quiero pavo con arroz, I want turkey with rice.

Exercise 2: What would you say before the words you hear: *el, la, los* or *las*?: 1. *la* sal, the salt; 2. *el* pescado, the fish; 3. *los* filetes, the steaks; 4. *las* botellas, the bottles; 5. *los* espaguetis, the spaghetti; 6. *el* atún, the tuna; 7. *la* carne, the meat; 8. *los* platos, the dishes; 9. *el* salmón, the salmon; 10. *el* arroz, the rice.

Exercise 3: Complete each sentence with one of the following missing words: 1. ¿Tiene una mesa *para* cuatro?, Do you have a table for four?; 2. ¿Pueden volver dentro *de* dos horas?, Can you come back in two hours?; 3. ¿Qué van *a* tomar?, What are you going to have?; 4. Quiero un filete *con* patatas fritas, I want a steak with chips; 5. Están *a* la derecha, They're on the right; 6. ¿Nos puede traer la carta *de* vinos?, Can you bring us the wine list?; 7. Hay un teléfono *en* la habitación, There's a telephone in the room; 8. ¿Tienen habitaciones *con* baño?, Do you have rooms with bathroom?; 9. El desayuno se sirve *de* siete a diez, Breakfast is served from seven till ten; 10. ¿Me puede dar la llave *de* la habitación?, Can you give me the room key?

Exercise 4: How would you translate these sentences?: 1. ¿Tiene radio?, Does it have a radio?; 2. ¿Podemos ver la carta de vinos?, Can we see the wine list?; 3. ¿Me puede decir dónde están las botellas de agua?, Can you tell me where the bottles of water are? (you = ud); 4. Tenemos carne asada, We have roast meat; 5. Les recomiendo el pollo frito, I recommend the fried chicken (to you - you = uds); 6. Tenemos un amigo en Inglaterra, We have a friend in England; 7. Vamos a ver a Margarita, We're going to see Margaret; 8. ¿Me puede traer el desayuno?, Can you bring me breakfast? (you = ud); 9. ¿Me puede dar un pollo?, Can you give me a chicken? (you = ud); 10. ¿Dónde están las patatas?, Where are the potatoes?

Lesson 5: The alphabet

Exercise 2: Which of the two letters is being said?: 1. e; 2. t; 3. g; 4. i; 5. c; 6. s; 7. f; 8. q; 9. b; 10. j.

Exercise 3: Write down the letters you hear: 1. v; 2. a; 3. z; 4. g; 5. f; 6. h; 7. c; 8. e; 9. j; 10. q.

Exercise 4: Write down the names being spelt out: 1. Hannah; 2. Jacob; 3. Alexis; 4. Joshua; 5. Rachel; 6. Christopher; 7. Natalie; 8. Joseph; 9. Rebecca; 10. Benjamin.

Lesson 6: Ordering drinks

Exercise 1: Say these sentences in Spanish: 1. Quiero dos cafés con leche, I want two white coffees; 2. No nos queda jerez, We don't have any sherry left; 3. ¿Me puede traer otra copa de vino tinto?, Can you [ud] bring me another glass of red wine?; 4. ¿Tienen vino blanco?, Do you [uds] have white wine?; 5. Voy a tomar una caña, I'm going to have a small beer [colloquial]; 6. Vamos a beber naranjada, We're going to drink orangeade; 7. Tenemos cuatro botellas de cerveza, We have four bottles of beer; 8. ¿Me puede decir dónde está el ron?, Can you [ud] tell me where the rum is?; 9. La sopa está caliente, The soup is hot; 10. ¿Tienen agua mineral sin gas?, Do you [uds] have still mineral water?

Exercise 2: Which of the two words is being said?: 1. cafés, coffees; 2. batidos, milk shakes; 3. zumo, juice; 4. euros, euros; 5. cerveza, beer; 6. jarra, jug; 7. vaso, glass; 8. cañas, small beers; 9. copa, glass; 10. limones, lemons.

Exercise 3: Match the Spanish sentences with their English translations: 1. Quiero cuatro cervezas grandes, I want four large beers; 2. Quiero cuatro cervezas pequeñas, I want four small beers; 3. Quieren cuatro cervezas grandes, You want four large beers; 4. Quieren cuatro cervezas pequeñas, You want four small beers; 5. Tenemos cuatro cervezas grandes, We have four large beers; 6. Tenemos cuatro cervezas pequeñas, We have four small beers; 7. Tienen cuatro cervezas grandes, You have four large beers; 8. Tienen cuatro cervezas pequeñas, You have four small beers; 9. Tengo cuatro cervezas grandes, I have four large beers; 10. Tengo cuatro cervezas pequeñas, I have four small beers.

Exercise 4: Dictation: write down the words you hear. You will hear each set of words twice: 1. Vamos a cenar, We're going to have dinner; 2. ¿A qué hora?, At what time?; 3. Un vaso de agua, A glass of water; 4. ¿Dónde está el chocolate?, Where is the chocolate?; 5. ¿Tienen cerveza?, Do you have beer?; 6. Hay nueve botellas, There are nine bottles; 7. Un descafeinado, One decaf; 8. Quiero té, I want tea; 9. Voy a beber vino, I'm going to drink wine; 10. Ahora mismo, Right away.

Lesson 7: At the apartment

Exercise 1: Say these sentences in Spanish: 1. Hay una cama grande en el salón, There is a large bed in the sitting room; 2. ¿Podemos ver la terraza del apartamento?, Can we see the apartment balcony?; 3. Tienen una cocina pequeña, They have a small kitchen; 4. ¿Dónde están las mantas?, Where are the blankets?; 5. ¿Cuándo abren la piscina?, When do they open the swimming pool?; 6. ¿Hay algún garaje cerca de aquí?, Are there any garages near here?; 7. ¿Qué día vienen los niños?, What day do the children come?; 8. ¿Qué quieren cenar?, What do you [uds] want to have for dinner?; 9. ¿Tienen coche?, Do you [uds] have a car?; 10. Abren a las nueve de la mañana, They open at nine in the morning.

Exercise 2: Which phrase is the answer to each question you hear?: 1. ¿A qué hora abren la piscina por la mañana?, A las ocho. (What time do they open the swimming pool in the morning? At eight.) 2. ¿Dónde están las toallas?, En el armario del baño. (Where are the towels?, In the bathroom cupboard.) 3. ¿Cuándo cierran el supermercado?, A las nueve de la noche. (When do they close the supermarket?, At 9.00pm.) 4. ¿Qué día vienen José y Rocío?, El jueves por la mañana. (What day are Joseph and Rocio coming?, On Thursday morning.) 5. ¿Qué van a beber?, Una tónica y un zumo de naranja. (What are you going to drink?, A tonic water and an orange juice.) 6. ¿Me puede decir cuánto es todo?, Doce euros y veinte céntimos. (Can you tell me how much everything is?, Twelve euros and twenty cents.) 7. ¿Tiene una mesa para dos?, Lo siento, está completo. (Do you have a table for two?, I'm sorry, it's full.) 8. ¿Dónde se deja la basura?, En el cubo de la entrada. (Where should we leave the rubbish?, In the bin at the entrance.) 9. ¿Hay algún hotel cerca de aquí?, Sí, hay dos. (Are there any hotels near here?, Yes, there are two.) 10. ¿Qué van a cenar?, Sopa de pescado y espaguetis. (What are you going to have for dinner?, Fish soup and spaghetti.)

Exercise 3: What is the odd one out in each group?: 1. el coche (the car is not a part of the day); 2. nombre (name is not a number); 3. el pavo (the turkey is not a part of the house); 4. la botella (the bottle is not a kitchen appliance); 5. el pollo (the chicken is not a drink); 6. la mayonesa (the mayonnaise is not a drink); 7. el vaso (the glass is not a dish); 8. Inglaterra

(England is not a person's name); 9. la caña (a small beer is not a fish); 10. la manta (the blanket is not a drink).

Exercise 4: What would you put before each of the words below: *el* or *la*?: 1. *el* nombre (the name) 2. *el* salón (the sitting room) 3. *la* habitación (the room) 4. *el* congelador (the freezer) 5. *la* noche (the night) 6. *la* tarde (the afternoon, the evening) 7. *el* coche (the car) 8. *el* garaje (the garage) 9. *la* información (the information) 10. *el* café (the coffee)

Lesson 8: At the supermarket 1

Exercise 1: Say these sentences in Spanish: 1. ¿Dónde están las uvas?, Where are the grapes?; 2. El azúcar está junto al aceite, The sugar is next to the oil; 3. ¿Cuánto cuestan las galletas?, How much are the biscuits?; 4. Tenemos champiñones en lata, We have tinned mushrooms; 5. Sólo tengo dos euros, I only have two euros; 6. Necesito el coche, I need the car; 7. No me quedan toallas, I don't have any towels left; 8. ¿Cuándo puedo ver el apartamento?, When can I see the apartment?; 9. ¿Me puede poner dos kilos de fresas?, Can you [ud] give me two kilos of strawberries?; 10. ¿Quién es Margarita?, Who is Margaret?

Exercise 2: Which of the two words is being said?: 1. los carritos, the trolleys; 2. la cesta, the basket; 3. la fresa, the strawberry; 4. el plátano, the banana; 5. las manzanas, the apples; 6. las uvas, the grapes; 7. el kilo, the kilo; 8. las cajas, the boxes; 9. las cebollas, the onions; 10. las lechugas, the lettuces.

Exercise 3: Match the English with the Spanish expressions: 1. yo también, me too; 2. eso es todo, that's everything; 3. cómo no, of course; 4. quédese con el cambio, keep the change; 5. ahora mismo, right away; 6. vamos a ver, let's see; 7. como pueden ver, as you can see; 8. cerca de aquí, near here; 9. al fondo, at the end; 10. de nada, you're welcome.

Exercise 4: How would you translate these sentences?: 1. ¿Puedo ver las cestas?, Can I see the baskets?; 2. ¿Dónde están los espárragos en lata?, Where are the tinned asparagus?; 3. Hay diez niños en la piscina, There are ten children in the swimming pool; 4. La fruta está en la nevera, The fruit is in the fridge; 5. Vamos a tomar fresas, We're going to have strawberries; 6. Quiero un zumo de manzana, I want an apple juice; 7. ¿Cuándo vienen al supermercado?, When do they (or you) come to the supermarket?; 8. La carne está en el congelador, The meat is in the freezer; 9. ¿Qué día vamos a cenar con mi amigo?, What day (or when) are we going to have dinner with my friend?; 10. No me quedan sandías grandes, I don't have any large watermelons left.

Lesson 9: The family

Exercise 1: Say these sentences in Spanish: 1. Vivo en un apartamento con mi mujer, I live in a flat with my wife; 2. Mi hermana se llama Clara, My sister is called Clare; 3. Mi tío Juan está casado, My uncle John is married; 4. ¿Cómo se llama tu sobrina?, What's your niece called?; 5. El lunes tenemos que ir al supermercado, On Monday we have to go to the supermarket; 6. ¿Dónde está el perro de tu amigo?, Where is your friend's dog?; 7. ¿Cuánto cuestan las fresas?, How much are the strawberries?; 8. No me quedan galletas, I don't have any biscuits left; 9. ¿Hay algún pimiento en la nevera?, Are there any peppers in the fridge?; 10. ¿Podemos ver a la abuela?, Can we see grandmother?

Exercise 2: Which sentence is the question for each answer you hear?: 1. ¿Qué día es la boda de Juana?, el lunes (What day is Joanna's wedding?, Monday); 2. ¿Cómo se llama el primo de tu amiga?, Ricardo. (What's your friend's cousin called?, Richard); 3. ¿Cómo se llama la prima de tu amigo?, Susana. (What's your friend's cousin called?, Susanna); 4. ¿Dónde están las toallas?, En el armario. (Where are the towels?, In the wardrobe); 5. ¿Cuánto cuestan los plátanos?, Dos euros el kilo. (How much are the bananas?, Two euros per kilo); 6. ¿Dónde está el coche de Luis?, En el garaje. (Where is Louis's car?, In the garage); 7. ¿Con quién está casado Javier?, Con Juana. (Who is Javier married to?, Joanna); 8. ¿Dónde vive el marido de tu sobrina?, En una casa con jardín. (Where does your niece's husband live?, In a house with a garden); 9. ¿Vamos a ir en coche? Sí. (Are we going by car?, Yes); 10. ¿Cuándo abren el supermercado? A las ocho. (When does the supermarket open?, At eight).

Exercise 3: Complete these sentences with the missing words given: 1. ¿Me puede decir cómo se *llama* su tía?, Can you tell me her aunt's name?; 2. ¿Me puede *poner* tres kilos de manzanas?, Can you give me three kilos of apples?;

3. Las copas están en el *armario* de la cocina, The glasses are in the kitchen cupboard; 4. ¿Dónde están las *mantas* de los niños?, Where are the children's blankets?; 5. ¿A qué *hora* podemos ir a su casa?, What time can we go to her house?; 6. ¿Hay algún supermercado *cerca* de aquí?, Are there any supermarkets near here?; 7. ¡*Qué* lío!, What a mess!; 8. Menos *mal* que tenemos coche, It's just as well that we have a car; 9. Voy a tomar té *con* leche, I'm going to have tea with milk; 10. No sé *cómo* se llama su hermana, I don't know what her sister's called.

Exercise 4: Write down the plurals of these words: 1. el sobrino, los sobrinos (the nephews); 2. la sobrina, las sobrinas (the nieces); 3. soltero, solteros (single); 4. separada, separadas (separated); 5. el padre, los padres (the fathers); 6. la madre, las madres (the mothers); 7. principal, principales (main); 8. el lavaplatos, los lavaplatos (the dishwashers); 9. el salón, los salones (the sitting rooms); 10. grande, grandes (big).

Lesson 10: Numbers 31-100

Exercise 1: Read these numbers out loud in Spanish: a. Treinta y siete (37); b. Cuarenta y nueve (49); c. Cincuenta y tres (53); d. Sesenta y seis (66); e. Catorce (14); f. Setenta y uno (71); g. Ochenta y cuatro (84); h. Cero (0); i. Noventa y nueve (99); j. Cien (100).

Exercise 2: Which numbers have not been said in the recordings?: a. veintiuno (21); b. treinta y nueve (39); c. once (11); d. cuarenta y cuatro (44); e. cincuenta y uno (51); f. sesenta y siete (67); g. sesenta y seis (66); h. ochenta y nueve (89); i. cuarenta y dos (42); j. doce (12).

Exercise 3: Write down the figures for the numbers you hear: a. 89 (ochenta y nueve); b. 15 (quince); c. 56 (cincuenta y seis); d. 27 (veintisiete); e. 44 (cuarenta y cuatro); f. 98 (noventa y ocho); g. 77 (setenta y siete); h. 38 (treinta y ocho); i. 62 (sesenta y dos); j. 12 (doce).

Exercise 4: Write down the telephone numbers you hear: a. 93 892 44 76; b. 954 28 98 01; c. 968 34 080; d. 953 01 370; e. 00 44 0131 380 31 92; f. 00 34 91 809 121 02; g. 906 365 024; h. 00 1 0980 46 81; i. 00 49 38 094 341; j. 00 33 1 903 45 67.

Lesson 11: Telling the time

Exercise 1: Say these sentences in Spanish: a. Son las tres y media de la tarde, It's 3.30pm; b. Es la una y cuarto de la mañana, It's 1.15am; c. Son las diez y cinco de la noche, It's 10.05pm; d. Son las once y diez de la mañana, It's 11.10am; e. Son las cuatro menos cuarto de la tarde, It's 3.45pm; f. Son las dos y diez de la tarde, It's 2.10pm; g. Son las cinco menos veinticinco de la tarde, It's 4.35pm; h. Son las once y veinte de la noche, It's 11.20pm; i. Es la una menos cuarto de la tarde, It's 12.45pm; j. Son las siete menos veinte de la tarde, It's 6.40pm.

Exercise 2: Which time has been said in each case?: a. Son las dos y cuarto (2.15); b. Son las tres y veinte (3.20); c. Son las cuatro menos veinticinco (3.35); d. Son las cinco menos diez (4.50); e. Son las seis menos cinco (5.55); f. Son las once y cinco (11.05); g. Son las doce y media (12.30); h. Es la una y diez (1.10); i. Son las siete menos diez (6.50); j. las ocho menos veinte (7.40).

Exercise 3: Match the Spanish sentences with their English translations: a. La una y diez, Ten past one; b. Las dos y cuarto, Quarter past two; c. Las dos menos veinticinco, Twenty-five to two; d. Las tres y cinco, Five past three; e. Las tres y veinte, Twenty past three; f. Las cinco y media, Half past five; g. Las siete menos diez, Ten to seven; h. Las siete menos cuarto, Quarter to seven; i. Las once menos veinte, Twenty to eleven; j. Las doce menos cinco, Five to twelve.

Exercise 4: Write down the following times: a. Son las dos menos veinticinco de la mañana (1:35); b. Son las seis menos cuarto de la tarde (17:45); c. Son las doce de la noche (24:00); d. Son las once y cuarto de la mañana (11:15); e. Son las dos y veinte de la mañana (2:20); f. Son las tres y diez de la mañana (3:10); g. Son las tres y veinticinco de la tarde (15:25); h. Son las seis y cinco de la tarde (18:05); i. Son las siete menos cinco de la mañana (6:55); j. Son las diez y media de la noche (22:30).

Lesson 12: Ordering tapas

Exercise 1: Say these sentences in Spanish: 1. ¿Te gustan las manzanas?, Do you like apples?; 2. A mí no me gustan las empanadillas, I, myself, don't like pasties; 3. No me quedan huevos duros, I don't have any hard boiled eggs left; 4. ¿Qué otras verduras tienes?, What other vegetables do you have?; 5. Quiero cuatro anchoas y tres aceitunas, I want four anchovies and three olives; 6. Vamos a pedir dos cañas y un pincho de tortilla, We're going to order two small beers and a small portion of Spanish potato omelette; 7. ¿Os gustan las berenjenas fritas?, Do you like fried aubergines?; 8. Tenemos jamón serrano y queso, We have Spanish cured ham and cheese; 9. Los calamares están muy buenos, The squid is very good; 10. Tampoco tenemos mejillones, We don't have mussels either.

Exercise 2: Which phrase is the answer to each question you hear?: 1. ¿Te gustan las setas?, Sí, me gustan mucho. (Do you like mushrooms?, Yes, I like them very much); 2. ¿Qué vais a beber?, Dos descafeinados y un batido. (What are you going to drink?, Two decafs and a milk shake); 3. ¿Qué otra fruta tienes?, Tengo plátanos y fresas. (What other fruit do you have?, I have bananas and strawberries); 4. ¿Qué hora es?, Las once menos cuarto. (What time is it?, Quarter to eleven); 5. ¿A qué hora vamos a ir?, A las cinco y media. (When are we going?, At half past five); 6. ¿Qué día vienen?, El jueves. (Which day are they coming?, On Thursday); 7. ¿Dónde están los mejillones?, En la nevera. (Where are the mussels?, In the fridge); 8. ¿Con quién estás?, Con mi prima Clara. (Who are you with?, With my cousin Clare); 9. ¿Hay algún vaso en el armario?, Sí, hay dos. (Are there any glasses in the cupboard?, Yes, there are two); 10. ¿Cómo se llama tu sobrina?, Margarita. (What's your niece's name?, Margaret).

Exercise 3: According to the dialogue on p. 86, is each statement true or false?: 1. Voy a tomar un pincho de tortilla, T (I'm going to have a small portion of Spanish potato omelette); 2. Voy a pedir pimientos rellenos de bonito, F (I'm going to order tuna stuffed peppers); 3. No me quedan croquetas de jamón y queso, T (I don't have any ham and cheese croquettes left); 4. Tengo anchoas, chorizos, pinchos de queso ..., F (I have anchovies, spicy sausages, cheese snacks ...); 5. Quiero una ración de patatas fritas, F (I want a portion of french fries); 6. Tengo calamares a la romana, F (I have batter-fried squid); 7. Las patatas alioli no están buenas, F (The potatoes in garlic mayonnaise aren't good); 8. No tenemos morcillas de arroz, T (We don't have rice blood sausages); 9. Prefiero las empanadillas, F (I prefer pasties); 10. Quieren beber cerveza, T (They want to drink beer);

Exercise 4: What would you put before each of the words below: el, la, los or las?: 1. el jamón, the ham; 2. los canapés, the canapés; 3. el atún, the tuna; 4. la ración, the portion; 5. los calamares, the squid; 6. los riñones, the kidneys; 7. los caracoles, the snails; 8. los mejillones, the mussels; 9. el limón, the lemon; 10.el jerez, the sherry.

Lesson 13: Transport

Exercise 1: Say these sentences in Spanish: 1. Quiero un billete de ida y vuelta a Barcelona, I want a return ticket to Barcelona; 2. ¿Cuántas manzanas hay en la nevera?, How many apples are there in the fridge?; 3. Somos las hermanas de Bárbara, We are Barbara's sisters; 4. Hacemos un descuento del quince por ciento, We give a fifteen per cent discount; 5. ¿Cuándo sale el próximo tren para la playa?, When does the next train to the beach leave?; 6. Tienen que esperar veinte minutos, They have to wait twenty minutes; 7. ¿Me puede dar dos, por favor?, Can you give me two, please? (you = ud); 8. ¿Qué autobús tenemos que coger para ir al hotel?, Which bus do we have to take to go to the hotel?; 9. ¿Cuánto cuesta la leche?, How much is the milk?; 10. No me gustan los autobuses, I don't like buses.

Exercise 2: Which of the two sentences is being said?: 1. Quieren dos billetes de ida y vuelta, They want two return tickets; 2. Somos los primos de Ana, We are Anne's (male) cousins; 3. Tienen que ir al hotel en autobús, They have to go to the hotel by bus; 4. ¿Me puede dar siete asientos de no fumador?, Can you give me seven non smoking seats?; 5. ¿Qué tren tienen que coger?, Which train do they have to take?; 6. ¿Cuánto cuesta el billete?, How much is the ticket?; 7. ¿Os gustan las patatas fritas?, Do you like chips?; 8. Son las cuatro menos cuarto, It's quarter to four; 9. La prima de mi madre se llama Juana, My mother's cousin is called Joanna; 10. ¿Me puede traer otra cerveza?, Can you bring me another beer?

Exercise 3: Complete each sentence with one of the missing words: 1. Quieren dos billetes de ida y *vuelta*, They want two return tickets; 2. ¿Cuántas manzanas *hay* en la nevera?, How many apples are there in the fridge?; 3. Hacemos un descuento del doce por *ciento*, We give a twelve per cent discount; 4. ¿Qué autobús tengo que *coger* para ir al apartamento?, Which bus do I have to take to go to the apartment?; 5. ¿Cuánto *cuesta* el zumo de naranja?, How much is the orange juice?; 6. ¿Cuánto *cuestan* las galletas?, How much are the biscuits?; 7. No me quedan *mejillones*, I don't have any mussels left; 8. No me queda *café*, I don't have any coffee left; 9. Los abuelos *quieren* ir a la playa, The grandparents want to go to the beach; 10. El abuelo *quiere* ir a la playa, Grandfather wants to go to the beach.

Exercise 4: How would you translate these sentences into Spanish?: 1. Quieren un kilo de almejas, They want a kilo of clams; 2. Quiero dieciséis empanadillas de atún, I want sixteen tuna pasties; 3. Quiere diez albóndigas, He wants ten meatballs; 4. Somos los amigos de Francisco, We are Frank's friends; 5. Soy el padre de Luis, I'm Louis's father; 6. ¿Eres la madre de María?, Are you Mary's mother?; 7. Es el tío de José, He's Joseph's uncle; 8. ¿Sois hermanas?, Are you sisters?; 9. Son los hijos de Pablo, They're Paul's sons; 10. Va a ser mi tía, She's going to be my aunt.

Lesson 14: Shops and eating places

Exercise 1: Say these sentences in Spanish: 1. ¿Hay muchos regalos en la tienda?, Are there many gifts in the shop?; 2. En esta calle, a la izquierda, On this street, on the left; 3. No sé, creo que vamos a ir hoy, I don't know, I think we're going today; 4. Las botellas están entre la fruta y el pescado, The bottles are between the fruit and the fish; 5. ¿Dónde hay una tienda de deportes?, Where is there a sports shop?; 6. No hay ningún coche en el garaje, There aren't any cars in the garage; 7. No hay ninguna farmacia en mi calle, There aren't any chemist's on my street; 8. Mis amigos están en la carnicería, My friends are at the butcher's; 9. Tus primos quieren ir a la librería, Your (male) cousins want to go to the bookshop; 10. ¿Cuánto cuestan los bocadillos?, How much are the sandwiches?

Exercise 2: Which phrase is the answer to each question you hear?: 1. ¿Hay muchos autobuses en la parada?, Si, hay cinco. (Are there many buses at the bus stop?, Yes, there are five); 2. ¿Dónde está la agencia de viajes?, En la próxima calle, a la derecha. (Where is the travel agency?, On the next street, on the right); 3. ¿Cuándo vienen los abuelos?, No sé, creo que vienen mañana. (When are the grandparents coming?, I don't know, I think they're coming tomorrow); 4. ¿Hay alguna toalla en el baño?, No, no hay ninguna. (Are there any towels in the bathroom?, No, there aren't any); 5. ¿Quién es?, Es mi tío. (Who is it?, It's my uncle); 6. ¿Cuándo sale el próximo autobús?, A las cinco y veinticinco. (When does the next bus leave?, At twenty-five past five); 7. ¿Cuánto cuesta el metrobús?, Cinco euros y veinte céntimos. (How much is the 10-journey ticket?, Five euros and twenty cents); 8. ¿Cuánto cuestan los apartamentos?, Mucho. (How much do the apartments cost?, A lot); 9. ¿Qué van a tomar?, Un descafeinado y un café con leche. (What are you going to have?, A decaf and a white coffee); 10. ¿Qué hora es?, Las seis y media. (What time is it?, Half past six);

Exercise 3: Match the Spanish sentences with their English translations: 1. Mi sobrino está en esta tienda, My nephew is in this shop; 2. Mi sobrina está en esta tienda, My niece is in this shop; 3. Mis sobrinos están en esta tienda, My nephews are in this shop; 4. Mis sobrinas están en esta tienda, My nieces are in this shop; 5. Tu sobrino está en esta tienda, Your nephew is in this shop; 6. Tu sobrina está en esta tienda, Your niece is in this shop; 7. Tus sobrinos están en esta tienda, Your nephews are in this shop; 8. Tus sobrinas están en esta tienda, Your nieces are in this shop; 9. Su sobrino está en esta tienda, His nephew is in this shop; 10. Su sobrina está en esta tienda, His niece is in this shop.

Exercise 4: What would you put before each of the words below: *el* or *la*?: 1. *la* calle, the street; 2. *el* viaje, the trip; 3. *el* día, the day; 4. *el* billete, the ticket; 5. *el* tren, the train; 6. *el* autobús, the bus; 7. *el* metrobús, the 10-journey ticket; 8. *la* ración, the portion; 9. *la* carne, the meat; 10. *la* información, the information.

Lesson 15: At the chemist's

Exercise 1: Say these sentences in Spanish: 1. ¿Puedo comprar kiwis en el mercado?, Can I buy kiwis at the market?; 2. ¿Puede darme dos kilos de tomates?, Can you [ud] give me two kilos of tomatoes?; 3. Estos pepinos no son buenos, These cucumbers aren't good; 4. No me gustan estas cremas, I don't like these creams; 5. Tengo varios apartamentos donde elegir, I have several flats to choose from; 6. También quiero llevarme una caja de aspirinas, I also want to take a box of aspirins with me; 7. Prefiero las mesas grises, I prefer grey tables; 8. ¿Te gustan estos cepillos?, Do you like these hairbrushes?; 9. Esta zapatería está cerrada, This shoe shop is closed; 10. No hay ninguna peluquería en mi calle, There aren't any hairdressers' on my street.

Exercise 2: Which of the two words is being said?: 1. esta, this (feminine); 2. este, this (masculine); 3. estas, these (f); 4. prefiero, I prefer; 5. recomiendo, I recommend; 6. recomendar, to recommend; 7. mucha, much (f); 8. muchas, many (f); 9. muchos, many (m); 10. mucha, much (f).

Exercise 3: Complete each sentence with one of the missing words: 1. *Estos* pañales no son buenos, (These nappies aren't good); 2. *Estas* lentillas son muy buenas, (These contact lenses are very good); 3. *Este* suavizante no me gusta, (I don't like this conditioner); 4. ¿Cuánto cuesta *esta* crema?, (How much is this cream?); 5. La tienda *está* cerrada, (The shop is closed); 6. Los grandes almacenes *están* abiertos, (The department store is closed); 7. Los cepillos *son* grandes, (The hairbrushes are big); 8. El peine *es* pequeño, (The comb is small); 9. Tenemos *mucho* donde elegir, (We have a lot to choose from); 10. Tienen *mucha* pasta de dientes, (They have a lot of toothpaste).

Exercise 4: Translate these sentences into Spanish: 1. Estoy en la farmacia con mi amigo Gabriel, I'm at the chemist's with my friend Gabriel; 2. ¿Estás casado? or ¿estás casada?, Are you (tú) married?; 3. Está cerrado hasta el lunes, It's closed till Monday; 4. Están de vacaciones con los niños, They're on holiday with the children; 5. Soy amigo de tu hermano or soy el amigo de tu hermano, I'm your [you=tú] brother's friend; 6. ¿Eres Juana, la amiga de mi prima?, Are you (tú) Joanna, my (female) cousin's friend?; 7. Es tarde,

It's late; 8. Somos los padres de Cristina, We are Christine's parents; 9. ¿Sois primas? or ¿sois primos?, Are you (vos) cousins?; 10. Son amigas or son amigos, They're friends.

Lesson 16: On holiday

Exercise 1: Say these sentences in Spanish: 1. Están de vacaciones, They're on holiday; 2. Vamos a estar aquí cuatro días, We're going to be here for four days; 3. Queremos alquilar una sombrilla, We want to hire a beach umbrella; 4. ¿Por qué no vamos a la tienda de deportes?, Why don't we go to the sports shop?; 5. ¿Cuánto tiempo lleváis en el hotel?, How long have you (vos) been in the hotel for?; 6. Hay demasiadas tumbonas en la piscina, There are too many sun loungers at the swimming pool; 7. Hoy hace demasiado calor, Today it's too hot; 8. Primero tenemos que cenar, First we have to have dinner; 9. ¿Te gusta tomar el sol?, Do you (tú) like sunbathing?; 10. ¿Te gustan los helados?, Do you (tú) like ice creams?

Exercise 2: Which of the two words is being said?: 1. estás, you [tú] are; 2. estáis, you [vos] are; 3. estás, you [tú] are; 4. estar, to be; 5. estáis, you [vos] are; 6. quiere, he/she/it wants, you [ud] want; 7. quiero, I want; 8. quieren, you [uds]/they want; 9. queréis, you [vos] want; 10. pollo, chicken.

Exercise 3: Match the questions with the appropriate answers: 1. ¿Cuánto tiempo vais a estar aquí?, Tres días (How long are you going to be here for?, 3 days.); 2. ¿Tenemos que pagar ahora?, No, pueden pagar más tarde (Do we have to pay now?, No, you can pay later.); 3. ¿Hay algún pepino en la nevera?, Sí, hay uno (Are there any cucumbers in the fridge?, Yes, there is one.); 4. ¿Hay alguna tumbona en la piscina?, Sí, hay una (Are there any sun loungers at the swimming pool?, Yes, there is one.); 5. ¿Qué vais a hacer mañana?, Vamos a ir al lago (What are you doing tomorrow?, We're going to the lake.); 6. ¿Te gustan los trenes?, No, prefiero los autobuses (Do you like trains?, No, I prefer buses.); 7. ¿Te gusta la fruta?, No, prefiero las verduras (Do you like fruit?, No, I prefer vegetables.); 8. ¿Tiene chupetes?, Lo siento, no me quedan (Do you have dummies?, I'm sorry, I don't have any left.); 9. ¿Cuánto cuestan las vendas?, Un euro (How much are the bandages?, One euro.); 10. ¿A qué hora vienen?, A la una (What time are they coming?, At one o'clock.).

Exercise 4: What would you put before each of the words below: *el, la, los* or *las*?: 1. *las* vacaciones, the holidays; 2. *el* sol, the sun; 3. *las* fotos, the photographs; 4. *el* calor, the heat; 5. *los* carretes, the films; 6. *el* flotador, the rubber ring; 7. *los* calmantes, the painkillers; 8. *la* fiebre, the temperature; 9. *los* chupetes, the dummies; 10. *el* biberón, the feeding bottle.

Lesson 17: At the supermarket 2

Exercise 1: Say these sentences in Spanish: 1. ¿Me puede poner una docena de mejillones?, Can you [ud] give me a dozen mussels?; 2. Me voy a llevar medio kilo de salchichas, I'm going to take half a kilo of sausages; 3. Dame tres cuartos de kilo de carne picada, Give me three quarters of a kilo of mince; 4. ¿Me puede dar un poco de arroz?, Can you give me a bit of rice?; 5. Los guisantes están congelados, The peas are frozen; 6. Las botellas de aceite están detrás del pan, The bottles of oil are behind the bread; 7. ¿Te gustan los yogures de piña?, Do you like pineapple yoghurts?; 8. Me quedan cuatro habitaciones con baño, I have four rooms with bathroom left; 9. ¿Por qué quieren ir hoy?, Why do they want to go today?; 10. ¿Cuánto cuesta el salami?, How much is the salami?

Exercise 2: Which of the two sentences is being said?: 1. Quiero doce, I want twelve; 2. Tenemos dos horas y media, We have two and a half hours; 3. ¿Dónde está el congelador?, Where is the freezer; 4. No me gusta el chocolate, I don't like chocolate; 5. Quieren un poco de té, They want some tea; 6. Son gratis, They're free; 7. Cierran a las dos, They close at two; 8. Prefiere los pomelos, He prefers grapefruit; 9. Les recomiendo las judías verdes, I recommend the French beans (to you - you = uds); 10. Esta casa está en Inglaterra, This house is in England.

Exercise 3: According to the dialogue on p. 132, is each phrase true or false?: 1. Es por la mañana, T (It's the morning). 2. La señora Álvarez quiere cien gramos de carne picada, F (Mrs Alvarez wants 100 grams of mince). 3. El dependiente no tiene salami, T (The shop assistant doesn't have salami). 4. La señora Álvarez no va a comprar salchichón, T (Mrs Alvarez isn't going to buy salami-type sausage). 5. Las mandarinas vienen mañana, T (The tangerines are coming tomorrow). 6. La señora Álvarez no quiere berenjenas, T (Mrs Alvarez doesn't want aubergines). 7. El perejil cuesta mucho, F (Parsley is very expensive). 8. En el supermercado no hay congelados, F (There's no frozen food in the supermarket). 9. Las bolsas de patatas fritas están junto a los bollos, T (The bags of crisps are next to the buns). 10. No hay ni mantequilla ni margarina en el supermercado, F (There's neither butter nor margarine in the supermarket).

Exercise 4: Write down the plurals of these words (using *los* or *las*): 1. el albaricoque, los albaricoques (the apricots) 2. el bote, los botes (the jars) 3. el cereal, los cereales (the cereals) 4. la coliflor, las coliflores (the cauliflowers) 5. el melocotón, los melocotones (the peaches) 6. el yogur, los yogures (the yoghurts) 7. el salchichón, los salchichones (the salami-type sausages) 8. la vez, las veces (the times) 9. el jardín, los jardines (the gardens) 10. el guisante, los guisantes (the peas).

Lesson 18: Days, months and dates

Exercise 1: Say these sentences in Spanish: 1. El miércoles por la tarde vamos al cine, On Wednesday afternoon we're going to the cinema; 2. El mes que viene van a comprar una televisión, Next month they're going to buy a TV; 3. Su madre prefiere ir en coche, Her mother prefers to go by car; 4. ¿Qué día es el cumpleaños de su hijo?, What day is their son's birthday?; 5. Este ordenador es mío, This computer is mine; 6. Esta jarra es mía, This jug is mine; 7. El viernes por la noche tenemos que ver a Juan, On Friday night we have to see John; 8. Mañana por la mañana vienen a limpiar, Tomorrow morning they're coming to clean; 9. Hoy es jueves, quince de enero, Today is Thursday, 15 January; 10. Los abuelos van a pasar las Navidades con nosotros, The grandparents are going to spend Christmas with us.

Exercise 2: Which phrase is the answer to each question you hear?: 1. ¿Qué día es hoy?, Martes. (What day is it today?, Tuesday.) 2. ¿Cuántos días se va a quedar la prima Begoña?, Hasta el sábado. (How long is cousin Begoña going to stay for?, Till Saturday.) 3. ¿Qué vais a hacer hoy?, Vamos a ir de compras. (What are you doing today?, We're going shopping.) 4. ¿Os gusta la casa nueva?, Sí, nos gusta mucho.(Do you like the new house?, Yes, we like it a lot.) 5. ¿Os gustan los flotadores nuevos?, No, no nos gustan. (Do you like the new rubber rings?, No, we don't like them.) 6. ¿Te gusta la habitación de Ana?, Sí, me gusta mucho. (Do you like Anne's room?, Yes, I like it a lot.) 7. ¿Te gustan las cerezas?, No, no me gustan. (Do you like cherries?, No, I don't like them.) 8. ¿Cuántos años tiene tu hija?, Cuarenta. (How old is your daughter?, Forty.) 9. ¿No tiene hoy ciruelas?, No, no me quedan. (Don't you have plums today?, No, I don't have any left.) 10. ¿Puedo comprar salchichón?, No, tenemos muchas cosas en la nevera. (Can I buy salami-type sausage?, No, we have plenty of things in the fridge.)

Exercise 3: Complete each sentence using the following missing words and phrases: 1. (Yo) *tengo que* ir con mi hermano a ver a mi padre, I have to go with my brother to see my father; 2. (Ella) *tiene que* ir con su hermano a ver a su padre, She has to go with her brother to see their father; 3. (Nosotros) *tenemos que* ir con vosotros, We have to go with you; 4. (Ellos) *tienen que* ir con nosotros, They have to go with us; 5. (Yo) *tengo* veinticuatro años, I am twenty-four years old; 6. (Ella) *tiene* una casa en la playa, She has a house on the beach; 7. (Nosotros) *tenemos* dos colchonetas, We have two air beds; 8. (Ellos) *tienen* cuatro regalos, They have four presents; 9. (Él) *viene* mañana, He's coming tomorrow; 10. (Ellos) *vienen* el lunes que viene, They're coming next Monday.

Exercise 4: Finish each new sentence using the describing word from the examples given: 1. El coche es nuevo ⇒ La nevera es nueva (The car is new ⇒ The fridge is new); 2. Las lentillas son nuevas ⇒ Los cepillos son nuevos (The lenses are new ⇒ The hairbrushes are new); 3. El billete es mío ⇒ La manta es mía (The ticket is mine ⇒ The blanket is mine); 4. Patricia es pequeña ⇒ Emilio es pequeño (Patricia is small ⇒ Emile is small); 5. Los botes son pequeños ⇒ Las camas son pequeñas (The jars are small ⇒ The beds are small); 6. El peine es grande ⇒ La plaza es grande (The comb is big ⇒ The square is big); 7. Los calamares son grandes ⇒ Las almejas son grandes (The squid is big ⇒ The clams are big); 8. Mi tía está soltera ⇒ Mi tío está soltero (My aunt is single ⇒ My uncle is single); 9. Mis primos están solteros ⇒ Mis primas están solteras (My [male] cousins are single ⇒ My [female] cousins are single); 10. Mi abuela está viuda ⇒ Mi abuelo está viudo (My grandmother is a widow ⇒ My grandfather is a widower).

Lesson 19: Asking for directions

Exercise 1: Say these sentences in Spanish: 1. ¿Tienes un plano pequeño?, Do you have a small map?; 2. Tienes que comprar un billete de tren, You have to buy a train ticket; 3. Vivo en la calle Segovia número once, I live at 11 Segovia Street; 4. ¿Cómo se va a la oficina de Correos?, How do you get to the post office?; 5. La estación de autobuses está muy cerca de mi casa, The bus station is very close to my house; 6. Me gusta bastante este restaurante, I quite like this restaurant; 7. Hoy es viernes, trece de mayo, Today is Friday, 13 May; 8. La estación de metro está demasiado lejos de aquí, The underground station is too far from here; 9. ¿Qué parada está más cerca?, Which stop is closer?; 10. Tenemos que seguir todo recto, We have to continue straight ahead.

Exercise 2: Fill in the missing words when you hear them?: 1. *todo* recto, straight ahead; 2. *a* pie, on foot; 3. *más* despacio, slower; 4. al final *de*, at the end of; 5. al otro *lado* de, on the other side of; 6. el *fin* de semana, the weekend; 7. tres *cuartos* de kilo de, 3/4 of a kilo of; 8. no *es* necesario, it's not necessary; 9. todo *el* día, all day; 10. *a* la izquierda, on the left.

Exercise 3: Match the Spanish sentences with their English translations: 1. Hay demasiados restaurantes en esta plaza, There are too many restaurants in this square; 2. Hay demasiadas tiendas en esta calle, There are too many shops on this street; 3. Hace demasiado calor en la terraza, It's too hot in the balcony; 4. El viaje dura demasiado, The trip is too long; 5. Tenemos demasiado que hacer, We have too much to do; 6. Hay demasiadas oficinas en este edificio, There are too many offices in this building; 7. Tienes demasiada leche en la nevera, You have too much milk in the fridge; 8. Los grandes almacenes son demasiado pequeños, The department store is too small; 9. Tenemos demasiadas maletas en el coche, We have too many suitcases in the car; 10. Me quedan demasiados botes de mermelada, I have too many jam jars left.

Exercise 4: What would you put before each of the words below: *el* or *la*?: 1. *el* final, the end; 2. *el* pie, the foot; 3. *la* estación, the station; 4. *el* mar, the sea; 5. *el* restaurante, the restaurant; 6. *el* cumpleaños, the birthday; 7. *el* mes, the month; 8. *el* yogur, the yoghurt; 9. *el* perejil, the parsley; 10. *el* viaje, the trip.

Lesson 20: 101 to 1000, and more

Exercise 1: Read these numbers out loud in Spanish: a. 147, ciento cuarenta y siete; b. 251, doscientos cincuenta y uno; c. 313, trescientos trece; d. 460, cuatrocientos sesenta; e. 511, quinientos once; f. 628, seiscientos veintiocho; g. 706, setecientos seis; h. 895, ochocientos noventa y cinco; i. 919, novecientos diecinueve; j. 1000, mil.

Exercise 2: Extra speaking exercise. Read these numbers out loud in Spanish: a. primero, 1° (1st); b. segundo, 2° (2nd); c. tercera, 3^{a} (3rd); d. cuarta, 4^{a} (4th); e. quinto, 5° (5th); f. sexta, 6^{a} (6th); g. séptimo, 7° (7th); h. octava, 8^{a} (8th); i. noveno, 9° (9th); j. décima, 10^{a} (10th).

Exercise 3: Which of the two numbers is being said?: a. seiscientos setenta y seis, 676; b. quinientos cincuenta y cuatro, 554; c. novecientos ochenta y nueve, 989; d. trescientos ochenta y tres, 383; e. doscientos doce, 212; f. novecientos diecisiete, 917; g. ciento setenta y siete, 177; h. cuatrocientos trece, 413; i. seiscientos cuarenta y cinco, 645; j. ciento cinco, 105.

Exercise 4: Match the Spanish words with the correct figures: a. setecientos cuarenta y cinco, 745; b. setecientos cincuenta y cuatro, 754; c. seiscientos cuarenta y cinco, 645; d. seiscientos cincuenta y cuatro, 654; e. setecientos sesenta y cuatro, 764; f. setecientos setenta y cuatro, 774; g. seiscientos setenta y cuatro, 674; h. seiscientos sesenta y cuatro, 664; i. setecientos cuarenta y siete, 747; j. seiscientos cuarenta y seis, 646.

Exercise 5: Write down the numbers you hear: a. ciento noventa y cuatro, 194; b. doscientos noventa y tres, 293; c. trescientos cuarenta y uno, 341; d. cuatrocientos dos, 402; e. quinientos nueve, 509; f. seiscientos doce, 612; g. seiscientos sesenta y uno, 661; h. setecientos setenta y tres, 773; i. ochocientos cuarenta y seis, 846; j. novecientos veinte, 920.

Lesson 21: At the tourist office

Exercise 1: Say these sentences in Spanish: 1. Las camas son muy baratas, The beds are very cheap; 2. Mi casa está lejos de la iglesia, My house is far from the church; 3. No me gusta ir en barco a la isla, I don't like going to the island by boat; 4. ¿Cuáles son las excursiones más interesantes?, Which are the most interesting excursions?; 5. Creo que no tenemos entradas, I don't think we've got entrance tickets; 6. En general, ¿te gustan los museos?, In general, do you like museums?; 7. No sé si está cerca del centro, I don't know if it's close to the centre; 8. ¿Me puede dar dos folletos en inglés?, Can you give me two brochures in English?; 9. ¿En qué pueblo está el castillo?, Which small town is the castle in?; 10. ¿Me puede decir cómo se va a la catedral?, Can you tell me how you get to the cathedral?

Exercise 2: Which of the two words is being said?: 1. allí, there; 2. ahí, there; 3. barata, cheap; 4. español, Spanish; 5. gratuita, free; 6. inglesa, English; 7. interesante, interesting; 8. moderna, modern; 9. necesito, I need; 10. público, public.

Exercise 3: According to the dialogue on p. 164, is each of these statements true or false?: 1. Miguel quiere una habitación en un hotel barato, T (Michael wants a room in a cheap hotel); 2. El hotel Alicante cuesta menos que el Torrevieja, T (The Alicante Hotel costs less than the Torrevieja); 3. El hotel Torrevieja está al lado del monasterio, F (The Torrevieja Hotel is next to the monastery); 4. No nos quedan folletos sobre la zona, F (We don't have any brochures about the area left); 5. El Palacio Real es interesante, T (The Royal Palace is interesting); 6. Hay un castillo a menos de treinta kilómetros, T (There is a castle less than thirty kilometres away); 7. La entrada al castillo cuesta bastante, F (The entrance to the castle costs quite a bit); 8. El castillo abre por la tarde, F (The castle opens in the afternoon); 9. Muchos museos abren a las nueve, T (Many museums open at nine); 10. Los lunes no hay excursión a la isla, F (There's no excursion to the island on Mondays).

Exercise 4: Translate these sentences into Spanish: 1. Me gusta cenar en este restaurante, I like having dinner in this restaurant; 2. ¿Me puede recomendar un hotel bueno?, Can you recommend a good hotel (to me)?; 3. Las peras son más baratas que las fresas, The pears are cheaper than the strawberries; 4. El cine está a un kilómetro de mi casa, The cinema is one kilometre away from my house; 5. La iglesia está lejos del pueblo, The church is far from the village; 6. ¿Cuánto cuesta mandar un mensaje por correo electrónico?, How much does it cost to send an email message?; 7. ¿Cuánto cuestan los lavaplatos?, How much do the dishwashers cost?; 8. Todos los días vamos de compras al supermercado, Every day we go shopping in the supermarket; 9. Mi tío no es inglés, pero se llama Smith, My uncle is not English, but he's called Smith; 10. ¿De dónde son las mandarinas?, Where are the tangerines from?

Lesson 22: Clothes and shoes

Exercise 1: Say these sentences in Spanish: 1. Todavía no tienen coche, They still don't have a car; 2. No me gustan mucho los abrigos blancos, I don't like white coats very much; 3. ¿Cuánto cuesta la gorra amarilla del escaparate?, How much is the yellow cap in the shop window?; 4. Creo que no van a comprar toallas nuevas este año, I don't think they're going to buy new towels this year; 5. Los bolsos están en la quinta planta, The handbags are on the fifth floor; 6. No sé si las camisetas están de oferta, I don't know if the T-shirts are on offer; 7. Por cierto, ¿cuándo viene tu hermano?, By the way, when is your brother coming?; 8. Prefiero pagar en efectivo, I prefer to pay cash; 9. ¿Me puede decir en qué planta están los jerseys?, Can you tell me which floor the jumpers are on?; 10. Los pantalones negros no me quedan bien, The black trousers don't fit me.

Exercise 2: Which of the two sentences is being said?: 1. No me gustan mucho estas camisas, I don't like these shirts very much; 2. Prefiero los rojos, I prefer the red ones; 3. ¿Cuánto cuesta esta camisa?, How much is this shirt?; 4. Todos los lunes visitan a su abuela, They visit their grandmother every Monday; 5. No sé dónde está tu corbata negra, I don't know where your black tie is; 6. Las camisas blancas están de oferta, The white shirts are on offer; 7. Los abrigos están en la cuarta planta, The coats are on the fourth floor; 8. ¿Puedo probarme este vestido?, May I try this dress on?; 9. El pueblo de mi padre está a seis kilómetros, My father's small town is six kilometres away; 10. Mis amigas son inglesas, My [f] friends are English.

Exercise 3: Complete the sentences using the correct form of the words in brackets: 1. Tenemos dos billetes *azules*, We have two blue tickets; 2. ¿Cuántos autobuses *rojos* hay en la parada?, How many red buses are there at the bus stop?; 3. No me queda arroz *blanco*, I don't have any white rice left; 4. ¿Tiene chupetes *amarillos?*, Do you have any yellow dummies?; 5. No vendemos biberones *rosas*, We don't sell pink feeding bottles; 6. ¿No tienes flotadores *negros*?, Don't you have black rubber rings?; 7. En la estación hay dos trenes *grises*, There are two grey trains at the station; 8. Quiero comprar tres bikinis *blancos*, I want to buy three white bikinis; 9. Me gustan mucho estos pantalones *verdes*, I like these green trousers very much; 10. El helado de fresa es *rosa*, The strawberry ice cream is pink.

Exercise 4: Translate these sentences into Spanish: 1. Todavía no queremos cenar, We don't want to have dinner yet; 2. No me gustan mucho los bañadores blancos, I don't like white swimming costumes very much; 3. ¿Cuántos cuestan los pantalones del escaparate?, How much are the trousers in the shop window?; 4. No sé cómo se llama, I don't know her name; 5. Las camisetas blancas están de oferta, The white T-shirts are on offer; 6. Ya tienen demasiadas gorras, They already have too many caps; 7. ¿En qué planta están los zapatos?, Which floor are the shoes on?; 8. ¿Puedo pagar con Visa?, Can I pay by Visa?; 9. Los grandes almacenes están cerca de la playa, The department store is close to the beach; 10. Estas islas son muy interesantes, These islands are very interesting.

Lesson 23: Renting a car

Exercise 1: Say these sentences in Spanish: 1. Queremos alquilar este modelo por una semana, We want to hire this model for a week; 2. Las corbatas de esta tienda son demasiado caras, The ties in this shop are too expensive; 3. ¿Cuándo tengo que devolver el coche?, When do I have to return the car?; 4. Por cierto, ¿cómo te llamas?, By the way, what's your name?; 5. Nuestros hijos no van a pasar las Navidades en un hotel, Our children aren't going to spend Christmas in a hotel; 6. Es mejor esperar una hora, It's better to wait an hour; 7. Todavía no sé a qué hora vienen, I still don't know what time they're coming; 8. Creo que tengo tres tarjetas de crédito, I think I have three credit cards; 9. ¿Me puedes dar cambio para un café?, Can you [tú] give me change for a coffee?; 10. ¿Cuánto cuesta la oferta especial de este mes?, How much is this month's special offer?

Exercise 2: Which phrase is the answer to each question you hear?: 1. ¿De qué color es la falda de Mercedes? Roja. (What colour is Mercedes' skirt? Red); 2. ¿Te gustan los pantalones verdes? Sí, me gustan mucho. (Do you like the green trousers? Yes, I like them very much); 3. ¿Os gustan las zapatillas de mi hermano? No, no nos gustan mucho. (Do you like my brother's trainers? No, we don't like them very much); 4. ¿Qué día vais a ir al cine? El viernes que viene. (When are you going to the cinema? Next Friday); 5. ¿A qué hora vais a visitar a la abuela? A las siete y media. (What time are you going to visit grandmother? At half past seven); 6. ¿Qué hora es? Las cuatro y veinte. (What time is it? Twenty past four); 7. ¿Cuánto cuestan las gorras verdes? Tres euros y veinte céntimos. (How much are the green caps? Three euros and twenty cents); 8. ¿Tienes alguna camisa roja? No, no tengo ninguna. (Do you have any red shirts? No, I don't have any); 9. ¿Tienes algún bolso negro? Sí, tengo uno. (Do you have any black handbags? Yes, I have one); 10. ¿Tenéis alguna sombrilla? Sí, tenemos dos. (Do you have any beach umbrellas? Yes, we have two).

Exercise 3: Match the English with the Spanish expressions: 1. está mal, it's not bad; 2. por allí, around there; 3. por supuesto, of course; 4. por si acaso, just in case; 5. todavía no, not yet; 6. no me queda bien, it doesn't fit me; 7. en efectivo, cash; 8. por cierto, by the way; 9. todo recto, straight ahead; 10. a pie, on foot.

Exercise 4: Translate these sentences into Spanish: 1. Quieren alquilar un coche pequeño, They want to hire a small car; 2. Los jerseys de esta tienda son demasiado caros, The jumpers in this shop are too expensive; 3. Los zapatos marrones no me quedan bien, The brown shoes don't fit me; 4. Hoy vamos a cenar con nuestras amigas inglesas, Today we're going to have dinner with our English (female) friends; 5. ¿Me puede dar un plano de la ciudad?, Can you [ud] give me a map of the city?; 6. Es mejor comprar la fruta en la frutería, It's better to buy fruit at the fruit shop; 7. Todavía no tienen los regalos de los niños, They still don't have the children's presents; 8. Prefiero ver un museo interesante, I'd prefer to see an interesting museum; 9. Las mantas están hoy de oferta, The blankets are on offer today; 10. ¿En qué planta están los microondas?, Which floor are the microwaves on?

Lesson 24: At the bank

Exercise 1: Say these sentences in Spanish: 1. Quiero cambiar cincuenta libras esterlinas a euros, I want to change fifty pounds sterling into euros; 2. Vamos a ir en seguida, We are going to go at once; 3. ¿Podemos cobrar cheques de viaje en esta sucursal?, Can we cash in traveller's cheques at this branch?; 4. Tu carné de conducir está en la mesa de la cocina, Your driving licence is on the kitchen table; 5. No sé dónde está el resto, I don't know where the rest is; 6. Los servicios están junto a las salidas internacionales, The toilets are next to the international departures; 7. Quiero a mandar este paquete por correo certificado, I want to send this parcel by registered mail; 8. Casi no me queda agua, I have almost no water left; 9. ¿Dónde podemos sacar dinero?, Where can we take money out?; 10. Lo siento, no me quedan sellos de un euro, I'm sorry, I don't have any one euro stamps left.

Exercise 2: Which of the words below completes each sentence you hear?: 1. Quiero *cambiar* doscientas libras esterlinas a euros, I want to change two hundred pounds sterling into euros; 2. Aquí no pueden cobrar *cheques* de viaje, You can't cash in traveller's cheques here; 3. *Casi* no me quedan billetes de cinco euros, I have almost no five euro notes left; 4. ¿Me puede decir dónde están las *salidas* internacionales?, Can you tell me where the international departures are?; 5. Todavía tengo que comprar dos *paquetes* de tabaco, I still have to buy two packets of cigarettes; 6. ¿Por qué no vamos a *sacar* dinero ahora?, Why don't we go take money out now?; 7. ¿Dónde está mi *carné* de conducir?, Where is my driving licence?; 8. Creo que hay un *cajero* automático en la otra calle, I think there's a cash dispenser on the other street; 9. Hay un buzón a la *entrada* de la estación, There's a letter box at the entrance of the station; 10. ¿Lo quiere mandar por *correo* certificado?, Do you want to send it by registered mail?

Exercise 3: According to the dialogue on p. 192, is each statement true or false?: 1. Almudena quiere cambiar 140 libras, F (Almudena wants to change 140 pounds); 2. El dólar vale 0,89 euros, T (The dollar costs 0.89 euros); 3. Almudena quiere cobrar dos cheques de viaje, F (Almudena wants to cash in two traveller's cheques); 4. Almudena quiere seis billetes de diez euros, F (Almudena wants six ten euro notes); 5. No hay ningún cajero automático cerca de la playa, F (There are no cash dispensers near the beach); 6. Hay una sucursal en el aeropuerto, T (There's one branch at the airport); 7. Borja quiere tres sellos, T (Borja wants three stamps); 8. La empleada no sabe dónde hay un buzón, F (The employee doesn't know where there's a letter box); 9. Borja quiere pagar en efectivo, F (Borja wants to pay cash); 10. Borja tiene que sacar dinero, T (Borja has to take money out).

Exercise 4: Translate these sentences into Spanish: 1. No sé dónde cobrar este cheque de viaje, I don't know where to cash in this traveller's cheque; 2. Prefiero sacar dinero en mi sucursal, I prefer to take money out at my branch; 3. Vamos a coger el autobús en seguida, We're going to take the bus at once; 4. No tengo ni sellos ni postales, I have neither stamps nor postcards; 5. En esta ciudad no hay casi ninguna zapatería, In this city there are almost no shoe shops; 6. ¿Me puede dar dos paquetes de tabaco?, Can you [ud] give me two packets of cigarettes?; 7. Los abrigos de esta tienda son demasiado caros, The coats in this shop are too expensive; 8. Por cierto, ¿cómo se va al aeropuerto?, By the way, how do you get to the airport?; 9. Es mejor sacar dinero por la mañana, It's better to take money out in the morning; 10. ¿Cuánto valen/cuánto cuestan los encendedores?, How much are the lighters?

Nicholas's family tree

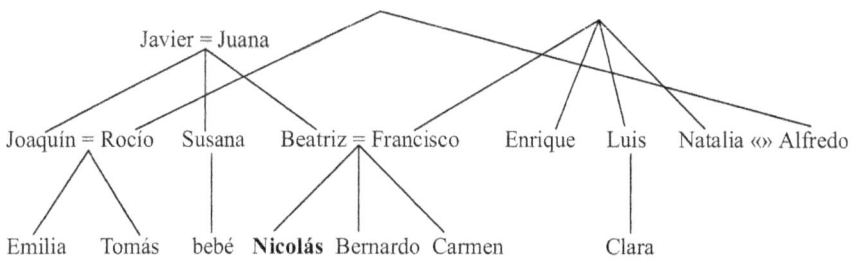

Clothes and shoe sizes

Women's dresses and Suits	Women's shoes
European 34 36 38 40 42 44 46 48 UK 6 8 10 12 14 16 18 20 USA 4 6 8 10 12 14 16 18	European 37$_{1/2}$ 38 38$_{1/2}$ 39 40 40$_{1/2}$ UK 4$_{1/2}$ 5 5$_{1/2}$ 6 6$_{1/2}$ 7 USA 7 7$_{1/2}$ 8 8$_{1/2}$ 9 9$_{1/2}$
Men's suits and Overcoats	**Men's shirts**
European 46 48 50 52 54 56 58 UK 36 38 40 42 44 46 48 USA 36 38 40 42 44 46 48	European 36 37 38 39 41 42 43 UK 14 14$_{1/2}$ 15 15$_{1/2}$ 16 16$_{1/2}$ 17 USA 14 14$_{1/2}$ 15 15$_{1/2}$ 16 16$_{1/2}$ 17
Men's shoes	**Children's clothes**
European 41 42 43 44 45 46 UK 7 7$_{1/2}$ 8$_{1/2}$ 9$_{1/2}$ 10$_{1/2}$ 11 USA 8 8$_{1/2}$ 9$_{1/2}$ 10$_{1/2}$ 11$_{1/2}$ 12	European 125 135 150 155 160 UK 43 48 55 58 60 USA 4 6 8 10 12

Map of Spain

Map of the world

1. Canadá	Canada	18. Argelia	Algeria	Suecia	Sweden
2. Estados Unidos	US	19. Libia	Libya	Finlandia	Finland
3. México	Mexico	20. Turquía	Turkey	Noruega	Norway
4. Cuba	Cuba	21. Egipto	Egypt	Dinamarca	Denmark
5. Colombia	Colombia	22. Etiopía	Ethiopia	Islandia	Iceland
6. Brasil	Brazil	23. Somalia	Somalia	Francia	France
7. Venezuela	Venezuela	24. Asia	Asia	Suiza	Switzerland
8. Uruguay	Uruguay	25. India	India	Alemania	Germany
9. Chile	Chile	26. China	China	Holanda	Holland
10. Argentina	Argentina	27. Japón	Japan	Bélgica	Belgium
11. Paraguay	Paraguay	28. Australia	Australia	Austria	Austria
12. Bolivia	Bolivia	29. Nueva Zelanda	New Zealand	Polonia	Poland
13. Perú	Peru	30. Europa:	Europe:	Hungría	Hungary
14. Ecuador	Ecuador	Inglaterra	England	Grecia	Greece
15. Rusia	Russia	Gales	Wales	Italia	Italy
16. África	Africa	Escocia	Scotland	Portugal	Portugal
17. Marruecos	Morocco	Irlanda	Ireland	31. España	Spain

Verb tables

Regular verbs[1] ending in -ar: present tense.

Example: COMPRAR (TO BUY)

(yo)	compr**o**	I buy
(tú)	compr**as**	you [sing., coll] buy
(él/ella/usted)	compr**a**	he/she/it/you [sing., formal] buy(s)
(nosotros/nosotras)	compr**amos**	we buy
(vosotros/vosotras)	compr**áis**	you [plural, coll.] buy
(ellos/ellas/ustedes)	compr**an**	they/you [plural, formal] buy

Other '-ar' verbs which follow this pattern and have come up in this book: necesitar (to need), aceptar (to accept), cenar (to have dinner), limpiar (to clean), alquilar (to hire), pagar (to pay), firmar (to sign), cobrar (to charge).

Regular verbs ending in -er: present tense

Example: VENDER (TO SELL)

(yo)	vend**o**	I sell
(tú)	vend**es**	you [sing., coll] sell
(él/ella/usted)	vend**e**	he/she/it/you [sing., formal] sell(s)
(nosotros/nosotras)	vend**emos**	we sell
(vosotros/vosotras)	vend**éis**	you [plural, coll.] sell
(ellos/ellas/ustedes)	vend**en**	they/you [plural, formal] sell

Other '-er' verbs which follow this pattern: comer (to eat), beber (to drink).

Regular verbs ending in -ir: present tense

Example: VIVIR (TO LIVE)

(yo)	viv**o**	I live
(tú)	viv**es**	you [sing., coll] live
(él/ella/usted)	viv**e**	he/she/it/you [sing., formal] live(s)
(nosotros/nosotras)	viv**imos**	we live
(vosotros/vosotras)	viv**ís**	you [plural, coll.] live
(ellos/ellas/ustedes)	viv**en**	they/you [plural, formal] live

Other '-ir' verbs which follow this pattern: escribir (to write).

---

[1] Regular verbs are those that follow the patterns for the verbs given on this page.

How to build regular verb forms from the previous patterns:

Let's see how you get the forms for *necesitar* (to need), *comer* (to eat) and *escribir* (to write), for example:

→ *Necesitar* is a regular -ar verb, so it follows the pattern for *comprar*.

→ Remove the letters 'ar' from *necesitar*.

→ To get the forms for the six persons, add the letters in bold in *comprar*, the example for -ar verbs, to 'necesit'.

→ The six forms you get are:

necesito	I need
necesitas	you [sing., coll] need
necesita	he/she/it/you [sing., formal] need(s)
necesitamos	we need
necesitáis	you [plural, coll] need
necesitan	they/you [plural, formal] need

→ To get the forms for *comer* (to eat), add the letters in bold in *vender*, the example for -er verbs, to 'com'.

→ Here's what you get:

como	I eat
comes	you [sing., coll] eat
come	he/she/it/you [sing., formal] eat(s)
comemos	we eat
coméis	you [plural, coll] eat
comen	they/you [plural, formal] eat

→ To get the forms for *escribir* (to write), add the letters in bold in *vivir*, the example for -ir verbs, to 'escrib'.

→ Here's what you get:

escribo	I write
escribes	you [sing., coll] write
escribe	he/she/it/you [sing., formal] write(s)
escribimos	we write
escribís	you [plural, coll] write
escriben	they/you [plural, formal] write

IRREGULAR VERBS[2]

Dar (to give). Irregular verb: present tense

(yo)	doy	I give
(tú)	das	you [sing., coll] give
(él/ella/usted)	da	he/she/it/you [sing., formal] give(s)
(nosotros/nosotras)	damos	we can
(vosotros/vosotras)	dais	you [plural, coll.] give
(ellos/ellas/ustedes)	dan	they/you [plural, formal] give

Estar (to be). Irregular verb: present tense

(yo)	estoy	I am
(tú)	estás	you [sing., coll] are
(él/ella/usted)	está	he/she/it/you [sing., formal] is/are
(nosotros/nosotras)	estamos	we are
(vosotros/vosotras)	estáis	you [plural, coll.] are
(ellos/ellas/ustedes)	están	they/you [plural, formal] are

Hacer (to do, to make). Irregular verb: present tense

(yo)	hago	I do, make
(tú)	haces	you [sing., coll] do, make
(él/ella/usted)	hace	he/she/it/you [sing., formal] do(es), make(s)
(nosotros/nosotras)	hacemos	we do, make
(vosotros/vosotras)	hacéis	you [plural, coll.] do, make
(ellos/ellas/ustedes)	hacen	they/you [plural, formal] do, make

Ir (to go). Irregular verb: present tense

(yo)	voy	I go
(tú)	vas	you [sing., coll] go
(él/ella/usted)	va	he/she/it/you [sing., formal] go(es)
(nosotros/nosotras)	vamos	we go
(vosotros/vosotras)	vais	you [plural, coll.] go
(ellos/ellas/ustedes)	van	they/you [plural, formal] go

[2]Irregular verbs are those that do not follow the patterns for regular verbs.

Poder (to able to, can). Irregular verb: present tense

(yo)	puedo	I can
(tú)	puedes	you [sing., coll] can
(él/ella/usted)	puede	he/she/it/you [sing., formal] can
(nosotros/nosotras)	podemos	we can
(vosotros/vosotras)	poséis	you [plural, coll.] can
(ellos/ellas/ustedes)	pueden	they/you [plural, formal] can

Poner (to put). Irregular verb: present tense

(yo)	pongo	I put
(tú)	pones	you [sing., coll] put
(él/ella/usted)	pone	he/she/it/you [sing., formal] put(s)
(nosotros/nosotras)	ponemos	we put
(vosotros/vosotras)	ponéis	you [plural, coll.] put
(ellos/ellas/ustedes)	ponen	they/you [plural, formal] put

Querer (to want). Irregular verb: present tense

(yo)	quiero	I want
(tú)	quieres	you [sing., coll] want
(él/ella/usted)	quiere	he/she/it/you [sing., formal] wants(s)
(nosotros/nosotras)	queremos	we want
(vosotros/vosotras)	queréis	you [plural, coll.] want
(ellos/ellas/ustedes)	quieren	they/you [plural, formal] want

Saber (to know). Irregular verb: present tense

(yo)	sé	I know
(tú)	sabes	you [sing., coll] know
(él/ella/usted)	sabe	he/she/it/you [sing., formal] know(s)
(nosotros/nosotras)	sabemos	we know
(vosotros/vosotras)	sabéis	you [plural, coll.] know
(ellos/ellas/ustedes)	saben	they/you [plural, formal] know

Ser (to be). Irregular verb: present tense

(yo)	soy	I am
(tú)	eres	you [sing., coll] are
(él/ella/usted)	es	he/she/it/you [sing., formal] is/are
(nosotros/nosotras)	somos	we
(vosotros/vosotras)	sois	you [plural, coll.] are
(ellos/ellas/ustedes)	son	they/you [plural, formal] are

Tener (to have). Irregular verb: present tense

(yo)	tengo	I have
(tú)	tienes	you [sing., coll] have
(él/ella/usted)	tiene	he/she/it/you [sing., formal] has/have
(nosotros/nosotras)	tenemos	we have
(vosotros/vosotras)	tenéis	you [plural, coll.] have
(ellos/ellas/ustedes)	tienen	they/you [plural, formal] have

Volver (to come back, to return). Irregular verb: present tense

(yo)	vuelvo	I come back
(tú)	vuelves	you [sing., coll] come back
(él/ella/usted)	vuelve	he/she/it/you [sing., formal] come(s) back
(nosotros/nosotras)	volvemos	we come back
(vosotros/vosotras)	volvéis	you [plural, coll.] come back
(ellos/ellas/ustedes)	vuelven	they/you [plural, formal] come back

Spanish - English Glossary

The numbers after the English translations refer to the page where each Spanish word first appears.

a	to, at, 20
a cinco minutos	five minutes away, 152
a cuánto está	how much is, 194
a esta hora	at this hour, at this time of day, 184
a la derecha	on the right, 30
a la entrada	at the entrance, 194
a la gallega	Galician-style, 88
a la izquierda	on the left, 108
a la madrileña	Madrid-style, 88
a la romana	batter-fried, 88
a las siete	at seven o'clock, 50
a mí	to me, 88
a mediodía	at lunchtime, 108
a pie	on foot, 152
a qué hora	at what time, 20
año (m)	year, 142
abiertas	open (f/pl), 108
abre	he/she/it opens, you [ud] open, 50
abren	you [uds]/they open, 50
abrigo (m)	coat, 176
abril	April, 142
abuela (f)	grandmother, 66
abuelo (m)	grandfather, 66
abuelos (m/pl)	grandparents, grandfathers, 66
aceite (m)	oil, 58
aceituna (f)	olive, 88
aceptáis	you [vos] accept, 176
aceptamos	we accept, 194
adiós	goodbye, 10
adulto (m)	adult, 98
aeropuerto (m)	airport, 184
agencia (f)	agency, 108
agencia (f) de viajes	travel agency, 108
agosto	August, 142
agua (f)	water, 30
ahí	there, over there, 166
ahora	now, 42
ahora mismo	right away, right now, 42

aire acondicionado (m)	air conditioning, 20
al	to the (m), 30
al ajillo	with garlic, 88
al final	at the end, 152
al fondo	at the end, 30
al otro lado	on the other side, 152
al vapor	steamed, 88
albóndiga (f)	meatball, 88
albaricoque (m)	apricot, 134
Alejandro	Alexander, 184
Alfredo	Alfred, 66
algún	any, some (m), 30
algo	something, anything, 30
alguna	any, some (f), 58
Alicante	Alicante, 166
Alicia	Alice, 142
alioli (m)	garlic mayonnaise, 88
allí	there, over there, 134
almeja (f)	clam, 88
alquila	he/she/it hires (out), you [ud] hire (out), 126
alquilamos	we rent (out), we hire (out), 184
alquilar	to hire (out), to rent (out), 126
amarillo	yellow (m), 176
americano	American (m), 194
amigo (m)	friend, 10
Ana	Anne, 10
anchoa (f)	anchovy, 88
antes de	before, 20
Antonio	Anthony, 30
aparcamiento (m)	car park, 184
aparcar	to park, 50
apartamento (m)	apartment, flat 50
aquí	here, 20
aquí mismo	right here, 98
Argentina	Argentina, 166
armario (m)	wardrobe, cupboard, 50
arroz (m)	rice, 30
arte (m)	art, 166
asadas	grilled, baked, roasted (f/pl), 30
asado	grilled, baked, roasted (m), 30
asiento (m)	seat, 98
aspirina (f)	aspirin, 118
atún (m)	tuna, 30

atienden	you [uds]/they serve,	176
autobús (m)	bus, 98	
automático	automatic (m), 184	
autoservicio (m)	self-service restaurant, 108	
autovía (f)	dual carriageway, 184	
avenida (f)	avenue, 152	
ayudar	to help, 118	
ayudarla	to help you [ud/f], to help her,	118
azúcar (m)	sugar, 58	
azul	blue (m and f), 176	
bañador (m)	swimming costume, 176	
bañarnos	(us) to bathe, 126	
baño (m)	bathroom, 20	
bacalao (m)	cod, 88	
bailar	to dance, 126	
bajarnos	(us) to get off, 98	
banco (m)	bank, 194	
banderilla (f)	banderilla, 88	
barato	cheap (m), 166	
Barcelona	Barcelona, 98	
barco (m)	boat, ship, 166	
bastante	quite, 152	
basura (f)	rubbish, 50	
batido (m)	milk shake, 42	
Beatriz	Beatrice, 42	
bebé (m)	baby, 66	
beber	to drink, 30	
berenjena (f)	aubergine, 88	
Bernardo	Bernard, 66	
biberón (m)	feeding bottle, 118	
bien	fine, well, 10	
bikini (m)	bikini, 176	
billete (m)	note, ticket, 194	
billete (m)	ticket, 98	
blanco	white (m), 176	
blanco	white (m), 42	
blusa (f)	blouse, 176	
bocadillo (m)	sandwich, 108	
boda (f)	wedding, 66	
Bolivia	Bolivia, 152	
bollo (m)	bun, 134	
bolsa (f)	bag, 134	
bolso (m)	handbag, 176	

bonito (m)	tuna, 88
bote (m)	jar, 134
botella (f)	bottle, 30
buñuelo (m)	fritter, 88
buenas	good (f/pl), 118
buenas	good (f/pl), 10
buenas noches	good evening, good night, 10
buenas tardes	good afternoon, good evening, 10
bueno	good (m), 118
buenos	good (m/pl), 88
buenos días	good morning, 10
buzón (m)	letterbox, mailbox, 194
café (m)	coffee, 42
café solo (m)	black coffee, 42
cafetería (f)	cafeteria, 20
caja (f)	till, box, 58
caja (f)	box, till, 118
cajero automático (m)	cash dispenser, 194
calamar (m)	squid, 88
caliente	hot (m and f), 42
calle (f)	street, 108
callos (m/pl)	tripe, 88
calmante (m)	painkiller, 118
calor (m)	heat, 126
calzas	you [tú] wear, 176
cama (f)	bed, 50
cámara (f)	camera, 126
camarera (f)	waitress, 30
camarero (m)	waiter, 30
cambiar	to change, 194
cambio (m)	exchange, change, 194
cambio (m)	change, 42
camisa (f)	shirt, 176
camiseta (f)	T-shirt, 176
canapé (m)	canapé, 88
caña (f)	small beer, 42
cara (f)	face, 118
caracol (m)	snail, 88
carné (m)	identity card, membership card, 184
carné (m) de identidad	identity card, 194
carné (m) de conducir	driving licence, 184
carne (f)	meat, 30
carne picada (f)	mince, 134

carnicería (f)	butcher's,	108
caro	expensive (m),	184
Carolina	Caroline,	142
carrete (m)	film,	126
carretera (f)	road,	184
carrito (m)	trolley,	58
carta (f)	letter,	194
carta (f)	menu,	30
casa (f)	house,	30
casado	married (m),	66
caseras	homemade (f/pl),	88
casi	almost,	194
casi no	hardly,	194
castillo (m)	castle,	166
catedral (f)	cathedral,	166
categoría (f)	category,	184
catorce	fourteen,	3
cebolla (f)	onion,	58
cenar	to have dinner,	30
céntimo (m)	cent,	42
central	central (m and f),	58
centro (m)	centre,	108
centro comercial (m)	shopping centre,	108
cepillo (m)	hairbrush,	118
cerca	near, nearby, close,	50
cerca de	near, close to,	50
cercana	close, near (f),	184
cerdo (m)	pork,	88
cereal (m)	cereal,	134
cereza (f)	cherry,	134
cerilla (f)	match,	194
cero	zero,	3
cerramos	we close,	126
cerveza (f)	beer,	42
cesta (f)	basket,	58
champú (m)	shampoo,	118
champiñón (m)	mushroom,	58
chaqueta (f)	jacket,	176
cheque (m)	cheque,	194
cheque (m) de viaje	traveller's cheque,	194
chocolate (m)	chocolate,	42
chocolatina (f)	chocolate bar,	134
chorizo (m)	spicy sausage,	88

chupete (m)	(baby's) dummy, 118
cien	one hundred, 74
ciento uno	one hundred and one (m/pl), 158
cierran	you [uds]/they close, 50
cinco	five, 3
cincuenta	fifty, 74
cine (m)	cinema, 142
ciruela (f)	plum, 134
ciudad (f)	city, town, 184
Clara	Clare, 66
claro	of course, 20
cobramos	we charge, 194
cobran	you [uds]/they charge, 194
cobrar	to charge, to cash in, 194
Coca-Cola (f)	Coke, 42
coche (m)	car, 50
cocina (f)	kitchen, cooker, 50
cocina (f) de gas	gas cooker, 50
coge	take (a command) [tú], 152
coger	to take, to catch, 98
colchoneta (f)	air bed, 126
coliflor (f)	cauliflower, 134
color (m)	colour, 176
coma (f)	comma, 194
comisión (f)	commission, 194
como	as, 50
cómo	how, 10
cómo no	of course, 30
cómo se va a	how do you go to, how does one go to, 152
completo	full (m), 30
compra (f)	shopping, purchase, 142
comprar	to buy, 118
comprarlo	to buy it, 118
compresa (f)	sanitary towel, 118
con	with, 20
con gas	sparkling, fizzy, 30
con tarjeta	by Visa, 176
conducir	to drive, 184
congelador (m)	freezer, 50
congelados	frozen (m/pl), 134
congelados (m/pl)	frozen food, 134
consume	he/she/it takes/consumes, you [ud] take/consume, 184
copa (f)	glass, 42

corbata (f)	tie, 176
correo (m)	mail, post, 20
correo (m) certificado	registered mail, 194
Correos	post office, 152
cosa (f)	thing, 58
crema (f)	cream, 118
crema (f) hidratante	moisturising cream, 118
creo	I believe/think, 108
Cristina	Christine, 108
croqueta (f)	croquette, 88
cruce (m)	crossing, 152
cuál	which, which one, 118
cuáles	which, 166
cuándo	when, 50
cuántas	how many (f/pl), 20
cuánto	how much (m), 42
cuánto cuesta	how much is, 98
cuánto cuestan ...	how much are ..., 58
cuánto tiempo	how long, 126
cuántos	how many (m/pl), 142
cuántos días	how long, how many days, 142
cuarenta	forty, 74
cuarta	fourth (f), 152
cuarto	fourth (m), 152
cuatro	four, 3
cuatrocientos	four hundred (m/pl), 152
cubo (m)	bin, 50
cuenta (f)	bill, 30
cuestan	they cost, 58
cumpleaños (m)	birthday, 142
dame	give me [tú], 134
Daniel	Daniel, 152
dar	to give, 20
darle	to give him/her/it/you(ud), 118
de	from, of, 10
de al lado	next, next door, 126
de nada	you're welcome, 58
de primero	as a starter, 30
de segundo	for the main course, 30
de vacaciones	on holiday, on vacation, 126
décimo	tenth (m), 152
decir	to tell, to say, 30
deja	he/she/it leaves, you [ud] leave, 50

dejar	to leave, 20
del	of the (m), 50
demasiado	too, 184
demasiados	too many (m/pl), 126
dentro de	in, 30
dependienta (f)	shop assistant, 58
dependiente (m)	shop assistant, 126
deporte (m)	sport, 108
derecha (f)	right, 30
desayuno (m)	breakfast, 20
descafeinado (m)	decaf, 42
descuento (m)	discount, 98
desea	he/she/it wishes, you [ud] wish, 118
desean	you [uds]/they wish, 42
desodorante (m)	deodorant, 118
despacio	slowly, 152
detrás de	behind, 134
devolver	to return, to give back, 184
día (m)	day, 10
diálogo (m)	dialogue, 10
diciembre	December, 142
dieciséis	sixteen, 3
diecinueve	nineteen, 3
dieciocho	eighteen, 3
diecisiete	seventeen, 3
diente (m)	tooth, 118
diez	ten, 3
dinero (m)	money, 194
discoteca (f)	club, nightclub, disco, 126
disculpe	excuse me [ud], 58
divorciada	divorced (f), 66
doble	double, 20
doce	twelve, 3
docena (f)	dozen, 134
dólar (m)	dollar, 194
domingo	Sunday, 142
donde	where, 118
dónde	where, 10
dormir	to sleep, 126
dormir la siesta	to have a nap, 126
dos	two, 3
doscientos	two hundred (m/pl), 152
doy	I give, 194

dura	it lasts,	98
duros	hard (m/pl),	88
edificio (m)	building,	152
el	the (m),	10
él	he,	66
electrónico	electronic (m),	20
elegir	to choose,	118
Elena	Helen,	108
ella	she,	66
Emilia	Emily,	66
Emilio	Emile,	108
empanadilla (f)	pasty,	88
empieza	he/she/it starts, you [ud] start,	166
empiezan	you [uds]/they start,	176
empleada (f)	(female) employee,	98
empleado (m)	(male) employee,	98
en	in, at, on,	10
en efectivo	cash,	176
en gabardina	in batter,	88
en general	in general,	166
en seguida	right away,	194
encantada	pleased (f),	10
encantado	pleased (m),	10
encendedor (m)	lighter,	194
encontrar	to find,	58
enero	January,	142
Enrique	Henry,	66
ensalada (f)	salad,	30
enseñar	to show,	176
enseño	I show,	50
entonces	then,	10
entrada (f)	(entrance) ticket,	166
entrada (f)	entrance,	50
entre	between, among,	108
equipaje (m)	luggage,	20
eres	you [tú] are,	10
es	he/she/it is, you [ud] are,	20
escaparate (m)	shop window,	176
ese	that (m),	126
eso	that,	20
espaguetis (m/pl)	spaghetti,	30
español (m)	Spanish language,	166
espárrago (m)	asparagus,	58

especial	special (m and f), 184
esperar	to wait, 98
esquí acuático (m)	water-skiing, 126
esquina (f)	corner, 152
esta	this (f), 108
ésta	this, this one (f), 50
está	he/she/it is, you [ud] are, 20
está de oferta	it's on offer, 176
estáis	you [vos] are, 126
están	you [uds]/they are, 30
estar	to be, 126
estas	these (f/pl), 118
estás	you [tú] are, 10
esta noche	tonight, 126
estación (f)	station, 152
estación (f) de autobuses	bus station, 152
estación (f) de metro	metro station, underground station, 152
estación (f) de tren	train station, 152
este	this (m), 120
éste	this one, this (m), 118
Estefanía	Stephanie, 142
éste otro	this other one (m), 176
estos	these (m/pl), 176
éstos	these ones (m/pl), 176
estoy	I am, 66
euro (m)	euro, 42
ex	ex, 66
excursión (f)	excursion, 166
Extremadura	Extremadura, 152
falda (f)	skirt, 176
familia (f)	family, 66
farmacéutica (f)	pharmacist (female), 118
farmacia (f)	chemist's, pharmacy, 108
febrero	February, 142
Federico	Frederick, 142
Felipe	Philip, 88
Fernando	Ferdinand, 126
fiebre (f)	temperature, fever, 118
fiesta (f)	party, 126
filete (m)	steak, 30
fin (m)	end, 142
fin (m) de semana	weekend, 142
final (m)	end, 152

firma	sign (a command) (you[tú]), 176
firme	sign (a command) (you[ud]), 20
flotador (m)	rubber ring, 126
folleto (m)	brochure, 166
foto (f)	photograph, picture, 126
francesa	French (f), 30
Francisco	Frank, 58
frente a	in front of, opposite, 98
fresa (f)	strawberry, 58
fritas	fried (f/pl), 30
fritos	fried (m/pl), 88
fruta (f)	fruit, 58
frutería (f)	fruit shop, 108
fumador (m)	smoker, 98
Gabriel	Gabriel, 108
galleta (f)	biscuit, 58
gamba (f)	prawn, 88
garaje (m)	garage, 50
gasolina (f)	petrol, 184
gasolinera (f)	petrol station, gas station, 184
gato (m)	cat, 66
Gerardo	Gerard, 98
girar	to turn, 152
gorra (f)	cap, 176
gracias	thank you, 10
gramo (m)	gram, 134
grande	big, large (m), 42
grandes almacenes (m/pl)	department store, 98
gratis	free (m and f/sing and pl), 134
gratuita	free (f), 166
Gregorio	Gregory, 152
gris	grey (m and f), 50
guía (f)	guide (female), guidebook, 126
guisante (m)	pea, 134
habitación (f)	room, bedroom, 20
hace	he/she/it makes, you [ud] make, 126
hace mucho calor	it's very hot, 126
hacemos	we make/do, 98
hacen	you [uds] make/do, they make/do, 98
hacer	to make/do, 98
hacer esquí acuático	to water-ski, 126
hacer submarinismo	to go scuba diving, 126
hasta	until, till, 10

hasta la vista	see you,	10
hasta pronto	see you soon,	10
hay	there is, there are,	20
helado (m)	ice cream,	126
hermana (f)	sister,	66
hermano (m)	brother,	66
hermanos (m/pl)	brothers and sisters, siblings, brothers,	66
hielo (m)	ice,	42
hija (f)	daughter,	66
hijo (m)	son,	66
hijos (m/pl)	children, sons,	66
históricos	historical (m/pl),	166
hola	hello, hi,	10
hora (f)	time, hour,	20
horario (m)	timetable,	166
hotel (m)	hotel,	10
hoy	today,	88
huevo (m)	egg,	88
ida (f)	outward journey,	98
ida y vuelta (f)	round trip,	98
iglesia (f)	church,	166
ilimitado	unlimited (m),	184
incluyen	you [uds]/they include,	184
indicarme	to show me,	152
individual	individual, single (m and f),	20
información (f)	information,	50
inglés (m)	English language,	166
Inglaterra	England,	10
instrucciones (f/pl)	instructions,	50
interés (m)	interest,	166
interesante	interesting (m and f),	166
internacional	international (m and f),	194
ir	to go,	66
ir de compras	to go shopping,	142
Irlanda	Ireland,	194
Isabel	Elizabeth,	108
isla (f)	island,	166
IVA (m)	VAT,	184
izquierda (f)	left,	108
jabón (m)	soap,	118
Jaime	Jaime,	126
jamón (m)	ham,	88
jamón serrano (m)	Spanish cured ham,	88

jardín (m)	garden, 66
jarra (f)	jug, 42
jerez (m)	sherry, 42
jersey (m)	jumper, 176
Joaquín	Joachim, 66
Jorge	George, 42
José	Joseph, 10
Juan	John, 10
Juana	Joanna, 66
judías verdes (f/pl)	French beans, 134
jueves	Thursday, 50
jueves	Thursday, 142
Julián	Julian, 152
julio	July, 142
junio	June, 142
junto a	next to, 58
junto al	next to, 108
kilo (m)	kilo, 58
kilometraje (m)	mileage, 184
kiwi (m)	kiwi, 58
kleenex (m)	tissue, paper handkerchief, 118
la	the (f), 10
lado (m)	side, 126
lago (m)	lake, 126
lata (f)	tin, can, 58
Laura	Laura, 88
lavadora (f)	washing machine, 50
lavaplatos (m)	dishwasher, 50
leche (f)	milk, 42
lechuga (f)	lettuce, 58
lejos	far, 152
lentilla (f)	contact lens, 118
les	to you [uds], to them, 30
libra (f)	pound, 194
libra (f) esterlina	pound sterling, 194
librería (f)	bookshop, 108
libres	free (m/pl and f/pl), 20
limón (m)	lemon, 42
limpiar	to clean, 50
línea (f)	line, 98
líquido (m)	solution, liquid, 118
llave (f)	key, 20
llegar	to get to, to arrive, 152

lleváis	you [vos] take, 126
llevarme	to take (with me), 118
lo	it, 176
lo siento	I'm sorry, 20
los	them (m), the (m/pl), 176
luego	then, later, 152
lugar (m)	place, 166
Luis	Louis, 66
Luisa	Louise, 118
lunes	Monday, 142
lunes	Monday, 50
madre (f)	mother, 66
mal	bad, 184
maleta (f)	suitcase, 20
maletero (m)	(car) boot, 184
mamá (f)	mum, 66
mandar	to send, 20
mandarina (f)	tangerine, 134
manta (f)	blanket, 50
mantequilla (f)	butter, 134
manzana (f)	apple, 58
mañana	tomorrow, 66
mañana (f)	morning, 50
mapa (m)	map, 166
mar (m)	sea, 152
María	Mary, 10
margarina (f)	margarine, 134
Margarita	Margaret, 10
marido (m)	husband, 66
marisco (m)	shellfish, 30
marrón	brown (m and f), 176
Marta	Martha, 50
martes	Tuesday, 142
marzo	March, 142
más	more, 30
más despacio	more slowly, 152
matrícula (f)	number plate, licence plate, 184
mayo	May, 142
mayonesa (f)	mayonnaise, 30
me gusta mucho ...	I like ... very much (sing), 126
me gustan	I like (pl), 88
me llamo	my name is, 10
me puedes decir	can you [tú] tell me, 152

mediana	medium(-sized),	134
medio	half (m), 58	
mejillón (m)	mussel, 88	
mejor	better, 184	
melocotón (m)	peach, 134	
melón (m)	melon, 58	
menos	minus, to, 80	
menos mal	it's just as well, 66	
mensaje (m)	message, 20	
mercado (m)	market, 108	
mermelada (f)	jam, marmalade, 134	
mes (m)	month, 142	
mesa (f)	table, 30	
metro (m)	underground, metro, 98	
metro (m)	metre, 184	
metrobús (m)	10-journey ticket, 98	
mi	my (m and f), 10	
microondas (m)	microwave, 50	
miércoles	Wednesday, 142	
Miguel	Michael, 166	
mil	one thousand, 152	
mineral	mineral (m and f), 30	
minuto (m)	minute, 30	
mío	mine (m), 142	
mismo	same (m), 42	
mixta	mixed (f), 30	
modelo (m)	model, 184	
moderno	modern (m), 166	
momento (m)	moment, 20	
monólogo (m)	monologue, 66	
monasterio (m)	monastery, 166	
moneda (f)	coin, 194	
monovolumen (m)	people carrier, 184	
montaña (f)	mountain, 126	
monumento (m)	monument, 166	
morcilla (f)	blood sausage, 88	
mosquito (m)	mosquito, 126	
moto (f)	motorbike, 184	
muchas	many (f/pl), 108	
muchas gracias	thank you very much, 20	
mucho	much, a lot (m), 88	
muchos	many (m/pl), 166	
muebles (m/pl)	furniture, 108	

mujer (f)	wife, woman, 66
museo (m)	museum, 166
muy	very, 88
muy bien	very well, 184
naranja (f)	orange, 42
naranjada (f)	orangeade, 42
Natalia	Natalie, 66
Navidades (f/pl)	Christmas, Christmas season, 142
necesario	necessary (m), 126
necesita	he/she/it needs, you [ud] need, 166
necesitan	you [uds]/they need, 50
necesito	I need, 58
negro	black (m), 176
nevera (f)	fridge, 50
ni ... ni	not ... or, neither ... nor, 88
Nicolás	Nicholas, 66
nieta (f)	granddaughter, 66
nieto (m)	grandson, 66
nietos (m/pl)	grandchildren, grandsons, 66
ninguno	none (m), 108
niño (m)	child, boy, 50
niños (m/pl)	children, 98
no	no, 20
no está mal	it's not bad, 184
no fumador (m)	non-smoker, 98
no me queda bien	it doesn't fit/suit me, 176
no nos queda ...	we don't have any ... left, 42
no sé	I don't know, 66
noche (f)	night, 10
nombre (m)	name, 20
nos	us, to us, 30
nosotras	we (all females), 126
nosotros	we, 142
novecientos	nine hundred (m/pl), 152
noveno	ninth (m), 152
noventa	ninety, 74
novia (f)	fiancée, girlfriend, 66
noviembre	November, 142
novio (m)	fiancé, boyfriend, 66
nuestra	our (f), 184
nueva	new (f), 142
nueve	nine, 3
número (m)	(shoe) size, number, 176

número (m)	number, 50
número de matrícula (m)	registration no., 184
o	or, 176
ochenta	eighty, 74
ocho	eight, 3
ochocientos	eight hundred (m/pl), 152
octavo	eighth (m), 152
octubre	October, 142
ocupado	full, busy (m), 20
oferta (f)	offer, 176
oficina (f)	office, 152
oficina (f) de turismo	tourist office, 166
oficina (f) de Correos	post office, 152
once	eleven, 3
ordenador (m)	computer, 20
os gustan	you [vos] like (pl), 88
otra	another, another one (f), 42
otras	other, others (f/pl), 88
otro	another, another one (m) 152
Pablo	Paul, 88
padre (m)	father, 66
pagar	to pay, 126
pago	I pay, 58
palacio (m)	palace, 166
pan (m)	bread, 134
panadería (f)	bakery, 108
pantalones (m/pl)	trousers, 176
pañal (m)	nappy, 118
papá (m)	dad, 66
papel (m)	paper, 118
papel (m) higiénico	toilet tissue, 118
paquete (m)	packet, parcel, 194
para	for, 20
parada (f)	stop, bus stop, 98
parador (m)	state-owned hotel, 166
parque (m)	park, 166
parquímetro (m)	parking meter, 184
pasaporte (m)	passport, 20
pasar	to spend, to pass, 142
pasillo (m)	aisle, corridor, 58
pasta (f) de dientes	toothpaste, 118
pastelería (f)	pastry shop, 108
pastilla (f)	tablet, pill, 118

patata (f)	potato, 30
patatas bravas (f/pl)	spicy potatoes, 88
patatas fritas (f/pl)	crisps, french fries, chips 134
pato (m)	duck, 30
Patricia	Patricia, 126
pavo (m)	turkey, 30
pedir	to ask for, to order, 88
Pedro	Peter, 10
peine (m)	comb, 118
peluquería (f)	hairdresser's, 108
pepino (m)	cucumber, 58
pequeña	small (f), 42
pera (f)	pear, 134
perdona	excuse me [tú], I'm sorry, 108
perejil (m)	parsley, 134
pero	but, 66
perro (m)	dog, 66
pescadería (f)	fishmonger's, 108
pescado (m)	fish, 30
pimienta (f)	pepper (spice), 30
pimiento (m)	pepper, capsicum, 58
pincho (m)	snack, small portion, 88
piña (f)	pineapple, 134
piscina (f)	swimming pool, 50
pizzería (f)	pizzeria, 108
plano (m)	street map, 98
planta (f)	floor, plant, 176
plátano (m)	banana, 58
plato (m)	dish, plate 30
playa (f)	beach, 10
plaza (f)	square, 108
plomo (m)	lead (the metal), 184
podemos	we can, 20
pollo (m)	chicken, 30
polo (m)	ice lolly, 126
pomelo (m)	grapefruit, 134
poner	to put, 58
pongo	I put, 42
por	for, through, 20
por allí	around there, 184
por aquí	around here, this way, 108
por aquí	this way, 30
por ciento	per cent, 98

por cierto	by the way, 176
por favor	excuse me, 42
por favor	please, 20
por qué	why, 126
por semana	per week, 184
por si acaso	just in case, 184
por supuesto	of course, 184
postal (f)	postcard, 194
potito (m)	jar of baby food, 118
precio (m)	price, 184
prefiere	he/she/it prefers, you [ud] prefer, 118
prefiero	I prefer, 88
pregunta	he/she/it asks, you [ud] ask, 126
presento	I introduce, 10
prima (f)	(female) cousin, 66
primera	first (f), 126
primero	first (m), 152
primo (m)	(male) cousin, 66
principal	main (m and f), 58
probador (m)	changing room, 176
probar	to try, to try on, 176
probarme	to try on (me), 176
protector solar (m)	sun block, 118
próxima	next (f), 108
próximo	next (m), 98
público	public (m), 166
pueblo (m)	small town, village, 166
puede	he/she/it can, you [ud] can, 20
pueden	you [uds]/they can, 30
puedes	you [tú] can, 126
puedo	I can, 20
pues	then, 30
puesto (m)	stall, 58
pulpo (m)	octopus, 88
que	that, 20
qué	what, which, 10
qué día	what day, when, 50
qué día es hoy	what day is it today?, 142
qué lío	what a mess, 66
qué más	what else, 58
qué pena	what a pity, 88
qué tal estás	how are you [tú], 10
que viene	next, 142

quedarse	to stay, 142
quédese	keep (a command) (ud), 42
queréis	you [vos] want, 126
queremos	we want, 126
queso (m)	cheese, 88
quién	who, 58
quiere	he/she/it wants, you [ud] want, 98
quieren	you [uds]/they want, 30
quieres	you [tú] want, 176
quiero	I want, 20
quince	fifteen, 3
quinientos	five hundred (m/pl), 152
quinto	fifth (m), 152
ración (f)	portion, 88
radio (f)	radio, 20
real	royal (m and f), 166
rebajas (f/pl)	sales, 176
recepcionista (f)	receptionist, 20
recepcionista (m)	receptionist, 20
receta (f)	prescription, 118
recibo (m)	receipt, 176
recomendar	to recommend, 118
recomienda	he/she/it recommends, you [ud] recommend, 30
recto	straight (m), 152
regalo (m)	present, gift, 108
región (f)	region, 166
rellenos	stuffed (m/pl), 88
reserva (f)	reservation, 20
reservada	reserved (f), 20
reservado	reserved (m), 50
reservar	to book, to reserve, 166
restaurante (m)	restaurant, 152
resto (m)	rest, 194
revelar	to develop, 126
Ricardo	Richard, 10
riesgo (m)	risk, 184
riñón (m)	kidney, 88
rojo	red (m), 176
ron (m)	rum, 42
ropa (f)	clothes, 108
Rosa	Rose, 20
rosa	pink (m and f), 176
rosado	rosé (m), 42

sábado	Saturday, 142
sabe	he/she//it knows, you [ud] know, 58
sabes	you [tú] know, 108
sacar	to take out, 126
sal (f)	salt, 30
salón (m)	sitting room, 50
salami (m)	salami, 134
salchicha (f)	sausage, 134
salchichón (m)	salami-type sausage, 134
sale	he/she/it leaves, you [ud] leave, 98
salida (f)	departure, exit, 194
salmón (m)	salmon, 30
sandía (f)	watermelon, 58
sangría (f)	sangria, 42
sardina (f)	sardine, 30
sé	I know, 66
se casa	he/she/you get(s) (is/are getting) married, 66
se deja	one leaves, 50
se escribe	one writes, 36
se llama	he/she/it is called, you [ud] are called, 66
se paga	is paid, one pays, 58
séptimo	seventh (m), 152
se queda	he/she/it stays, you [ud] stay, 142
se sirve	is served 20
señor (m)	man, gentleman, 20
señora (f)	woman, lady, 20
seguir	to continue, to go on, 152
segundo	second (m), 152
seguro (m)	insurance, 184
seguro (m) a todo riesgo	comprehensive insurance, 184
seis	six, 3
seiscientos	six hundred (m/pl), 152
sello (m)	stamp, 194
semana (f)	week, 126
separado	separated (m), 66
septiembre	September, 142
ser	to be, 66
servicios (m/pl)	toilets, 30
sesenta	sixty, 74
seta (f)	mushroom, 88
setecientos	seven hundred (m/pl), 152
setenta	seventy, 74
Sevilla	Seville, 142

sexto	sixth (m), 152
si	if, 30
sí	yes, 10
siesta (f)	nap, 126
siete	seven, 3
siguiente	next (m and f), 58
Silvia	Sylvia, 88
sin	without, 42
sin plomo	unleaded, 184
sitio (m)	place, 166
sobre	on, about, on top of, 50
sobre (m)	envelope, 194
sobrina (f)	niece, 66
sobrino (m)	nephew, 66
sol (m)	sun, 10
solo	on its own, alone (m), 42
sólo	only, 58
soltero	single (m), 66
sombrero (m)	hat, 176
sombrilla (f)	beach umbrella, 126
somos	we are, 98
son	you [uds]/they are, 80
sopa (f)	soup, 30
soy	I am, 66
Sr	Mr, 20
Sra	Mrs, Ms, 20
su	his, her, its, your [ud/uds], their, 20
suavizante (m)	conditioner, 118
submarinismo (m)	scuba diving, 126
sucursal (f)	branch, 194
supermercado (m)	supermarket, 50
sus	his, her, its, your [ud/uds], their, 142
Susana	Susan, 66
tabaco (m)	tobacco, cigarettes, 194
talla (f)	(clothes) size, 176
también	too, also, 10
tampoco	not ... either, neither, 88
tampón (m)	tampon, 118
tapa (f)	tapa, small dish, snack, 88
tarde	late 30
tarde (f)	afternoon, evening, 10
tarifa (f)	tariff, 184
tarjeta (f)	card, 176

tarjeta (f) de crédito	credit card, 184
te	to you [tú], 10
té (m)	tea, 42
te gustan	you [tú] like (pl), 88
teléfono (m)	telephone, 20
televisión (f)	television, 20
tenemos	we have, 20
tenemos que	we have to, 20
tengo	I have, 20
tengo que	I have to, 98
tercero	third (m), 152
Teresa	Theresa, 30
terraza (f)	balcony, 50
tía (f)	aunt, 66
tiempo (m)	time, 126
tienda (f)	shop, store, 108
tiene	he/she/it has, you [ud] have, 20
tiene que	he/she/it has to, you [ud] have to, 98
tienen	you [uds]/they have, 20
tienen que	you [uds]/they have to, 98
tienes	you [tú] have, 88
tienes que	you [tú] have to, 152
tinto	red (wine) (m), 30
tío (m)	uncle, 66
tirita (f)	plaster, 118
toalla (f)	towel, 50
toda	all (f), 50
todas	all (f/pl), 20
todavía	yet, still, 176
todo	all (m), 20
todo recto	straight ahead, 152
todos	all (m/pl), 66
tomar	to take, to have, 30
tomar el sol	to sunbathe, 126
Tomás	Thomas, 66
tomate (m)	tomato, 58
tónica (f)	tonic water, 42
tortilla (f)	Spanish potato omelette, 88
tortilla (f)	omelette, 30
traer	to bring, 30
tráfico (m)	traffic, 184
traigo	I bring, 176
transbordo (m)	change, 98

trece	thirteen, 3
treinta	thirty, 3
tren (m)	train, 98
tres	three, 3
tres cuartos	three quarters, 134
trescientos	three hundred (m/pl), 152
tu	your [tú], 36
tú	you (singular, colloquial), 10
tumbona (f)	sun lounger, 126
turismo (m)	tourism, 166
último	last (m), 98
un poco de	a bit of, some, 134
uno	one (m), 3
unos	some (m/pl), 30
usas	you [tú] use, 176
uva (f)	grape, 58
va	he/she/it goes/is going, you [ud] go/are going, 66
vaca (f)	beef, cow 30
vacaciones (f/pl)	holidays, 10
vais	you [vos] go, 88
vale	it is worth, it costs, 194
vale	OK, 20
vamos	we go/are going, 30
vamos a ver	let's see, 42
van	you [uds]/they go, are going, 30
varias	several (f/pl), 108
varios	several (m/pl), 50
vaso (m)	glass, 42
vegetariano	vegetarian (m), 30
veinte	twenty, 3
veinticinco	twenty-five, 3
veinticuatro	twenty-four, 3
veintidós	twenty-two, 3
veintinueve	twenty-nine, 3
veintiocho	twenty-eight, 3
veintiséis	twenty-six, 3
veintisiete	twenty-seven, 3
veintitrés	twenty-three, 3
veintiuno	twenty-one (m/pl), 3
venda (f)	bandage, 118
vendemos	we sell, 118
Venezuela	Venezuela, 194
venimos	we come, 126

venir	to come,	126
ver	to see,	20
verde	green (m and f),	176
verdes	green (m/pl and f/pl),	58
verdulería (f)	vegetable shop,	108
verduras (f/pl)	vegetables,	58
vestido (m)	dress,	176
vez (f)	time, occasion,	126
viaje (m)	trip, journey,	98
Víctor	Victor,	152
victoria (f)	victory,	166
viene	he/she/it comes, you [ud] come,	142
vienen	you [uds]/they come,	50
viernes	Friday,	142
vino (m)	wine,	30
virgen (f)	virgin,	166
Visa	Visa,	176
visitar	to visit,	166
vitamina (f)	vitamin,	118
viudo	widowed, widower (m),	66
vivo	I live,	66
vodka (m)	vodka,	42
volver	to come back,	30
voy	I go/am going,	30
vuelta (f)	return,	98
vuelvo	I return, I come back,	194
whisky (m)	whisky,	42
y	and, past,	80
y	and,	10
ya	already,	176
yo	I, me,	10
yogur (m)	yoghurt,	134
zanahoria (f)	carrot,	58
zapatería (f)	shoe shop,	108
zapatilla (f)	trainer, sports shoe,	176
zapato (m)	shoe,	176
zona (f)	area, zone,	50
zumo (m)	juice,	42

English - Spanish Glossary

The numbers after the Spanish translations refer to the page where each word first appears.

a bit of	un poco de, 134
a lot	mucho, 88
about	sobre, 50
accept (we)	aceptamos, 194
accept (you [vosotros])	aceptáis, 176
adult	adulto (m), 98
afternoon	tarde (f), 10
agency	agencia (f), 108
air bed	colchoneta (f), 126
air conditioning	aire acondicionado (m), 20
airport	aeropuerto (m), 184
aisle	pasillo (m), 58
Alexander	Alejandro, 184
Alfred	Alfredo, 66
Alicante	Alicante, 166
Alice	Alicia, 142
all (f)	toda, 50
all (m), (f/pl)	todo, todas, 20
all (m/pl)	todos, 66
almost	casi, 194
alone (m)	solo, 42
already	ya, 176
also	también, 10
am (I)	soy, estoy, 66
American (m)	americano, 194
among	entre, 108
anchovy	anchoa (f), 88
and	y, 10
Anne	Ana, 10
another (f)	otra, 42
another (m)	otro, 152
another one (f)	otra, 42
Anthony	Antonio, 30
any (m)	algún, 30
any (f)	alguna, 58
anything	algo, 30
apartment	apartamento (m), 50
apple	manzana (f), 58

apricot	albaricoque (m), 134
April	abril, 142
are (you [tú])	eres, estás, 10
are (you [uds])	están, 30
are (you [vosotros])	estáis, 126
are (they)	son, 80
are (we)	somos, 98
are (you [uds])	son, 80
are called (you [ud])	se llama, 66
are going (they)	van, 30
are going (you [uds])	van, 30
area	zona (f), 50
Argentina	Argentina, 166
around here	por aquí, 108
around there	por allí, 184
arrive (to)	llegar, 152
art	arte (m), 166
as	como, 50
as a starter	de primero, 30
ask (you [ud])	pregunta, 126
ask for (to)	pedir, 88
asks (he/she/it)	pregunta, 126
asparagus	espárrago (m), 58
aspirin	aspirina (f), 118
at	en, 10
at	a, 20
at lunchtime	a mediodía, 108
at seven o'clock	a las siete, 50
at the end	al final, 152
at the end	al fondo, 30
at the entrance	a la entrada, 194
at this hour	a esta hora, 184
at this time of day	a esta hora, 184
at what time	a qué hora, 20
aubergine	berenjena (f), 88
August	agosto, 142
aunt	tía (f), 66
automatic (m)	automático, 184
avenue	avenida (f), 152
baby	bebé (m), 66
bad	mal, 184
bag	bolsa (f), 134
baked (m)	asado, 30

bakery	panadería (f), 108
balcony	terraza (f), 50
banana	plátano (m), 58
bandage	venda (f), 118
banderilla	banderilla (f), 88
bank	banco (m), 194
Barcelona	Barcelona, 98
basket	cesta (f), 58
bathe (to) (ourselves)	bañarnos, 126
bathroom	baño (m), 20
batter-fried	a la romana, 88
be (to)	ser, 66
be (to)	estar, 126
beach	playa (f), 10
beach umbrella	sombrilla (f), 126
Beatrice	Beatriz, 42
bed	cama (f), 50
bedroom	habitación (f), 20
beef	vaca (f), 30
beer	cerveza (f), 42
before	antes de, 20
behind	detrás de, 134
believe (I)	creo, 108
Bernard	Bernardo, 66
better	mejor, 184
between	entre, 108
big (m and f)	grande, 42
bikini	bikini (m), 176
bill	cuenta (f), 30
bin	cubo (m), 50
birthday	cumpleaños (m), 142
biscuit	galleta (f), 58
black (m)	negro, 176
black coffee	café solo (m), 42
blanket	manta (f), 50
blood sausage	morcilla (f), 88
blouse	blusa (f), 176
blue (m and f)	azul, 176
boat	barco (m), 166
Bolivia	Bolivia, 152
book (to)	reservar, 166
bookshop	librería (f), 108
boot (car)	maletero (m), 184

bottle	botella (f), 30
box	caja (f), 118
boy	niño (m), 50
boyfriend	novio (m), 66
branch	sucursal (f), 194
bread	pan (m), 134
breakfast	desayuno (m), 20
bring (to)	traer, 30
bring (I)	traigo, 176
brochure	folleto (m), 166
brother	hermano (m), 66
brothers	hermanos (m/pl), 66
brothers and sisters	hermanos (m/pl), 66
brown (m and f)	marrón, 176
building	edificio (m), 152
bun	bollo (m), 134
bus	autobús (m), 98
bus station	estación (f) de autobuses, 152
bus stop	parada (f), 98
busy (m)	ocupado, 20
but	pero, 66
butcher's	carnicería (f), 108
butter	mantequilla (f), 134
buy (to)	comprar, 118
buy it (to)	comprarlo, 118
by the way	por cierto, 176
by Visa	con tarjeta, 176
cafeteria	cafetería (f), 20
camera	cámara (f), 126
can (you [uds])	pueden, 30
can (I)	puedo, 20
can	lata (f), 58
can (you [tú])	puedes, 126
can (you [ud])	puede, 20
can (he/she/it)	puede, 20
can (they)	pueden, 30
can (we)	podemos, 20
can you [tú] tell me	me puedes decir, 152
canapé	canapé (m), 88
cap	gorra (f), 176
capsicum	pimiento (m), 58
car	coche (m), 50
car park	aparcamiento (m), 184

card	tarjeta (f), 176
Caroline	Carolina, 142
carrot	zanahoria (f), 58
cash	en efectivo, 176
cash dispenser	cajero automático (m), 194
cash in (to)	cobrar, 194
castle	castillo (m), 166
cat	gato (m), 66
catch (to)	coger, 98
category	categoría (f), 184
cathedral	catedral (f), 166
cauliflower	coliflor (f), 134
cent	céntimo (m), 42
central (m and f)	central, 58
centre	centro (m), 108
cereal	cereal (m), 134
change	transbordo (m), 98
change	cambio (m), 42
change (to)	cambiar, 194
changing room	probador (m), 176
charge (to)	cobrar, 194
charge (we)	cobramos, 194
charge (you [uds])	cobran, 194
charge (they)	cobran, 194
cheap (m)	barato, 166
cheese	queso (m), 88
chemist's	farmacia (f), 108
cheque	cheque (m), 194
cherry	cereza (f), 134
chicken	pollo (m), 30
child	niño (m), 50
children	niños (m/pl), 98
children	hijos (m/pl), 66
chips	patatas fritas (f/pl), 30
chocolate	chocolate (m), 42
chocolate bar	chocolatina (f), 134
choose (to)	elegir, 118
Christine	Cristina, 108
Christmas	Navidades (f/pl), 142
Christmas season	Navidades (f/pl), 142
church	iglesia (f), 166
cigarettes	tabaco (m), 194
cinema	cine (m), 142

city	ciudad (f), 184
clam	almeja (f), 88
Clare	Clara, 66
clean (to)	limpiar, 50
close (f)	cercana, 184
close	cerca, 50
close (we)	cerramos, 126
close (you [uds])	cierran, 50
close (they)	cierran, 50
close to	cerca de, 50
clothes	ropa (f), 108
club	discoteca (f), 126
coat	abrigo (m), 176
cod	bacalao (m), 88
coffee	café (m), 42
coin	moneda (f), 194
Coke	Coca-Cola (f), 42
colour	color (m), 176
comb	peine (m), 118
come (to)	venir, 126
come (we)	venimos, 126
come (you [ud])	viene, 142
come (you [uds])	vienen, 50
come (they)	vienen, 50
come back (I)	vuelvo, 194
come back (to)	volver, 30
comes (he/she/it)	viene, 142
comma	coma (f), 194
commission	comisión (f), 194
comprehensive insurance	seguro (m) a todo riesgo, 184
computer	ordenador (m), 20
conditioner	suavizante (m), 118
consume (you [ud])	consume, 184
consumes (he/she/it)	consume, 184
contact lens	lentilla (f), 118
continue (to)	seguir, 152
cooker	cocina (f), 50
corner	esquina (f), 152
corridor	pasillo (m), 58
cost (they)	cuestan, 58
costs (it)	vale, 194
cousin (male)	primo (m), 66
cousin (female)	prima (f), 66

cow	vaca (f), 30
cream	crema (f), 118
credit card	tarjeta (f) de crédito, 184
crisps	patatas fritas (f/pl), 134
croquette	croqueta (f), 88
crossing	cruce (m), 152
cucumber	pepino (m), 58
cupboard	armario (m), 50
dad	papá (m), 66
dance (to)	bailar, 126
Daniel	Daniel, 152
daughter	hija (f), 66
day	día (m), 10
decaf	descafeinado (m), 42
December	diciembre, 142
deodorant	desodorante (m), 118
department store	grandes almacenes (m/pl), 98
departure	salida (f), 194
develop (to)	revelar, 126
dialogue	diálogo (m), 10
discount	descuento (m), 98
dish	plato (m), 30
dishwasher	lavaplatos (m), 50
divorced (f)	divorciada, 66
do (to)	hacer, 98
do (you [uds])	hacen, 98
do (they)	hacen, 98
do (we)	hacemos, 98
doesn't fit me (it)	no me queda bien, 176
doesn't suit me (it)	no me queda bien, 176
dog	perro (m), 66
dollar	dólar (m), 194
don't have any ... left (we)	no nos queda ..., 42
don't know (I)	no sé, 66
double	doble, 20
dozen	docena (f), 134
dress	vestido (m), 176
drink (to)	beber, 30
drive (to)	conducir, 184
driving licence	carné (m) de conducir, 184
dual carriageway	autovía (f), 184
duck	pato (m), 30
dummy (baby's)	chupete (m), 118

egg	huevo (m), 88
eight	ocho, 3
eight hundred (m/pl)	ochocientos, 152
eighteen	dieciocho, 3
eighth (m)	octavo, 152
eighty	ochenta, 74
electronic (m)	electrónico, 20
eleven	once, 3
Elizabeth	Isabel, 108
Emile	Emilio, 108
Emily	Emilia, 66
employee (male)	empleado (m), 98
employee (female)	empleada (f), 98
end	final (m), 152
end	fin (m), 142
England	Inglaterra, 10
English (language)	inglés (m), 166
entrance	entrada (f), 50
envelope	sobre (m), 194
euro	euro (m), 42
evening	tarde (f), 10
ex	ex, 66
exchange	cambio (m), 194
excursion	excursión (f), 166
excuse me	disculpe (ud), 58
excuse me	perdona (tú), 108
excuse me	por favor, 42
exit	salida (f), 194
expensive (m)	caro, 184
Extremadura	Extremadura, 152
face	cara (f), 118
family	familia (f), 66
far	lejos, 152
father	padre (m), 66
February	febrero, 142
feeding bottle	biberón (m), 118
Ferdinand	Fernando, 126
fever	fiebre (f), 118
fiancé	novio (m), 66
fiancée	novia (f), 66
fifteen	quince, 3
fifth (m)	quinto, 152
fifty	cincuenta, 74

film	carrete (m), 126
find (to)	encontrar, 58
fine	bien, 10
first (m)	primero, 152
first (f)	primera, 126
fish	pescado (m), 30
fishmonger's	pescadería (f), 108
five	cinco, 3
five hundred (m/pl)	quinientos, 152
five minutes away	a cinco minutos, 152
fizzy	con gas, 30
flat	apartamento (m), 50
floor	planta (f), 176
for	por, para 20
for the main course	de segundo, 30
forty	cuarenta, 74
four	cuatro, 3
four hundred (m/pl)	cuatrocientos, 152
fourteen	catorce, 3
fourth (f)	cuarta, 152
fourth (m)	cuarto, 152
Frank	Francisco, 58
Frederick	Federico, 142
free (m/pl and f/pl)	libres, 20
free (f)	gratuita, 166
free (m and f, sing and pl)	gratis, 134
freezer	congelador (m), 50
French (f)	francesa, 30
French beans	judías verdes (f/pl), 134
french fries	patatas fritas (f/pl), 134
Friday	viernes, 142
fridge	nevera (f), 50
fried (f/pl)	fritas, 30
fried (m/pl)	fritos, 88
friend	amigo (m), 10
fritter	buñuelo (m), 88
from	de, 10
frozen (m/pl)	congelados, 134
frozen food	congelados (m/pl), 134
fruit	fruta (f), 58
fruit shop	frutería (f), 108
full (m)	completo, 30
full (m)	ocupado, 20

furniture	muebles (m/pl), 108
Gabriel	Gabriel, 108
Galician-style	a la gallega, 88
garage	garaje (m), 50
garden	jardín (m), 66
garlic mayonnaise	alioli (m), 88
gas cooker	cocina de (f) gas, 50
gas station	gasolinera (f), 184
gentleman	señor (m), 20
George	Jorge, 42
Gerard	Gerardo, 98
get married (you [ud])	se casa, 66
get off (to) (us)	bajarnos, 98
get to (to)	llegar, 152
gets married (he/she/it)	se casa, 66
gift	regalo (m), 108
girlfriend	novia (f), 66
give (I)	doy, 194
give (to)	dar, 20
give back (to)	devolver, 184
give him/her/it/you (ud) (to)	darle, 118
give me (tú)	dame, 134
glass	copa (f), 42
glass	vaso (m), 42
go (to)	ir, 66
go (you [uds])	van, 30
go (they)	van, 30
go (you [vosotros])	vais, 88
go on (to)	seguir, 152
go scuba diving (to)	hacer submarinismo, 126
go shopping (to)	ir de compras, 142
go/am going (I)	voy, 30
go/are going (we)	vamos, 30
go/are going (you [ud])	va, 66
goes/is going (he/she/it)	va, 66
good (f/pl)	buenas, 10
good (m)	bueno, 118
good (m/pl)	buenos, 88
good afternoon	buenas tardes 10
good evening	buenas noches, 10
good evening	buenas tardes, 10
good morning	buenos días, 10
good night	buenas noches, 10

goodbye	adiós, 10	
gram	gramo (m), 134	
grandchildren	nietos (m/pl), 66	
granddaughter	nieta (f), 66	
grandfather	abuelo (m), 66	
grandfathers	abuelos (m/pl), 66	
grandmother	abuela (f), 66	
grandparents	abuelos (m/pl), 66	
grandson	nieto (m), 66	
grandsons	nietos (m/pl), 66	
grape	uva (f), 58	
grapefruit	pomelo (m), 134	
green (m and f)	verde, 176	
green (m/pl and f/pl)	verdes, 58	
Gregory	Gregorio, 152	
grey (m and f)	gris, 50	
grilled (m)	asado, 30	
guide (female)	guía (f), 126	
guidebook	guía (f), 126	
hairbrush	cepillo (m), 118	
hairdresser's	peluquería (f), 108	
half (m)	medio, 58	
ham	jamón (m), 88	
handbag	bolso (m), 176	
hard (m/pl)	duros, 88	
hardly	casi no, 194	
has (he/she/it)	tiene, 20	
has to (he/she/it)	tiene que, 98	
hat	sombrero (m), 176	
have (to)	tomar, 30	
have (you [tú])	tienes, 88	
have (you [uds])	tienen, 20	
have (I)	tengo, 20	
have (they)	tienen, 20	
have (we)	tenemos, 20	
have (you [ud])	tiene, 20	
have a nap (to)	dormir la siesta, 126	
have dinner (to)	cenar, 30	
have to (you [tú])	tienes que, 152	
have to (we)	tenemos que, 20	
have to (you [ud])	tiene que, 98	
have to (I)	tengo que, 98	
have to (they)	tienen que, 98	

have to (you [uds])	tienen que, 98
he	él, 66
he opens (he/she/it)	abre, 50
he opens (you)	abre, 50
heat	calor (m), 126
Helen	Elena, 108
hello	hola, 10
help (to)	ayudar, 118
help her (to)	ayudarla, 118
help you [ud/f]	ayudarla, 118
Henry	Enrique, 66
her	su, 20
her	su, sus, 142
here	aquí, 20
hi	hola, 10
hire (out) (you [ud])	alquila, 126
hire (to)	alquilar, 126
hire out (to)	alquilar, 126
hires (out) (he/she/it)	alquila, 126
his	su, 20
his	su, sus, 142
historical (m/pl)	históricos, 166
holidays	vacaciones (f/pl), 10
homemade (f/pl)	caseras, 88
hot (m and f)	caliente, 42
hotel	hotel (m), 10
hour	hora (f), 20
house	casa (f), 30
how	cómo, 10
how are you	qué tal estás, 10
how do you go to	cómo se va a, 152
how does one go to	cómo se va a, 152
how long	cuánto tiempo, 126
how long	cuántos días, 142
how many (f/pl)	cuántas, 20
how many (m/pl)	cuántos, 142
how many days	cuántos días, 142
how much (m)	cuánto, 42
how much are ...	cuánto cuestan ..., 58
how much is	a cuánto está, 194
how much is	cuánto cuesta, 98
husband	marido (m), 66
I	yo, 10

ice	hielo (m), 42
ice cream	helado (m), 126
ice lolly	polo (m), 126
identity card	carné (m) de identidad, 194
identity card	carné (m), 184
if	si, 30
I'm sorry	lo siento, 20
I'm sorry	perdona, 108
in	en, 10
in	dentro de, 30
in batter	en gabardina, 88
in front of	frente a, 98
in general	en general, 166
include (they)	incluyen, 184
include (you [uds])	incluyen, 184
individual (m and f)	individual, 20
information	información (f), 50
instructions	instrucciones (f/pl), 50
insurance	seguro (m), 184
interest	interés (m), 166
interesting (m and f)	interesante, 166
international (m and f)	internacional, 194
introduce (I)	presento, 10
Ireland	Irlanda, 194
is (he/she/it)	es, está, 20
is called (he/she/it)	se llama, 66
is getting married (he/she/it)	se casa, 66
is getting married (you [ud])	se casa, 66
is paid	se paga, 58
is served	se sirve, 20
is worth (it)	vale, 194
island	isla (f), 166
it	lo, 176
its	su, sus, 142
it's just as well	menos mal, 66
it's not bad	no está mal, 184
it's on offer	está de oferta, 176
it's very hot	hace mucho calor, 126
jacket	chaqueta (f), 176
Jaime	Jaime, 126
jam	mermelada (f), 134
January	enero, 142
jar	bote (m), 134

jar of baby food	potito (m), 118
Joachim	Joaquín, 66
Joanna	Juana, 66
John	Juan, 10
Joseph	José, 10
journey	viaje (m), 98
jug	jarra (f), 42
juice	zumo (m), 42
Julian	Julián, 152
July	julio, 142
jumper	jersey (m), 176
June	junio, 142
just in case	por si acaso, 184
keep (a command) (ud)	quédese, 42
key	llave (f), 20
kidney	riñón (m), 88
kilo	kilo (m), 58
kitchen	cocina (f), 50
kiwi	kiwi (m), 58
know (you [tú])	sabes, 108
know (I)	sé, 66
know (you [ud])	sabe, 58
knows (he/she/it)	sabe, 58
lady	señora (f), 20
lake	lago (m), 126
large (m and f)	grande, 42
last (m)	último, 98
lasts (it)	dura, 98
late	tarde, 30
later	luego, 152
Laura	Laura, 88
lead (the metal)	plomo (m), 184
leave (to)	dejar, 20
leave (you [ud])	deja, 50
leave (you [ud])	sale, 98
leaves (he/she/it)	deja, 50
leaves (he/she/it)	sale, 98
left	izquierda (f), 108
lemon	limón (m), 42
let's see	vamos a ver, 42
letter	carta (f), 194
letterbox	buzón (m), 194
lettuce	lechuga (f), 58

licence plate	matrícula (f), 184
lighter	encendedor (m), 194
like them (I)	me gustan, 88
like ... very much (I)	me gusta mucho ... 126
like them (you [tú])	te gustan, 88
like them (you [vosotros])	os gustan, 88
line	línea (f), 98
liquid	líquido (m), 118
live (I)	vivo, 66
Louis	Luis, 66
Louise	Luisa, 118
luggage	equipaje (m), 20
Madrid-style	a la madrileña, 88
mail	correo (m), 20
mailbox	buzón (m), 194
main (m and f)	principal, 58
make (to)	hacer, 98
make (you [ud])	hace, 126
make (you [uds])	hacen, 98
make (we)	hacemos, 98
make (they)	hacen, 98
makes (he/she/it)	hace, 126
man	señor (m), 20
many (m/pl)	muchos, 166
many (f/pl)	muchas, 108
map	mapa (m), 166
March	marzo, 142
Margaret	Margarita, 10
margarine	margarina (f), 134
market	mercado (m), 108
marmalade	mermelada (f), 134
married (m)	casado, 66
Martha	Marta, 50
Mary	María, 10
match	cerilla (f), 194
May	mayo, 142
mayonnaise	mayonesa (f), 30
me	yo, 10
meat	carne (f), 30
meatball	albóndiga (f), 88
medium(-sized)	mediana, 134
melon	melón (m), 58
membership card	carné (m), 184

menu	carta (f), 30
message	mensaje (m), 20
metre	metro (m), 184
metro	metro (m), 98
metro station	estación (f) de metro, 152
Michael	Miguel, 166
microwave	microondas (m), 50
mileage	kilometraje (m), 184
milk	leche (f), 42
milk shake	batido (m), 42
mince	carne picada (f), 134
mine (m)	mío, 142
mineral (m and f)	mineral, 30
minus	menos, 80
minute	minuto (m), 30
mixed (f)	mixta, 30
model	modelo (m), 184
modern (m)	moderno, 166
moisturising cream	crema (f) hidratante, 118
moment	momento (m), 20
monastery	monasterio (m), 166
Monday	lunes, 142
money	dinero (m), 194
monologue	monólogo (m), 66
month	mes (m), 142
monument	monumento (m), 166
more	más, 30
more slowly	más despacio, 152
morning	mañana (f), 50
mosquito	mosquito (m), 126
mother	madre (f), 66
motorbike	moto (f), 184
mountain	montaña (f), 126
Mr	Sr, 20
Mrs	Sra, 20
Ms	Sra, 20
much (m)	mucho, 88
mum	mamá (f), 66
museum	museo (m), 166
mushroom	champiñón (m), 58
mushroom	seta (f), 88
mussel	mejillón (m), 88
my (m and f)	mi, 10

my name is	me llamo, 10
name	nombre (m), 20
nap	siesta (f), 126
nappy	pañal (m), 118
Natalie	Natalia, 66
near (f)	cercana, 184
near	cerca, cerca de, 50
necessary (m)	necesario, 126
need (you [uds])	necesitan, 50
need (they)	necesitan, 50
need (you [ud])	necesita, 166
need (I)	necesito, 58
needs (he/she/it)	necesita, 166
neither	tampoco, 88
neither ... nor	ni ... ni, 88
nephew	sobrino (m), 66
new (f)	nueva, 142
next	que viene, 142
next (m and f)	siguiente, 58
next (m)	próximo, 98
next	de al lado, 126
next (f)	próxima, 108
next door	de al lado, 126
next to	junto a, 58
Nicholas	Nicolás, 66
niece	sobrina (f), 66
night	noche (f), 10
nightclub	discoteca (f), 126
nine	nueve, 3
nine hundred (m/pl)	novecientos, 152
nineteen	diecinueve, 3
ninety	noventa, 74
ninth (m)	noveno, 152
no	no, 20
none (m)	ninguno, 108
non-smoker	no fumador (m), 98
not ... either	tampoco, 88
not ... or	ni ... ni, 88
note (bank)	billete (m), 194
November	noviembre, 142
now	ahora, 42
number	número (m), 50
number plate	matrícula (f), 184

occasion	vez (f), 126
October	octubre, 142
octopus	pulpo (m), 88
of	de, 10
of course	cómo no, 30
of course	claro, 20
of course	por supuesto, 184
of the (m)	del, 50
offer	oferta (f), 176
office	oficina (f), 152
oil	aceite (m), 58
OK	vale, 20
olive	aceituna (f), 88
omelette	tortilla (f), 30
on	en, 10
on	sobre, 50
on foot	a pie, 152
on holiday	de vacaciones, 126
on its own (m)	solo, 42
on the left	a la izquierda, 108
on the other side	al otro lado, 152
on the right	a la derecha, 30
on top of	sobre, 50
on vacation	de vacaciones, 126
one (m)	uno, 3
one hundred	cien, 74
one hundred and one (m)	ciento uno, 158
one leaves	se deja, 50
one pays	se paga, 58
one thousand	mil, 152
one writes	se escribe, 36
onion	cebolla (f), 58
only	sólo, 58
open (you [uds])	abren, 50
open (f/pl)	abiertas, 108
open (they)	abren, 50
opens (he/she/it)	abre, 50
opposite	frente a, 98
or	o, 176
orange	naranja (f), 42
orangeade	naranjada (f), 42
order (to)	pedir, 88
other (f/pl)	otras, 88

others (f/pl)	otras, 88
our (f)	nuestra, 184
outward journey	ida (f), 98
over there	ahí, 166
over there	allí, 134
packet	paquete (m), 194
painkiller	calmante (m), 118
palace	palacio (m), 166
paper	papel (m), 118
paper handkerchief	kleenex (m), 118
parcel	paquete (m), 194
park	parque (m), 166
park (to)	aparcar, 50
parking meter	parquímetro (m), 184
parsley	perejil (m), 134
party	fiesta (f), 126
pass (to)	pasar, 142
passport	pasaporte (m), 20
past	y, 80
pastry shop	pastelería (f), 108
pasty	empanadilla (f), 88
Patricia	Patricia, 126
Paul	Pablo, 88
pay (to)	pagar, 126
pay (I)	pago, 58
pea	guisante (m), 134
peach	melocotón (m), 134
pear	pera (f), 134
people carrier	monovolumen (m), 184
pepper	pimiento (m), 58
pepper (spice)	pimienta (f), 30
per cent	por ciento, 98
per week	por semana, 184
Peter	Pedro, 10
petrol	gasolina (f), 184
petrol station	gasolinera (f), 184
pharmacist (female)	farmacéutica (f), 118
pharmacy	farmacia (f), 108
Philip	Felipe, 88
photograph	foto (f), 126
picture	foto (f), 126
pill	pastilla (f), 118
pineapple	piña (f), 134

pink (m and f)	rosa, 176
pizzeria	pizzería (f), 108
place	sitio (m), lugar (m), 166
plant	planta (f), 176
plaster	tirita (f), 118
plate	plato (m), 30
please	por favor, 20
pleased (f)	encantada, 10
pleased (m)	encantado, 10
plum	ciruela (f), 134
pork	cerdo (m), 88
portion	ración (f), 88
post	correo (m), 20
post office	oficina (f) de Correos, Correos, 152
postcard	postal (f), 194
potato	patata (f), 30
pound	libra (f), 194
pound sterling	libra (f) esterlina, 194
prawn	gamba (f), 88
prefer (you [ud])	prefiere, 118
prefer (I)	prefiero, 88
prefers (he/she/it)	prefiere, 118
prescription	receta (f), 118
present	regalo (m), 108
price	precio (m), 184
public (m)	público, 166
purchase	compra (f), 142
put (to)	poner, 58
put (I)	pongo, 42
quite	bastante, 152
radio	radio (f), 20
receipt	recibo (m), 176
receptionist	recepcionista (m), recepcionista (f), 20
recommend (to)	recomendar, 118
recommend (you [ud])	recomienda, 30
recommends (he/she/it)	recomienda, 30
red (m)	rojo, 176
red (wine) (m)	tinto, 30
region	región (f), 166
registered mail	correo (m) certificado, 194
registration number	número de matrícula (m), 184
rent (out) (we)	alquilamos, 184
reservation	reserva (f), 20

reserve (to)	reservar, 166
reserved (f)	reservada, 20
reserved (m)	reservado, 50
rest	resto (m), 194
restaurant	restaurante (m), 152
return	vuelta (f), 98
return (I)	vuelvo, 194
return (to)	devolver, 184
rice	arroz (m), 30
Richard	Ricardo, 10
right	derecha (f), 30
right away	ahora mismo, 42
right away	en seguida, 194
right here	aquí mismo, 98
right now	ahora mismo, 42
risk	riesgo (m), 184
road	carretera (f), 184
roasted (m)	asado, 30
room	habitación (f), 20
rosé (m)	rosado, 42
Rose	Rosa, 20
round trip	ida y vuelta (f), 98
royal (m and f)	real, 166
rubber ring	flotador (m), 126
rubbish	basura (f), 50
rum	ron (m), 42
salad	ensalada (f), 30
salami	salami (m), 134
salami-type sausage	salchichón (m), 134
sales	rebajas (f/pl), 176
salmon	salmón (m), 30
salt	sal (f), 30
same (m)	mismo, 42
sandwich	bocadillo (m), 108
sangria	sangría (f), 42
sanitary towel	compresa (f), 118
sardine	sardina (f), 30
Saturday	sábado, 142
sausage	salchicha (f), 134
say (to)	decir, 30
scuba diving	submarinismo (m), 126
scuba diving (to go)	hacer submarinismo, 126
sea	mar (m), 152

seat	asiento (m), 98
second (m)	segundo, 152
see (to)	ver, 20
see you	hasta la vista, 10
see you soon	hasta pronto, 10
self-service restaurant	autoservicio (m), 108
sell (we)	vendemos, 118
send (to)	mandar, 20
separated (m)	separado, 66
September	septiembre, 142
serve (you [uds])	atienden, 176
serve (they)	atienden, 176
seven	siete, 3
seven hundred (m/pl)	setecientos, 152
seventeen	diecisiete, 3
seventh (m)	séptimo, 152
seventy	setenta, 74
several (f/pl)	varias, 108
several (m/pl)	varios, 50
Seville	Sevilla, 142
shampoo	champú (m), 118
she	ella, 66
shellfish	marisco (m), 30
sherry	jerez (m), 42
ship	barco (m), 166
shirt	camisa (f), 176
shoe	zapato (m), 176
shoe shop	zapatería (f), 108
shop	tienda (f), 108
shop assistant	dependiente (m), 126
shop assistant	dependienta (f), 58
shop window	escaparate (m), 176
shopping	compra (f), 142
shopping centre	centro comercial (m), 108
show (I)	enseño, 50
show (to)	enseñar, 176
show me (to)	indicarme, 152
siblings	hermanos (m/pl), 66
side	lado (m), 126
sign (a command) (tú)	firma, 176
sign (a command) (ud)	firme, 20
single (m and f)	individual, 20
single (m)	soltero, 66

sister	hermana (f), 66
sitting room	salón (m), 50
six	seis, 3
six hundred (m/pl)	seiscientos, 152
sixteen	dieciséis, 3
sixth (m)	sexto, 152
sixty	sesenta, 74
size (clothes)	talla (f), 176
size (shoe)	número (m), 176
skirt	falda (f), 176
sleep (to)	dormir, 126
slowly	despacio, 152
small (f)	pequeña, 42
small beer	caña (f), 42
small dish	tapa (f), 88
small portion	pincho (m), 88
small town	pueblo (m), 166
smoker	fumador (m), 98
snack	tapa (f), 88
snack	pincho (m), 88
snail	caracol (m), 88
soap	jabón (m), 118
solution	líquido (m), 118
some	un poco de, 134
some (m/pl)	unos, 30
some (f)	alguna, 58
some (m)	algún, 30
something	algo, 30
son	hijo (m), 66
sons	hijos (m/pl), 66
soup	sopa (f), 30
spaghetti	espaguetis (m/pl), 30
Spanish (language)	español (m), 166
Spanish cured ham	jamón serrano (m), 88
Spanish potato omelette	tortilla (f), 88
sparkling	con gas, 30
special (m and f)	especial, 184
spend (to)	pasar, 142
spicy potatoes	patatas bravas (f/pl), 88
spicy sausage	chorizo (m), 88
sport	deporte (m), 108
sports shoe	zapatilla (f), 176
square	plaza (f), 108

squid	calamar (m), 88
stall	puesto (m), 58
stamp	sello (m), 194
start (you [uds])	empiezan, 176
start (they)	empiezan, 176
start (you [ud])	empieza, 166
starts (he/she/it)	empieza, 166
state-owned hotel	parador (m), 166
station	estación (f), 152
stay (to)	quedarse, 142
stay (you [ud])	se queda, 142
stays (he/she/it)	se queda, 142
steak	filete (m), 30
steamed	al vapor, 88
Stephanie	Estefanía, 142
still	todavía, 176
stop	parada (f), 98
store	tienda (f), 108
straight (m)	recto, 152
straight ahead	todo recto, 152
strawberry	fresa (f), 58
street	calle (f), 108
street map	plano (m), 98
stuffed (m/pl)	rellenos, 88
sugar	azúcar (m), 58
suitcase	maleta (f), 20
sun	sol (m), 10
sun block	protector solar (m), 118
sun lounger	tumbona (f), 126
sunbathe (to)	tomar el sol, 126
Sunday	domingo, 142
supermarket	supermercado (m), 50
Susan	Susana, 66
swimming costume	bañador (m), 176
swimming pool	piscina (f), 50
Sylvia	Silvia, 88
table	mesa (f), 30
tablet	pastilla (f), 118
take (a command) (tú)	coge, 152
take (you [ud])	consume, 184
take (to)	coger, 98
take (to)	tomar, 30
take (with me) (to)	llevarme, 118

take (you [vosotros])	lleváis,	126
take out (to)	sacar,	126
takes (he/she/it)	consume,	184
tampon	tampón (m),	118
tangerine	mandarina (f),	134
tapa	tapa (f),	88
tariff	tarifa (f),	184
tea	té (m),	42
telephone	teléfono (m),	20
television	televisión (f),	20
tell (to)	decir,	30
temperature	fiebre (f),	118
ten	diez,	3
10-journey ticket	metrobús (m),	98
tenth (m)	décimo,	152
thank you	gracias,	10
thank you very much	muchas gracias,	20
that	eso, que,	20
that (m)	ese,	126
the (f)	la,	10
the (m)	el,	10
their	su,	20
their	su, sus,	142
them	los,	176
then	luego,	152
then	pues,	30
then	entonces,	10
there	ahí,	166
there	allí,	134
there are	hay,	20
there is	hay,	20
Theresa	Teresa,	30
these (m/pl)	estos,	176
these (f/pl)	estas,	118
these ones (m/pl)	éstos,	176
they are	están,	30
thing	cosa (f),	58
think (I)	creo,	108
third (m)	tercero,	152
thirteen	trece,	3
thirty	treinta,	3
this (m)	este,	120
this (m)	éste,	118

this (f)	esta,	108
this (f)	ésta,	50
this one (m)	éste,	118
this one (f)	ésta,	50
this other one (m)	éste otro,	176
this way	por aquí,	30
Thomas	Tomás,	66
three	tres,	3
three hundred (m/pl)	trescientos,	152
three quarters	tres cuartos,	134
through	por,	20
Thursday	jueves,	142
ticket	billete (m),	98
ticket (entrance)	entrada (f),	166
tie	corbata (f),	176
till	hasta,	10
till	caja (f),	58
time	tiempo (m), vez (f),	126
time	hora (f),	20
timetable	horario (m),	166
tin	lata (f),	58
tissue	kleenex (m),	118
to	a,	20
to	menos,	80
to you (uds)	les,	30
to me	a mí,	88
to the (m)	al,	30
to them	les,	30
to us	nos,	30
tobacco	tabaco (m),	194
today	hoy,	88
toilet tissue	papel (m) higiénico,	118
toilets	servicios (m/pl),	30
tomato	tomate (m),	58
tomorrow	mañana,	66
tonic water	tónica (f),	42
tonight	esta noche,	126
too	demasiado,	184
too	también,	10
too many (m/pl)	demasiados,	126
tooth	diente (m),	118
toothpaste	pasta (f) de dientes,	118
tourism	turismo (m),	166

tourist office	oficina (f) de turismo, 166
towel	toalla (f), 50
town	ciudad (f), 184
traffic	tráfico (m), 184
train	tren (m), 98
train station	estación (f) de tren, 152
trainer	zapatilla (f), 176
travel agency	agencia (f) de viajes, 108
traveller's cheque	cheque (m) de viaje, 194
trip	viaje (m), 98
tripe	callos (m/pl), 88
trolley	carrito (m), 58
trousers	pantalones (m/pl), 176
try (to)	probar, 176
try on (to)	probar, 176
try on (to) (me)	probarme, 176
T-shirt	camiseta (f), 176
Tuesday	martes, 142
tuna	bonito (m), atún (m), 88
tuna	atún (m), 30
turkey	pavo (m), 30
turn (to)	girar, 152
twelve	doce, 3
twenty	veinte, 3
twenty-eight	veintiocho, 3
twenty-five	veinticinco, 3
twenty-four	veinticuatro, 3
twenty-nine	veintinueve, 3
twenty-one (m)	veintiuno, 3
twenty-seven	veintisiete, 3
twenty-six	veintiséis, 3
twenty-three	veintitrés, 3
twenty-two	veintidós, 3
two	dos, 3
two hundred (m/pl)	doscientos, 152
uncle	tío (m), 66
underground	metro (m), 98
underground station	estación (f) de metro, 152
unleaded	sin plomo, 184
unlimited (m)	ilimitado, 184
until	hasta, 10
us	nos, 30
use (you [tú])	usas, 176

VAT	IVA (m), 184
vegetable shop	verdulería (f), 108
vegetables	verduras (f/pl), 58
vegetarian (m)	vegetariano, 30
Venezuela	Venezuela, 194
very	muy, 88
very well	muy bien, 184
Victor	Víctor, 152
victory	victoria (f), 166
village	pueblo (m), 166
virgin	virgen (f), 166
Visa	Visa, 176
visit (to)	visitar, 166
vitamin	vitamina (f), 118
vodka	vodka (m), 42
wait (to)	esperar, 98
waiter	camarero (m), 30
waitress	camarera (f), 30
want (you [tú])	quieres, 176
want (you [ud])	quiere, 98
want (you [uds])	quieren, 30
want (I)	quiero, 20
want (we)	queremos, 126
want (you [vosotros])	queréis, 126
want(they)	quieren, 30
wants (he/she/it)	quiere, 98
wardrobe	armario (m), 50
washing machine	lavadora (f), 50
water	agua (f), 30
watermelon	sandía (f), 58
water-ski (to)	hacer esquí acuático, 126
water-skiing	esquí acuático (m), 126
we	nosotros, 142
we (all females)	nosotras, 126
wear (you [tú]) (shoes)	calzas, 176
wedding	boda (f), 66
Wednesday	miércoles, 142
week	semana (f), 126
weekend	fin (f) de semana, 142
welcome (you're)	de nada, 58
well	bien, 10
what	qué, 10
what a mess	qué lío, 66

what a pity	qué pena,	88
what day	qué día,	50
what day is it today?	qué día es hoy,	142
what else	qué más,	58
when	qué día,	50
when	cuándo,	50
where	dónde,	10
where	donde,	118
which	cuáles,	166
which	qué,	10
which	cuál,	118
which one	cuál,	118
whisky	whisky (m),	42
white (m)	blanco,	42
who	quién,	58
why	por qué,	126
widowed (m)	viudo,	66
widower	viudo,	66
wife	mujer (f),	66
wine	vino (m),	30
wish (you [ud])	desea,	118
wish (you [uds])	desean,	42
wish (they)	desean,	42
wishes (he/she/it)	desea,	118
with	con,	20
with garlic	al ajillo,	88
without	sin,	42
woman	mujer (f),	66
woman	señora (f),	20
year	año (m),	142
yellow (m)	amarillo,	176
yes	sí,	10
yet	todavía,	176
yoghurt	yogur (m),	134
you (sing/col)	tú,	10
you (tú)	te,	10
your (ud/uds)	su,	20
your (ud/uds)	su, sus,	142
your (tú)	tu,	36
you're welcome	de nada,	58
zero	cero,	3
zone	zona (f),	50

Index

a, 43, 195
addresses, 153
al, 32
algo vs algún, 53
allí vs ahí, 168
alphabet, 37
ar verbs, 233

cómo, 11
cómo te llamas, 12
casa, 143
cerca, 153
colours, 177
con, 43
cuál, 119
cuánto, 145
cuesta vs cuestan, 99

dar, 235
de, 32, 43
decimals, 196
del, 51
demasiado, 128
describing words, 14
    ending in e, 43
    ending in o, 67
    plural, 67, 68
double letters, 153
double negative, 90, 109

el, 32

el/la vs the, 168
en, 43, 195
er verbs, 233
eres vs estás, 12
es vs está, 51
está vs ésta, 51
estar, 235

gratis, 136
greetings, 8
gusta vs gustan, 127
gustan, 90

hacer, 235
hay, 22
hora, 78

introductions, 8
ir, 235
ir verbs, 233

joining words together, 11, 21, 31

la, 32, 119
le, 119
lejos, 153
lo, 119
los, 177
lunes, 143

mío, 143

mañana, 51
map of Spain, 230
map of the world, 231
me, 12, 119, 135
me queda vs se queda, 143
mi vs mis, 109

negative sentences, 68, 127
no, 68
nosotras vs nosotros, 145
nouns
    ending in e, 59
numbers
    0 - 30, 3
    building up, 159
    cien vs ciento, 160
    feminine, 75, 159
    un, 159

para, 43
plural, 21
poco, 135
poder, 236
poner, 236
por, 43
por vs para, 185
pronunciation
    ñ, 142
    a, 50
    b, 4, 127
    c, 98, 108
    ch, 108
    common mistakes, 184, 194
    d, 127
    e, 42
    f, 134
    g, 81
    h, 11

    i, 58
infinitives, 195
    j, 67
    k, 37
    l, 166
    ll, 88, 166
    m, 152
    n, 142, 152
    o, 74
    p, 127
    qu, 98
    r, 31
    rr, 21
    s, 118
    silent u, 81, 99, 158
    t, 127
    u, 158
    v, 4, 134
    w, 37
    x, 176
    y, 88
    z, 108

qué, 11
qué versus que, 167
queda, 143
queda vs quedan, 59
querer, 236

regular verbs, 234

sólo vs solo, 60
saber, 236
se, 153
ser, 237
siguiente, 135
soy vs estoy, 67
stress, 31, 60

su, 68
su vs sus, 145

tú, 12
tú vs usted, 89
tarde vs noche, 82
te, 12
tener, 237
tiene, 51
tiene vs tienen, 23
tienes vs tienen, 136
todavía vs ya, 178
tu vs tus, 109

un, 21
una, 21
uno, 21
usted, 23
ustedes, 23

viene, 143
volver, 237
vosotras vs vosotros, 145
vosotros vs ustedes, 89

word order, 167
    describing words, 22
written accent, 5, 111

y, 74
yo, 12, 68, 128

■ Where to find Maria Fernandez's courses ■

SPANISH COURSES BY MARIA FERNANDEZ

Over the years I've created a number of Spanish courses and other material. You can find their free samples at **kerapido.com/free**

My courses and lessons come in different formats to help you learn Spanish fast wherever you are. Here are their titles and where to find them:

Learn Spanish at Your Own Pace - Online: interactive course with everyday conversations, vocabulary audio flashcards, pronunciation lessons, speaking and listening drills, quizzes, and more. Get the free samples and details at kerapido.com/online

Learn Spanish at Your Own Pace - Book & recordings: this book plus the audio version of the course above. Get the free samples and details at kerapido.com/book

Spanish Verb Course - Online: step-by-step videos with clear explanations, speaking practice, and listening drills. To see how this verb course works, go to kerapido.com/verbs

Spanish Verb Series - Books & audiobooks: single topic publications with step-by-step explanations, speaking practice, and listening drills. Find out more: kerapido.com/verbs

Spanish Audio Lessons for Complete Beginners - Audiobook & transcript: step-by-step lessons where I encourage you to speak with me from day 1. Get the free samples at kerapido.com/audio

Spanish Online Lessons - Live: join my live online group classes. There you can practise speaking and listening; and you can ask me your questions. For more details, go to kerapido.com/class

Fluent in Spanish - Book & audiobook: a short guide on how to learn Spanish fast and efficiently. Written and read by me, Maria Fernandez. Get the free sample and more details at kerapido.com/fluent

Sherlock Holmes Bilingual Story - Book: my Spanish translation of the Sherlock Holmes story "A Scandal in Bohemia" (Un escándalo en Bohemia). A parallel text edition with glossary. For more details, go to kerapido.com/story

Sherlock Holmes in Spanish - Audiobook: Spanish recording of "Un escándalo en

Bohemia" (my translation of the Sherlock Holmes story "A Scandal in Bohemia"). Narrated by me, Maria Fernandez. To hear the free sample, go to kerapido.com/story

Spanish Video Lessons on YouTube: my short Spanish video lessons with speaking and listening drills. Watch them at kerapido.com/youtube

Speak Spanish with Maria Fernandez: my free podcast. Subscribe to it at kerapido.com/podcast

ENGLISH COURSES BY MARIA FERNANDEZ

All these English courses can be found at **learnenglishwithmaria.com**

30-Day English Speaking Challenge - Online course: thirty 2-minute videos to help you improve your spoken English fast and easily. Each video focuses on one common mistake. Find out more: learnenglishwithmaria.com/speaking

Get a Better English Accent in 1 Hour - Online course: 5 step-by-step videos that show you the mistakes you're making, and how to avoid them. Fun and easy practice that will make the biggest difference to your accent. Find out more: learnenglishwithmaria.com/accent

Complete British English Pronunciation Course - Online course: learn and practise the 45 British English sounds. Step by step lessons with tongue and lip images, interactive flashcards, speaking drills and listening exercises. Find out more: learnenglishwithmaria.com/pronunciation

30-Day English Writing Challenge - Online course: thirty 2-minute videos to help you improve your written English fast and easily. Write like a native with accurate grammar, vocabulary, word order, and spelling. Find out more: learnenglishwithmaria.com/writing

English Online Lessons - Live: join my live online group classes. There you can practise speaking and listening; and you can ask me your questions. Find out more: learnenglishwithmaria.com/live

English Video Lessons on YouTube: my short English video lessons with speaking and listening drills. Watch them at learnenglishwithmaria.com/youtube

www.ingramcontent.com/pod-product-compliance
Lightning Source LLC
Chambersburg PA
CBHW071857290426
44110CB00013B/1184